REASON TO BELIEVE

Rational Explanations of Orthodox Jewish Faith

זכרון דוד

MENORAH

Rabbi Chaim Jachter

REASON TO BELIEVE

RATIONAL EXPLANATIONS OF ORTHODOX JEWISH FAITH

זכרון דוד

Menorah Books

REASON TO BELIEVE
Rational Explanations of Orthodox Jewish Faith

First Edition, 2017

Menorah Books
An imprint of Koren Publishers Jerusalem Ltd.

POB 8531, New Milford, CT 06776-8531, USA
& POB 4044, Jerusalem 9104001, Israel
www.menorah-books.com

The publication of this book was made possible through the generous support of *Torah Education in Israel.*

ISBN 978 1 940516 71 4, *hardcover*

A CIP catalogue record for this title is available from the British Library

Printed and bound in the United States

לע"נ

דוד משה בן יוסף ז"ל

David Morris Wagner

Husband, Father, Grandfather, and Great-grandfather
A man of quiet faith who embodied the phrase

אמור מעט ועשה הרבה... (משנה אבות א טו)

His deeds for his family, his community, and *Klal Yisrael* were many.

Roselin S. Wagner

Barry and Marcia Wagner Levinson

Eliron and Devorah Levinson
Chava Bracha, Moshe Chaim
Golda Chana, Dovid Yisroel

Aviyam and Rina Levinson
Nesanel Eliyahu, Chana Malka,
Shmuel Dovid

Jonathan and Phyllis Wagner

Ariel and Matthew Levitan
Alexa, David

Lauren and Michael Rosman
Mila, William

Anna Wagner

Kenneth Wagner and Sarah Wagner

Simcha, Meira, Eliana

Reviews

Rabbi Chaim Jachter's extraordinary blend of scholarship, talent and experience makes him uniquely qualified to have authored this essential volume.

In Reason to Believe *Rabbi Jachter brings to bear vast Torah knowledge, decades as a master educator and sensitive personal insight; as he tackles the critical questions of faith and belief that confront young and old in today's world.*

Readers of all backgrounds and outlooks throughout the Jewish community will be amazed and reassured as the author openly raises the very questions that they themselves have been asking and as he provides an array of profound, convincing responses to those questions.

Rabbi Shmuel Goldin, Past President, Rabbinical Council of America; author, *Unlocking the Torah Text*; Rabbi, Congregation Ahavath Torah, Englewood, N.J.

Though the foundations of Jewish belief are immutable they require modern articulation and timely refreshment in the face of recent cultural shifts. Rabbi Jachter has skillfully addressed a wide range of issues including perceived clashes between Torah and science, the reconciliation of Torah and human morality, and the obscuring of God in our world. His insights stream through fresh explanations of Tanach, classic tenets of Jewish philosophy, perspectives upon recent shifts in Jewish history and modern voices of the Orthodox world. Thank you for providing a modern repository to help reinforce the integrity of Judaism and belief in an age of intellectual turbulence and existential tumult.

Rabbi Moshe Taragin, Rebbe, Yeshivat Har Etzion, Gush Etzion, Israel.

Rabbi Jachter, a masterful teacher and prolific writer, has once again produced an excellent work, the influence of which will be felt for years to come. In the past Rabbi Jachter has successfully focused on making Halakha accessible to the English-speaking community. His Halakhic works are masterpieces of clarity, allowing the reader access to the profundity of Jewish law.

In Reason to Believe *Rabbi Jachter has now used this same talent while addressing the philosophic issues of faith that confront and challenge modern man. With intellectual rigor Rabbi Jachter tackles the pressing issues offering answers that our youth and adults alike are desperate to hear.*

Rabbi Elazar Muskin, Senior Rabbi, Young Israel of Century City, Los Angeles, CA.

Reason to Believe *will strengthen the faithful and encourage our youth to keep the faith in an age of rampant doubt. Rabbi Jachter analyzes profound and perennial questions in a pleasant and accessible style. A masterful and timely contribution.*

Rav Mordechai Willig, Rosh Kollel at Yeshiva University; Segan Av Beth Din of the Beth Din of America; Rabbi, Young Israel of Riverdale, N.Y.

With the proliferation of a myriad of opinions, beliefs and ideas throughout the vast recesses of the internet, our youth are growing up in a most challenging time to develop a deep and steadfast Orthodox religious ideology and relationship with Hashem.

Rabbi Jachter's thoughtful yet straightforward answers to many of the most basic questions vexing modern skeptics will arm students and their teachers with the necessary tools to deepen and strengthen the religious commitment of the next generation of Orthodox Judaism. Mechanchim and parents owe Rabbi Jachter profound thanks for providing this valuable resource in the fight against intellectual apathy and confusion, written in an engaging style teenagers and adults can relate to.

Rabbi Yisroel Kaminetsky, Rosh Yeshiva, Hebrew Academy of Long Beach; Menahel, Davis Renov Stahler Yeshiva High School for Boys, Woodmere, N.Y.

The Pesach Haggadah instructs us to conduct the Seder in accordance with educational background and experience: a lesson for the Tam, the simple one, may not be appropriate for the Chacham, the wise one.

Rabbi Jachter's "Reason to Believe" is an exception to that principle. Topics dealing with faith, origins of Torah, identifying the presence of God in today's world are topics not typically discussed in the curriculum of most yeshiva high schools. Hence, not only would the child lacking the ability to ask or the simple one be challenged by these issues, but even the wise one, who is well equipped to discuss the debate between Ramban and Rabbeinu Tam as to what constitutes Bittul Chametz, is often lost and perplexed when dealing with elements of faith.

Rabbi Jachter provides a framework for adults, as well as modern-day yeshiva students, to begin a vast exploration of these issues. He is a master teacher and skilled writer, a combination that can only lead to success.

Rabbi Yosef Adler, Rav, Congregation Rinat Yisrael; Rosh HaYeshiva, Torah Academy of Bergen County, Teaneck, N.J.

Contents

Introduction

It is the question of all questions and the issue of all issues: Is there a God, and did He author the books of the Torah? We set forth in this book compelling reasons why Orthodox Jewish belief is far more reasonable than secular perspectives on the world and Torah. Our goal is to deepen the belief of Orthodox Jews and to motivate those outside the Orthodox Jewish community to further explore the best possible lifestyle and belief system available to mankind.

The nineteenth, twentieth and twenty-first centuries have posed great challenges to Orthodox belief, most of which are connected with the rise of the scientific, materialistic world-view. Scientists have investigated the history of the universe and the origins of life and have come up with a story which on the surface appears to contradict the account in Genesis. Secular scholars have "analyzed" the Torah and argued that it is a human document put together at different times. Archaeologists have dug the soil of the Holy Land and some claimed to find evidence contradicting the biblical history – a few, with an obvious political agenda, even going so far as to deny the existence of an Israelite kingdom! Humanists have questioned the ethical status of some of the Torah's provisions. On the level of history, the massive suffering of the Holocaust has led some to deny the existence of a just and merciful God. And finally, present-day

Western culture, with its cult of instant gratification, has caused many to view Torah restrictions as senseless and outmoded inconveniences.

Not all of these challenges are really new. Indeed, Jewish sages and scholars have been wrestling with the underlying issues for a long time, and have articulated compelling answers to them. In the contemporary era, leaders such as Rav Joseph B. Soloveitchik have updated those answers, and Orthodox scholars have responded to the challenges posed by secular scholars. In this book, after an introduction on the nature of faith itself, we will present a significant portion of their answers.

Our hope is that the arguments put forth in this book will convince those who are considering leaving or have already left the Orthodox Jewish fold, to reconsider their decision in favor of remaining loyal to the faith of our ancestors. We also hope that within the Orthodox community this book will serve as a game-changer, elevating many from what has been termed "social Orthodoxy" to a more committed "substantive Orthodoxy" in which devout actions and firm belief fully align.

Orthodox Jewish belief is far from antiquated. In fact, modern times offer *new reasons* to affirm the traditional belief system of the Jewish people. We hope that readers of all backgrounds will find many opportunities set forth in this work to deepen their level of belief and commitment to God and His Torah.

Chapter 1

Emuna: What is Faith?

E*muna* – faith, which for the Jew means belief in Hashem and in the divine origin of the Torah – is a rather straightforward concept that can be explained in five minutes or less. In fact, Charlie Harary does a fine job setting forth a simple formula in a brief yet compelling video available on Youtube.[1] I shall start by summarizing his presentation.

The Truth of Hashem and Torah: Basic Arguments

Song of Songs compares our relationship with Hashem to that of a bride and groom.[2] This endearing parable offers profound advice to help us properly approach our relationship with Hashem.

A marriage can succeed only if both parties actively *choose* to commit to one another. Since Hashem, indeed, desires this intimacy, we are given the opportunity to join Him. However, if Hashem would reveal Himself completely, surely we would be left with no choice but to

1. "*The Six Constant Mitzvos with Charlie Harary: Mitzva #1*," https://www.youtube.com/watch?v=dv2PgYw2W7g.
2. See Rashi's commentary on Song of Songs. This parable of the relationship between Hashem and the Jewish people is a recurring theme in Torah literature. Hos. 2 is an excellent example.

acknowledge Him, because His omniscience would be irrefutable.[3] This would rob us of our choice whether to enter into the relationship. Therefore Hashem elects to conceal Himself, challenging us to discover Him and exclaim, "Behold He stands behind our wall, He looks in through the windows, He peers through the lattice."[4]

On the other hand, Hashem must make it *possible* for us to discover Him in order for the relationship to be achievable. Thus, Hashem hides Himself but not to the extent that we are unable to encounter Him. In Deut. 32:11, Hashem is compared to "As an eagle stirs up her nest, broods over her young." Rashi explains that Hashem is *nogei'a ve'eino nogei'a*, "He touches but does not touch." Hashem hovers above us, making Himself known in a subtle manner. Though His presence is understated, intimate knowledge of His presence is accessible to all.

Charlie Harary outlines various phenomena through which we can recognize Hashem. The first is nature. While we generally know how the body works, we are overwhelmed by its complexity and amazed by how efficiently it operates. There are millions of parts in the body, all functioning seamlessly in sync. Could this just be a matter of chance? We should ask the same of the entire world! Why do all the billions and billions of parts all work together unfailingly? Could this be mere coincidence as well?[5]

3. See the *Meshekh Ḥokhma* (Rabbi Meir Simcha of Dvinsk [1843–1926]) on Ex. 19:17, citing the talmudic assertion (Shabbat 88a) that we were coerced into receiving the Torah at Sinai. This is a difficult statement in light of the fact that according to Ex. 19 and 24 we chose to accept the Torah. But the *Meshekh Ḥokhma* explains that at Sinai Hashem revealed Himself so starkly as to leave no room for choice, so that it was *as if* we were coerced. The Gemara states that we later accepted the Torah voluntarily during the time of Ahasuerus. This certainly fits with the *Meshekh Ḥokhma*'s idea. Only when Hashem reveals Himself in a subtle manner, as in the Book of Esther, can we enter into a voluntary relationship with Hashem.
4. Song. 2:9.
5. Maimonides (*Hilkhot Yesodei Torah* 2:2) observes that observing the vast beauty of the universe is a means to both respect and love Hashem. Ezra Ghazal, a member of Congregation Shaarei Orah of Teaneck, New Jersey, who has fifty years experience as an engineer, notes that as an engineer he knows that every system, no matter how well designed and built, will eventually fail. Engineers routinely plan for such failure. The universe, by contrast, never breaks down. The processes of sunrise and sunset, for example, function every day without fail. Mr. Ghazal views nature as an

The same applies to the history of the Jewish people. Just a glimpse into our nation's past reveals a relentlessly-persecuted people who managed not only to survive centuries of humiliation, but to emerge a strengthened and influential nation. How can we account for a nation that has escaped the threat of destruction time and again to build a thriving homeland? How can the State of Israel survive among a sea of hostile neighbors bent on its destruction? It is an ongoing Ḥanukka miracle of "the many in the hands of the few," unfolding right before our eyes![6]

Finally, the fact that Hashem revealed Himself not to an individual, but to an entire nation of our ancestors – which stands in stark contrast to every other belief-system in the world – is a precious piece of our story that strengthens our ability to believe in the authenticity of His words.

Two Ways of Recognizing Hashem: "General Recognition" and "Marks"

If acquiring *emuna* merely requires a brief physiology or history lesson, why the need for the extended discussions of *emuna* in this book?

In his book *Abraham's Journey*,[7] Rabbi Joseph B. Soloveitchik notes that there are two means of identifying an object. One is to describe the item by signs or marks *(simanim)*. The other means of identification is from a general recognition of its form, without knowing its marks. This type of recognition is called *tvi'at ayin.*

Rabbi Soloveitchik explains that in a situation where a person seeks to claim a lost item, "halakha considers general recognition to be far superior to identification by naming marks." This is because "configurative recognition is solid, a certainty"...whereas "identification by *simanim* is not instantaneous; it consists of an act of inferring," and

opportunity to marvel at the amazing nature of Hashem's work which never fails, which so dramatically exceeds the handiwork of human beings which inevitably fail.

6. When asked why, for all his skepticism, he still believed in God, Voltaire replied: "Had it not been for the miracle of the survival of the Jewish people, I would have given up this proof as well" (quoted in Walter Wurzburger, *God is Proof Enough* [New York: Devora Publishing, 2000], 62).
7. Joseph B. Soloveitchik, *Abraham's Journey: Reflections on the Life of the Founding Patriarch* (Jersey City: Ktav Publishing House, Inc, 2008), 29-31.

the decision of the court to accept this type of identification depends upon "probability and statistics." By contrast, "identification based upon a general impression of the configuration or the whole is spontaneous, instantaneous," which is why it is considered superior.

Many of us come to recognize Hashem through *tvi'at ayin*. It can come through the opportunities outlined by Charlie Harary. It can also come from recognizing the grandeur of Torah,[8] appreciating its profundity compared to all other disciplines. Anyone who had the privilege to hear a lecture delivered by Rav Aharon Lichtenstein or by his student Rabbi Michael Rosensweig has surely been in a position to acknowledge the depth of Torah. In the words of my colleague Rabbi Raphi Mandelstam, a devoted student of Rabbi Rosensweig, "Hearing Rabbi Rosensweig deliver an extended, in-depth *shiur* [lecture], in which he ties together all the various and nuanced aspects of a *sugya* [topic] is like experiencing the revelation of Torah at Har Sinai." Anyone who studies the majestic lectures delivered by Rav Joseph B. Soloveitchik in memory of his father, can relive the "Sinai revelation" experienced by the attendees of these lectures. Many other profound Torah works, such as the *Ketzot HaHoshen* and Nahmanides' commentary on the Torah, are masterpieces which offer the opportunity for a revelation experience.[9]

In an article entitled "The Source of Faith is Faith Itself,"[10] Rav Lichtenstein beautifully articulates his *tvi'at ayin* experience:

> The greatest source of faith, however, has been the Ribbono Shel Olam Himself.... Existentially...nothing has been more

8. Maimonides calls this "recognition of the crown of Torah" (*Hilkhot Issurei Biah* 21:32). The ignorant Jew, writes Maimonides, is not acquainted with the crown of Torah. One of the most important goals of a Jewish education is for students to acquire an appreciation of the crown of Torah.
9. An English-language opportunity to gain entry into the highest level of Talmud study is Rabbi Daniel Mann's *A Glimpse of Greatness: A Study in the Works of Giants of Lomdus* [halakhic analysis] (Jerusalem: Eretz Hemdah Institute for Advanced Jewish Studies, 2013).
10. *Jewish Action*, fall 1992. This essay was republished in April 2015 (https://www.ou.org/jewish_action/04/2015/the-source-of-faith-is-faith-itself/).

> authentic than the encounter with *Avinu Malkeinu* [our Father, our King], the source and ground of all being. Nothing more sustaining, nothing more strengthening, nothing more vivifying. Encounter, of course, has been varied. In part it has been channeled – primarily through Torah study, but also through prayer and the performance of the commandments; or if you will, by the halakhic regimen in its totality. In part, it has been random – moments of illumination while getting on a crowded bus or watching children play in a park at twilight. Obviously, it has also been greatly varied in intensity. In its totality, however, whatever the form and content, it has been the ultimate basis of spiritual life.[11]

Nonetheless, despite the superiority of *tvi'at ayin* as a way of recognizing Hashem and His Torah, when it comes to responding to the skeptic the Gemara engages in identification by *simanim*. Moreover, *simanim* can also serve to deepen and broaden the belief of those who intuitively recognize Hashem and the divine origin of the Torah.[12] As Rav Soloveitchik concludes: "Recognition of God is an art in itself. It is a double one: by *simanim* and by *tvi'at ayin*."[13]

---

11. In this essay Rav Lichtenstein writes how his teachers serve as a great inspiration for his belief in Hashem and Torah. As a student of Rav Lichtenstein, I find it difficult to express the depth of the impact he has had upon me and undoubtedly upon thousands of others in bolstering our faith. Rav Lichtenstein was a role model and pillar of faith for those who had the privilege to sit in his shadow. The depth of Rav Lichtenstein's commitment and spirituality was breathtaking. Most of all, the fact that this great man emerged from Harvard University as a spiritual luminary who was thoroughly devoted to Torah serves as an inspiration for anyone who doubts the authenticity of Hashem and our Torah. Since Rav Lichtenstein, a man with such brilliance, vast Torah and secular knowledge, integrity, dignity, kindness and morality, believed, it must be true.
12. Hullin 60b.
13. Rabbi Dr. Walter Wurzburger, a leading student of Rav Soloveitchik, presents a full, eloquent, and moving articulation of *tvi'at ayin* in his work *God is Proof Enough* (see note 6). A briefer but very compelling presentation of *emuna* generated by *tvi'at ayin* is Rav Aharon Lichtenstein's beautiful essay "The Source of Faith is Faith Itself" (see note 10). Rav Lichtenstein was another leading student of Rav Soloveitchik.

The Purpose of this Book: *Simanim* to Bolster the *Tvi'at Ayin*

It has been very gratifying to hear from many believing Jews, even many practicing rabbis, who enjoyed my writings on *emuna* because they helped strengthen their faith in Hashem and Torah.[14] These are people who already recognize the divine truth with a *tvi'at ayin* recognition; adding *simanim* served to concretize and enrich their appreciation.

An example from our writings will help illustrate this point. God-conscious individuals find it intuitive that God's hand was involved in Israel's establishment, the Six Day War and the Entebbe raid. One need not have a thorough knowledge of these events to arrive at this conclusion. However, a careful examination of these events, to which we devote a number of chapters in this book, strengthens and confirms the *tvi'at ayin* recognition of the miracle.

Why Some Do Not Believe: Noise Drowning Out the Subtle and Quiet Voice

Every human being is naturally inclined to believe in God. Hashem has given this capacity to everyone.[15] The *Meshekh Ḥokhma* adds that "the Jewish soul is naturally inclined with an intense desire to fulfill God's will."[16] If that is the case, then why do some who were raised in observant families and given a Jewish education choose to discard their belief and Torah observance?

I gained insight into this phenomenon while walking on a busy and loud street when my cell phone rang repeatedly. Unfortunately, I failed to hear the subtle ring of my mobile telephone. This was

14. My writings on *emuna* have been published in Torah Academy of Bergen County's weekly Torah bulletin, *Kol Torah*.

15. However, Hashem does not coerce as we said earlier, due to His desire for an authentic relationship with us.

16. The *Meshekh Ḥokhma* (Ex. 19:17) bases his assertion on the celebrated teaching of Maimonides (*Hilkhot Gerushin* 2:20) that every Jew fundamentally wishes to observe the Torah, but is swayed from doing so only due to the influence of his Yeitzer Hara (pleasure drive). Maimonides's source appears to be the Gemara (Nidda 30b), which tells us that when a child is in the womb, the child is taught the entire Torah and at birth forgets it all. This teaches that Hashem implants a natural love and proclivity for Torah in every Jew.

reminiscent of an incident recorded in Tanakh (the Bible) regarding the prophet Elijah.

In I Kings 18 Elijah essentially demands that Hashem reveal Himself in an absolute and indisputable manner at Mount Carmel in an effort to motivate the Jews of Northern Israel to return to His service. Elijah goes so far as to blame Hashem, attributing the Jews' lack of faith to His failure to provide sufficient evidence of His presence.[17]

When Hashem responded and proved His existence beyond a shadow of a doubt, the Northern Jews responded "Hashem is God, Hashem is God *(Hashem Hu HaElokim, Hashem Hu HaElokim)!*"[18] Surprisingly, the Jews' newly acquired faith quickly dissipated, and Elijah retreated to Sinai in deep despair.[19] Hashem then encountered Elijah to explain that He is not made apparent in fire, earthquake or hurricane. Rather, Hashem deliberately prefers to announce Himself in a "subtle and quiet voice *(kol dmama dakka).*"

When Hashem appears in an obvious manner, the impact is fleeting because it does not involve any effort on the part of the people. As the Mishna teaches, "the reward is commensurate with the effort invested *(lefum tza'ara agra).*"[20] Therefore, He interacts with the world in an unobtrusive, natural manner in order to require us to make an effort in order to discover Him. When man invests in this quest for the Divine, this will have a more lasting effect. Hashem told Elijah that the way to bring people closer to God is not by performing overt miracles, but rather by training people to appreciate His *kol dmama dakka.*

Unfortunately, the efforts made by parents and teachers to instill this appreciation do not always bear fruit. Sometimes various noises can overpower the *kol dmama dakka* and inhibit a person's ability to connect to it, just as I did not hear my cellular phone's soft ringtone on a

17. I Kings 18:37. See Berakhot 31b for the Gemara's criticism of Elijah's demand.
18. We echo these statements on Yom Kippur because one can reach the same level of certitude regarding Hashem's existence through the intense religious experience of Yom Kippur, even without witnessing a violation of the laws of nature such as occurred on Mount Carmel.
19. See the commentary of the Malbim (Rabbi Me'ir Leibush ben Yeḥiel Mikhel Wisser [March 7, 1809 – September 18, 1879]) on I Kings 19:2.
20. Avot 5:23.

busy street. The noise may be in the form of external negative influences such as a spiritually impoverished environment that is deaf to the call of the Almighty. Internal noise pollution can also overshadow the subtle voice of Hashem. The noise may present as unrestrained passions and desires for (a misleading) independence from halakhic discipline and from God, or as lingering, unresolved psychological tensions created by various traumatic situations. Whatever the form of the noise, it can prevent Jewish souls from tuning into the call of the Divine.

The return of those who have strayed depends only on them. "Hashem is close to those who sincerely reach out to Him (*karov Hashem lekhol korav, l'chol asher yikra'uhu ve'emet*)."[21] This means that Hashem will *respond* to man, but only if man initiates the conversation. Similarly, "Hashem is good to those who yearn for Him, to the soul that seeks Him."[22] Hashem proposes, "Open for Me an opening as narrow as the eye of the needle and I will open for you gates as wide as the entrances of palaces."[23] All the articles and arguments in the world cannot convince someone to connect to Hashem and Torah unless he is willing to take the first step to eliminate the noises that create a barrier between himself and the *kol dmama dakka*.

A comparison may be made to physical exercise. Hashem has created us to love exercise due to His concern for us. Those of us who make time to exercise know that once one makes the commitment, a momentum is created and he will naturally be drawn to exercise, most likely enjoying the experience. However, one must initiate an effort if he is to reap the natural benefit of the process.

Rav Lichtenstein, in his aforementioned article about faith, writes, "The motto I inscribed in my college notebook was David's plea: *Tuv ta'am vada'at lamdeni key b'mitzvotecha he'emanti* [teach me good discernment and knowledge; for I have believed Thy commandments]. Answers, I of course continued –and continue – to seek, and have found many."[24]

21. Ps. 145:18.

22. Lam. 3:25.

23. Song of Songs Rabba 5:2.

24. "The Source of Faith is Faith Itself" (see note 10). I have inserted the translation of Ps. 119:66.

Rav Lichtenstein took the first step and constructively dealt with his questions and concerns about Torah. We can all make the same life-altering decision. We can experience and encounter God as Rav Lichtenstein did, if we are willing to invest the effort.

Is *Emuna* More Difficult in the Contemporary Era?

A contradiction exists between the Gemara, which frequently mentions *shedim* (demons), and Maimonides, who utterly denies their existence.[25] Rabbi Yaakov Kaminetzky[26] brilliantly resolves the inconsistency by citing King Solomon to the effect that "God created the one as well as the other *(zeh le'umat zeh asah Elokim),*" i.e. God creates a level playing field.[27] This means that at a time when God's presence is quite apparent, He makes a spiritual counterpart in order that we have a choice about believing in Him.[28] Hence in Talmudic times, when Hashem revealed Himself through a heavenly voice and other miracles recorded in the Gemara, Hashem also introduced the spiritual counterweight of demons to challenge us. But in the time of Maimonides such miracles had ceased, and there was no need for Hashem to introduce counterbalances such as *shedim.*[29]

Undoubtedly it was easier to sense God's presence in pre-modern times. Medicine then was primitive, and therefore one felt very vulnerable and dependent on God. With the advent of modern medicine, man does not feel as reliant on Hashem. Thus, it is not surprising that Jews in the Eastern European shtetl (village) used to cry on Yom Kippur, while most contemporary pious Jews do not. Of course in truth, man's fate was and is entirely dependent on God in all situations, but the *perception* of man's circumstances is the differentiating factor.

---

25. *Perush HaMishnayot to Avoda Zara,* Chapter 4 Mishna 7.
26. *Emet L'Yaakov,* Ex. 7:22.
27. Eccl. 7:14.
28. As we explained earlier, if we have no choice but to believe, then we cannot have a relationship with Hashem, since a relationship involves choice.
29. This is also the deeper meaning behind the encounter between R. Ashi and Menasseh (Sanhedrin 102b) in which Menasseh told R. Ashi, "Had you lived during my times, you would have run after idolatry." During an era when the presence of God was very intensely felt, the pull toward idolatry was much greater in order for the service of Hashem to be challenging and therefore meaningful.

Moreover, the temptation to sin is far greater today than only fifteen years ago. Severe violations of the Torah, with all their spiritually corrosive impacts, are accessible with one click of a computer mouse. Although such activity is self-destructive and against one's long-term interest, the short-term attraction can be intense.

Nonetheless, King Solomon's principle of "God created the one as well as the other" still resonates in our time. With the enormous spiritual challenges of modernity, there is an equal abundance of spiritual prospects. Most prominently, the thriving State of Israel presents boundless spiritual opportunities. Whereas only a century ago a visit to the Western Wall was experienced only by a privileged few among our people, today it is routine for observant Jews to connect with this very holy space many times during their lives. After years of displacement and exile to the four corners of the earth, Biblical predictions of the Jewish mass return to our homeland have begun to materialize.

Conclusion

This book is intended to enrich its readers' belief in Hashem and Torah, and to spread awareness of opportunities to gain closeness to the Almighty. However, the most effective means of promoting belief in Hashem is the behavior of observant Jews. When Orthodox Jews relate to the broader society in a peaceful, moral and productive manner, this serves as the most compelling evidence of the divine origin of the Torah. When Orthodox Judaism is identified not only with ritual observance such as Kashrut and Shabbat, but also with honesty in business, well mannered comportment in all areas of life, and contributions to humanity, belief in Hashem and His Torah are confirmed and enhanced.

Isaiah teaches that we are Hashem's witnesses[30] and that Hashem should be glorified by us.[31] This is the collective mission statement of our people, as we embrace the challenge to lead satisfying and enjoyable lives while upholding the Torah's ideals. Fulfillment of this goal will serve as the most compelling testimony that the Torah is the divine plan for the ultimate way a human being can conduct himself.

30. Is. 43:10.

31. Is. 60:21.

SIMPLE FAITH OR PERFECT FAITH? ABRAHAM'S DISCOVERY OF GOD

The Debate – Age 3 or Age 40?

The Midrash records a debate regarding the age at which Abraham recognized Hashem's existence.[32] One opinion holds that he was three years old, and another opinion claims that he was forty.[33] This dispute continues to rage among scholars of subsequent generations. Maimonides and his contemporary Rabbi Avraham ben David (Ravad), for example, debated this issue.[34]

This argument is most peculiar. Why does it matter whether Abraham discovered Hashem at age three or age forty? The Gemara dismisses such issues with the comment "what was, was *(mai dehava hava)*," i.e. it is simply not worth the time and effort to debate the past if there are no ramifications for the present or future.[35]

One may suggest, however, that these sources are essentially debating the ideal type of *emuna*. Abraham was the pioneer who discovered Hashem and led the first campaign for belief in the Almighty; thus his path to achieving awareness of the Divine should serve as a blueprint for the rest of us. Accordingly, the opinion that Abraham's epiphany occurred at age three teaches that simple and straightforward faith *(emuna pshuta)* is the ideal prototype. According to this view, the truth of Hashem's existence is so obvious that it is apparent even to a young child; any further investigation is therefore unnecessary and perhaps even counterproductive.

The other opinion holds that such basic *emuna* – while representing a decent foundation – is hardly the optimal form of belief in Hashem. The optimal form of belief is *emuna shlema* – full and proper *emuna* – which requires careful, thorough, mature reasoning. Only when one reaches the age of wisdom is he capable of attaining full and proper *emuna*.[36]

32. Genesis Rabba 64:4.
33. See *Kesef Mishneh* on Maimonides' *Hilkhot Avodat Kokhavim* 1:3.
34. *Hilkhot Avodat Kokhavim* 1:3.
35. Yoma 5b.
36. The talmudic sages teach that one achieves *binah* (wisdom), only at the age of 40 (Avot 5:21).

Maimonides' Compromise

Interestingly, Maimonides presents a compromise approach to this issue. Maimonides argues that Abraham began to recognize Hashem at age three but did not reach a conclusion until he was forty. Maimonides sees great value in the *emuna pshuta* of the very young child; however, *emuna* is able to fully blossom only when one reaches the age of forty and can process God's involvement in a sophisticated way.

It is most surprising that the arch-rationalist Maimonides attaches great significance to the *emuna* of a three-year-old child. One would have expected Maimonides to unreservedly embrace the opinion that Abraham arrived at his conclusion at age forty. Maimonides, however, teaches us the invaluable lesson that meaningful *emuna* is accessible to all. One need not be able to formulate well-structured and logical arguments in order to be considered a proper *ma'amin* (believer).[37]

My wife Malca is fond of explaining Hashem to young children in the following manner: When visiting a park one sees people flying kites. They hold the string at the bottom and slowly let their kites out until they are so high that the tops of the kites are no longer visible because they have ascended high into the clouds. One sees only people holding a string. How do they know that their kites remain in the sky if they are no longer visible? The answer is that they can feel the tug of the kite as it flies in the clouds; though the kites cannot be seen, they are felt. Similarly, although we cannot see Hashem, we feel the tugs implying His constant presence. Rav Joseph B. Soloveitchik describes this phenomenon as "the metaphysical pull" that Hashem implants in all of us allowing us to connect with Him.[38]

The Gemara specifies that young children who comprehend that their blessings are directed to Hashem may be counted towards a *zimmun,* the required number for saying grace in company.[39]

37. This, in part, is the lesson of the sages when they teach (see *Ein Ya'akov* on *Berakhot* 63a) that even a thief calls out to Hashem right before he engages in theft. The natural connection to Hashem emerges in stressful situations; as people are wont to say, there are no atheists in foxholes.
38. Soloveitchik, *Abraham's Journey*, 42.
39. *Berakhot* 48a.

Rav Ovadiah Yosef similarly rules that Sephardic Jews[40] may count a child from the age of six as the third or tenth person for a *zimmun*[41]. To illustrate this point, the Gemara tells a charming and instructive story: When the great Abaye and Rava were children they met Rabba, who asked them to whom we recite blessings. Rava responded: "To the All-Merciful One." Rabba then asked where the All-Merciful One is, and Rava pointed to the ceiling. Abaye went outside[42] and pointed upwards.[43]

When learning this passage in the Morasha Kollel in the summer of 1978, our Rebbe, Rabbi Yitzchok Cohen, conducted this experiment on his very young son Yaakov, then age three, to see if he knew to whom he recites blessings. Yaakov pointed to the ceiling. In my experience, even children with significant developmental disabilities can grasp the role of Hashem in their lives at a very young age.

What If One Does Not Feel the Tug?

What about those who claim that they cannot feel the tug or experience the metaphysical pull? Referring to the analogy between our relationship with Hashem and the husband-wife relationship, we may cite a story related by Rabbi Ben Tzion Shafier: a student once told him that he did not find his wife attractive. Rabbi Shafier thought this strange in the light of a talmudic passage which categorically states, "Husbands find their wives attractive and charming *(ḥen isha al ba'alah)*"[44] – Hashem ensures that husbands find their wives attractive. Upon exploring further, Rabbi Shafier discovered that the husband had gotten into the destructive habit of looking at pornography. This ugly psychological baggage had polluted his soul and inhibited his appreciation for his wife, the great gift Hashem had bestowed upon him.

40. *Yeḥave Da'at* 4:13.
41. Ashkenazic practice does not allow a pre-Bar Mitzva child to count towards a *zimmun*.
42. Echoing Genesis 15:5, where Hashem instructs Abraham to go outside and gaze at the stars.
43. Rabba predicted that these two children would grow up to be rabbis. This childhood dispute was a foretaste of the many that Abaye and Rava would have as adults.
44. Sota 47a.

Similarly, Hashem has instilled within us a natural inclination to connect with Him.[45] As King David writes, "As the hart pants after the water brooks, so my soul pants after You, O God. My soul thirsts for God."[46] But poor habits and exposure to negative influences create a barrier that clogs the natural feelings that should exist. Psychological challenges such as an abusive experience with a parent or religious figure may also disable the natural attraction one should feel for Hashem.

King David writes: "Who can scale the mountain of Hashem.... One with clean hands...who has not taken My Name in vain."[47] One who has sullied his soul will find it difficult to scale the mountain of God. Proper spiritual and even psychological guidance is likely to be necessary to remove the grime obstructing his spiritual portals to Hashem.

Unfortunately for those with significant exposure to secular society, their personality and thought patterns may be influenced or even formed by television programs and advertisements, lyrics of popular songs, and the behavior of unfitting role models.[48] This poison needs to be removed from the soul in order to form a proper relationship with Hashem. This is similar to the experience of Abraham, who was able to receive prophecy only after he separated from Lot. Similarly, Maimonides writes of the spiritual negativity that surrounded Abraham before he fully recognized Hashem. Such influences might explain the long delay from age three until age forty when Abraham finally achieved complete recognition of the Master of the Universe.[49]

---

45. Rav Soloveitchik writes: "There is a natural desire, a natural yearning in every human being, Jew and gentile alike, who were all created in the image of God, to come as close as possible to the Master of the Universe." Rav Soloveitchik cites the *Tanya, (Likkutei Amarim* chapters 12, 19 and 38) which calls this drive "*ahava tivit*," the natural love for God (Soloveitchik, *Abraham's Journey,* 59).
46. Ps. 42:1-2.
47. Ps. 24:3-4.
48. Cf. Ḥagiga 15b, which attributes Elisha b. Abuya's downfall to his being steeped in Greek culture.
49. Rashi (Genesis 13:14) states that "as long as the wicked one was with Abraham, Hashem separated from him." Rav Soloveitchik writes that there are those who "repress the drive for God or are not cognizant of it due to the environment or friends who smother the still, small voice of the human personality" (Soloveitchik, *Abraham's Journey,* 59).

A Third Opinion: Abraham discovered Hashem at age 48.

Finally, we need to analyze a third opinion presented in the aforementioned Midrash – that Abraham recognized Hashem only at the age of forty-eight. One might reasonably ask what would have prompted Abraham to recognize God specifically at age forty-eight. The choice of this age seems arbitrary and without a basis in the *Ḥumash* (Pentateuch).

However, Rashi (Genesis 19:20) states that Abraham was forty-eight years old during the episode of the Tower of Babel." In other words, Abraham's transformation resulted from his witnessing, or at least hearing about, Hashem's dramatic disruption of the construction of the tower of Babel. Hearing of this astounding miracle radically changed Abraham and drew him closer to Hashem.[50]

Why did not many more people react in the same manner?[51] Perhaps there were indeed many who shared Abraham's reaction, and these are the people whom Abraham and Sarah deeply impacted in Charan.[52]

Alternatively, one may answer that it is hardly surprising Abraham acted alone. The Zohar *(Parashat Yitro* s.v. *Vayishma Yitro)* teaches that the entire world heard about the great miracles of Egypt and the revelation at Sinai, yet Yitro was the only non-Jew who joined the Jewish people as a result. For everyone else, life went on as usual.

In our times, how many people became religious as a result of the miracles of the 1948 and 1967 Arab wars against Israel? These were undoubtedly miraculous events, acknowledged as such even by many non-observant Jews. As recently as the summer of 2014, when hundreds of rockets fell on Israel and caused relatively little damage, how many changed their lives dramatically after witnessing this incredible manifestation of divine intervention?

Do Not Bother Me with Inconvenient Facts

Most individuals are not interested in hearing facts that make them uncomfortable, especially if they encourage a radical change in routine

50. http://www.tanach.org/breishit/noach/shiur1.htm.
51. Torah Academy of Bergen County student Tani Greengart posed this question.
52. Rashi (Genesis 12:5).

and belief. The Midrash[53] presents a remarkable dialogue between Nimrod and Abraham that epitomizes the phenomenon of people flippantly dismissing an inconvenient reality.

When Nimrod ordered Abraham to worship fire, Abraham asked, "Why not worship water which extinguishes fire?" Nimrod then ordered Abraham to worship water; Abraham replied, "Why not worship the clouds from which water comes?" Nimrod ordered Abraham to worship the clouds: Abraham replied, "Why not worship wind which moves the clouds?" Nimrod ordered him to worship the wind and Abraham then asked, "Why not worship man who can withstand the wind?" Nimrod, realizing that Abraham had proven that worshipping fire was senseless, responded, "You are playing word-games with me." Even after witnessing Abraham's miraculous survival in the fire, Nimrod does not change his way of life, as demonstrated by his throwing Abraham's brother Haran into the fire for expressing support for his brother's stance.

Abraham is characterized by intellectual honesty, flexibility, and courage to act on the truth. Nimrod simply dismissed the inconvenient fact which Abraham soundly demonstrated and faithfully upheld. Such is the intellectual ignorance of those like Nimrod who lack the courage to face and live up to the truth. Others produce incredibly far-fetched answers to escape the "inconvenience" of living a Torah life. For such people, demonstrating the truth is insufficient; they must also be shown and taught how the Torah is a divine recipe for leading the most spiritually and psychologically compelling life possible.

Haran as a Bad Example

The aforementioned Midrash records that Haran was watching this episode unfold and was unsure of whom to support – his brother or Nimrod. He decided that if Abraham emerged unscathed, he would tell Nimrod that he supported Abraham. If Abraham died, he would support Nimrod. Abraham was thrown into the furnace and came out unharmed. When Nimrod demanded that Haran pledge his allegiance, he said that he supported his brother. They threw Haran into the furnace, and he was burned to death.

53. Genesis Rabba 38:13.

Why did Hashem not save Haran, as He had saved Abraham minutes before from Nimrod's fire? After all, Haran did express his support for Abraham. The answer is that Haran hardly deserved a miracle due to the shallow nature of his commitment, which was immediately preceded by an expression of agnosticism. Hashem expects unwavering commitment, just as a spouse demands and deserves unconditional loyalty, not one born simply of crass opportunism.

In a case where one genuinely wonders if the Torah is true, we can consider the Jewish version of "Pascal's wager." According to this calculation, one reasons that if the Torah is true, he will receive considerable punishment in the afterlife if he fails to observe its statutes. Since there is no considerable downside to observance – the Torah way of life is meaningful and enjoyable – he chooses to act as if he believes, because the risk of punishment if he does *not* believe outweighs the possible advantages of believing otherwise.

We could argue that one who lives an Orthodox life due to this calculation is better off than one who does not observe Torah at all. After all, we believe in the potential of *mitokh shelo lishmah ba lishmah* (by doing something from impure motives one may come to do it from pure motives). If a person observes the Torah with flawed motives, this may eventually lead to his or his child's observance of the Torah for noble motives.

Nonetheless, Haran's tragic death sounds a jolting alarm for those who observe Torah out of doubt. Such an attitude did not save Haran from Nimrod's fire and may not motivate children, who will inevitably notice their parents' shallow commitment, to live observant lives as adults.

A healthy connection with a spouse cannot emerge when one marries due to a "Pascal's wager" reckoning. So too, a healthy and life-affirming relationship with Hashem is possible only when one is fully committed.

As Elijah said on Mount Carmel:[54] "How long will you go limping between two opinions? If the Lord is God, follow Him: but if Ba'al, then follow him." Elijah suggests that it may be preferable to worship

54. I Kings 18:21.

idols than to serve Hashem inconsistently. There is abundant reasoning to support a full commitment to observance of the commandments. A Torah life lived in doubt will ultimately fail, as did Haran's brand of vacillating spiritual commitment.[55]

Conclusion

Abraham set a powerful example by boldly following the truth and unconditionally committing to Hashem's command. *Ḥazal* (our sages)[56] say that "the acts of the fathers are a sign for the children (*ma'aseh avot siman labanim*),"[57] which means that we are both blessed with the ability and charged with the responsibility to follow the undiluted faith of our forefathers. This is the only assurance for a spiritually satisfying life.

SIMPLE FAITH

Simple Faith and Conventional Faith

Simple faith *(emuna pshuta)* must be carefully distinguished from the faith of someone who keeps the commandments "simply" out of convention, because he was raised that way.

Someone who keeps the commandments out of convention is the reverse image of what Maimonides called "a child taken captive by gentiles *(tinok shenishba bein hagoyim)*," i.e. a person who was captured and raised in a non-Jewish environment. Such a person is a victim of circumstances beyond his control, and therefore we do not condemn him harshly for his failure to adhere to traditional Jewish belief.[58]

If we do not make an effort to deepen our belief in Hashem and the divine origin of the Torah, we are creating a "reverse *tinok shenishba*" scenario.[59] The *tinok shenishba* is pardoned because he is merely a product

55. Nahmanides comments on Deut. 6:16 (in regards to the prohibition against testing Hashem): "It is improper to serve Hashem in a manner of doubt."

56. This term, an acronym for *hakhamenu zikhronam livrakha* (our sages of blessed memory) refers specifically to the Jewish sages of mishnaic and talmudic times.

57. This is the idea that our forefathers set the standard of behavior for future generations (Nahmanides on Gen. 12:6).

58. *Hilkhot Mamrim* 3:3.

59. This remark was made by Maurice Rabbenou, an alumnus of Torah Academy of Bergen County.

of his surroundings and is thus not entirely "responsible" for his actions. But by the same token, the person who believes and observes the commandment simply out of conformity to his social environment does not receive much credit for his actions. In order to make our actions meaningful and to avoid the situation of a "reverse *tinok shenishba*," it is highly worthwhile to invest the time to enhance and deepen one's *emuna*.

In contrast, one who finds belief in Hashem and other traditional Torah beliefs to be intuitive and obvious *(emuna pshuta)* is *not* a "reverse *tinok shenishba*." He or she readily and intuitively perceives the Light of Torah that draws us near to Hashem.[60] For such a person, every prayer and every encounter with Torah further deepens his or her faith without the need for the discussions in this book.

Strengthening *Emuna*

Nevertheless, even a person of *emuna pshuta*, simple faith, can benefit from thinking about matters of faith.

Many Torah educators throughout the ages have not discussed *emuna* with their students. Perhaps they feel that through serious study of Torah, their students will be exposed to its inherent majesty and independently arrive at the conclusion that the Torah is a divine document. And for some this is certainly true. I personally, from a young age, found it intuitive that the Torah is a divine document and understood that our history is so unusual that it must be guided by God's hand. In high school I studied two Shakespeare plays, *Hamlet* and *Macbeth*. I found them enthralling, magnificent, and far superior to any other secular literature I had ever encountered. But I recognized even then that while these were outstanding works, they paled in comparison to the Torah's depth, manifold interpretations, and continued relevance. It was obvious to me that while Shakespeare may represent the pinnacle of human achievement, the Torah is unparalleled because it is the product of a divine author.[61]

60. *Petiḥa* to Lamentations Rabba 1:2.
61. This experience is reminiscent of a Gemara passage (Berakhot 19b), which encourages taking the opportunity to see non-Jewish kings, for if one merits he will be able to distinguish between Jewish and non-Jewish kings.

However, an insight from the Book of Exodus supports delving into matters of *emuna.* The Book of Exodus records that after the splitting of the Red Sea we proclaimed our belief in God and Moses.[62] Now, it is clear that we trusted in Hashem even prior to the splitting of the Red Sea, as the Torah explicitly states that we believed in God and Moses much earlier in the Exodus process.[63] Thus it seems that Ex. 14:31 does not mean that *only* after the splitting of the Red Sea we believed in Hashem; rather, it means that our faith was enhanced and deepened as a result of that intense experience. Perhaps one of the reasons we recite this verse in our daily prayers is so that by reminding ourselves of this event we can once again enhance our faith and thereby deepen our commitment to meticulous Torah observance.

Maimonides writes that the commandment is to "know" that God exists.[64] One can know that God exists and that the Torah is a divine document based on rational arguments such as those we are setting forth in this book. One does not require a "leap of faith" to believe in the Torah; [65] reasonable arguments can lead one to know that Hashem revealed the Torah to our ancestors at Sinai.

Aviad Shely, a Torah Academy of Bergen County student and a voracious and insightful reader of fine literature, told me that he concluded that the Torah is a divine document based on the profundity of the *Humash* (Pentateuch): how else could every single story in a book written thousands of years ago yield such a rich and wide variety of interpretations with manifold and profound life lessons that are as relevant today as they were at the time they were written.

62. Ex. 14:31.

63. Ex. 4:31.

64. *Hilkhot Yesodei HaTorah* 1:1.

65. Rabbi Yehuda Amital noted that Judaism does not require us to believe in anything illogical. This is an application of the principle of *deracheha darchei noam* (the ways of the Torah are pleasant) (Prov. 3:17). Rav Amital believes that just as the Gemara (Sukka 32b) applies this verse to teach us that the Torah does not require us to take a stinging plant as part of the "four kinds" of Sukkot, so too the Torah does not force us to believe something which violates the laws of logic, the intellectual equivalent of a stinging plant. One may add that for this reason the Torah does not obligate us to believe in anything that contradicts a scientifically proven fact, as seen in Maimonides' *Guide to the Perplexed* (2:25), *The Kuzari* (1:67), Nahmanides (Gen. 9:12) and our chapters on Torah and science.

A Remedy for Shallow *Emuna*

Rashi surprisingly describes Noah's *emuna* as shallow.[66] He observes that even Noah did not enter the ark until the floodwaters overwhelmed him. The Steipler Gaon explains that although Noah believed in Hashem, he did not believe in the truth of Hashem's word on the same level as he believed in the reality of the mundane world.[67] Proper belief is when one trusts in Hashem and His Torah with the same conviction as he believes, for example, that the sun and the moon exist.

The Steipler Gaon explains that this is the essential lesson of the deathbed advice offered by Rabban Yoḥanan ben Zakai: "One's fear of Hashem should be the same as his fear of man."[68] The existence of Hashem and the truth of His Torah should be just as obvious as the existence of other people. Otherwise, one's *emuna* is shallow, and the resulting level of commitment to proper Torah observance is limited.

Engaging students in discussions of *emuna* has the potential to transform superficial *emuna* into deep-rooted belief that results in a firm, enduring commitment to Torah observance. Rabbi Moshe Wolfson remarked that Jews have *emuna* etched into their DNA just as a beaver's ability to make a dam or a bird's ability to make a nest is a part of its genetic makeup. However, given the considerable countervailing cultural forces that challenge us today, many can no longer rely only on this natural, intuitive foundation of *emuna*. By presenting healthy-minded Jews with the rational basis of Judaism, we can help to bolster their *emuna* during spiritually turbulent times.

Bava Batra 89b: To Speak or Not to Speak

Some will argue that it is better not to examine issues of *emuna* with students and young people because it may cause those who already believe – or at least have not questioned our core beliefs – to challenge those principles.

This concern is reminiscent of a dilemma recorded by Ḥazal: Honesty in weights and measures is forcefully commanded by the

---

66. Gen. 7:7.
67 Rabbi Yaakov Yisrael Kanievsky (the Steipler Gaon), *Birkat Peretz* on *Parashat Noaḥ*.
68. Berakhot 28b.

Torah and should be strictly enforced by the authorities in a Torah community. Ḥazal were aware of all the tricks a swindling merchant might do to deceive his customers, such as using metal weights worn out with use and employing heavy sticks to smooth out measured flour to the disadvantage of the buyer. R. Yoḥanan ben Zakkai agonized over whether or not to make this information public: "*Oi li im omar oi li im lo omar* (Woe to me if I speak, woe to me if I do not speak)."[69] If he reveals these strategies, there is a danger that swindlers will learn from him how to fool their unknowing customers. If he refrains, his silence may be interpreted as an indication that the sages are unaware of their tricks. R. Yoḥanan ben Zakkai finally resolved his dilemma in favor of revealing on the basis of Hosea: "for the ways of the Lord are right, and the just do walk in them: but the transgressors shall stumble in them.'"[70] The ways of Hashem must be made known to all, and it is up to the free will of man to utilize the information for good or for evil.

Will there be those who will react to discussions of *emuna* with contrived and unreasonable responses that employ tortured logic? Unfortunately, the answer may be yes. Measures should be taken to manage this concern properly, such as presenting the issues in an interactive yet intimate setting. Caution should be exercised, but this concern should not deprive the vast majority of Orthodox Jews of the benefit they will derive from an effective, well-presented, rational explanation of the basis for Torah living.

Conclusion – Mainstream Orthodox Education for *Emuna*

Discussions of the rational basis for belief in Hashem and the divine origin of the Torah have, generally speaking, been confined to Jews who engage in outreach to non-observant Jews. However, it is appropriate for rabbis, educators, and parents throughout the Orthodox community to discuss these matters occasionally with observant Jews. The risk of *refraining* from addressing the rational basis of our faith, in the hope that it will somehow be inculcated naturally, is readily apparent. Shallow or lapsed commitment is, regrettably, not a rare occurrence in

69. Bava Batra 89b.
70. Hos. 14:10.

all segments of the Orthodox community. Since the evidence for the existence of Hashem and the divine origin of the Torah is accessible and readily understood, it behooves every Jew who is concerned about preserving our national legacy to devote some time to strengthening his *emuna* and that of his fellow Jews. Even if one prefers to engage in substantive Torah study in lieu of mere discussion *about* the Torah, it is vital for us all to be able to articulate to ourselves, to those around us, and to the succeeding generations of our people, a rational basis for our faith and practices.

It is important to stress again that there are many portals to *emuna*. This book contains the arguments and sources that satisfy this author, but may not necessarily address all concerns. One who is not satisfied by the evidence we present should consult other rabbis, teachers, and texts that can provide alternative directions.[71]

71. A good source of essays and presentations on *emuna* appear online at www.simpletoremember.com. Rabbi Lawrence Keleman's *Permission to Believe* (Southfield, Michigan: Targum Press, 1990) and *Permission to Receive* (Southfield, Michigan: Targum Press, 1996) are good resources as well.

Chapter 2

The Rational Basis for Belief

FIVE RATIONAL PORTALS TO BELIEF IN HASHEM AND THE DIVINE ORIGIN OF THE TORAH

Introduction

It is important to clarify that we do not seek to "prove" Hashem's existence, because this is not a productive exercise.

Rav Soloveitchik recalls the Danish philosopher Søren Kierkegaard's reaction upon hearing that the medieval philosopher Anselm of Canterbury spent an entire evening in prayer beseeching God to help him formulate his celebrated "ontological proof" of God's existence. Kierkegaard asked rhetorically whether a bride in the embrace of her beloved bridegroom requires proof of his existence. Kierkegaard argued that Anselm's intense prayer constituted a more authentic "proof" of God than Anselm's ontological thesis.[1]

Moreover, modern philosophers – such as Descartes and Kant – have demonstrated that one can prove very little, if anything. Although we cannot prove that other people exist; nevertheless, I am one hundred

1. Joseph B. Soloveitchik, *The Lonely Man of Faith* (Northvale, New Jersey: Jason Aronson, 1997), 54.

percent convinced of their existence. Similarly, I am thoroughly convinced of the truth of Hashem and His Torah. Moreover, I believe that denying the existence of God and the divine origin of the Torah is as unreasonable and irrational as denying that other people exist.

As a philosophy major who completed graduate study of Jewish philosophy, I deeply respect philosophic discourse. However, one cannot utilize philosophic reasoning to arrive at the most important decisions in life, such as choosing a spouse, a career, a community, a physician or a financial investment. Instead, one uses intuition, common sense and experience to make sound decisions. It is therefore unreasonable to abandon intuition, common sense, and experience when considering the most important decision of all – whether to believe in Hashem and His Torah. In our discussion, we will be using these essential tools of life – intuition, common sense, and experience – rather than the tools of pure theory and philosophical discourse, to arrive at a reasonable decision regarding Hashem and His Torah.

We will point here to five rational "portals" to belief in Hashem and the divine origin of the Torah: argument from design and anthropic principle, the tradition, Jewish history, halakha and fulfilled prophecies.

Portal #1: Argument from Design, Anthropic Principle, Nature as Source of Love of Hashem

Rabbi Elchanan Wasserman[2] states that it is obvious that there is a God given the high degree of order in this world. Common sense teaches that it would be impossible for this to happen spontaneously! Regarding an exquisite painting, it would be absurd to say that it was created by a long series of fortunate coincidences. It is just as ludicrous to say that something as intricate and accurate as the human eye came about without a Creator. Philosophers have traditionally referred to this type of proof as the argument from design. Many earlier authorities, such as Rabbeinu Baḥya, also espoused this argument for Hashem's existence.[3]

---

2. *Kovetz Ma'amarim*, pp. 11-20.
3. *Ḥovot HaLevavot* (introduction to *Sha'ar HaBeḥina*) states: "Reflection on the wisdom evident in God's creations is the most accessible way of verifying His existence."

Rabbi Wasserman takes this argument one step further, claiming that it is also obvious that the Creator would provide a manual on how to function best in the world He created. Just as a car manufacturer provides a manual on how to operate the car it has designed, common sense tells us that Hashem would provide a manual – called the Torah – telling all human beings (both Jews and non-Jews) how to act and excel in His world.

Dr. Nathan Aviezer, in his important work *Fossils and Faith: Understanding Torah and Science*, summarizes and defends what is known as the anthropic principle.[4] He writes:

> It has become clear to many scientists that the universe appears as if it were specifically designed for the existence and well-being of man. This phenomenon, which has attracted considerable scientific attention, is known as the anthropic principle. The anthropic principle expresses itself in two ways: 1) very slight changes in the laws of nature would have made it impossible for life to exist, and 2) human life would not have been possible were it not for the occurrence in the past of a large number of highly improbable events.

The Midrash (Temura 5) attributes a similar idea to R. Akiva (translation from www.chabad.org): "A heathen once came to Rabbi Akiba, and asked him, 'Who created the world?' 'G-d created the world,' Rabbi Akiba replied. 'Prove it to me,' persisted the heathen. 'Come back tomorrow,' Rabbi Akiba told him. The following day the heathen came back, and Rabbi Akiba engaged him in conversation. 'What are you wearing?' Rabbi Akiba asked him. 'A cloak, as you see.' 'Who made it?' Rabbi Akiba asked. 'The weaver, of course.' 'I don't believe it; prove it to me!' Rabbi Akiba persisted. 'What proof do you want? Cannot you see that the weaver has made the cloth?' 'Then why do you ask for proof that G-d created the world? Cannot you see that the Holy One blessed be He created it.' And to his disciples Rabbi Akiba added, 'My children, just as the house is proof of the builder, and the cloth is proof of the weaver, and the door is proof of the joiner, so this world proclaims that G-d created it.'"

The Book of Psalms is replete with references to Creation as evidence of God's wisdom. Examples include 104:24 "O Lord, how manifold are Your works! In wisdom have You made them all," and 19:2 "The heavens declare the glory of God; and the firmament proclaims His handiwork."

4. Nathan Aviezer, *Fossils and Faith: Understanding Torah and Science* (Hoboken: KTAV Publishing House, Inc, 2001), 21. This chapter is also available online at http://www.simpletoremember.com/articles/a/anthropic-principle/.

The first example Dr. Aviezer cites is the potency of the sun.[5]

> If the nuclear force were only a *few percent* weaker…there would be no solar fuel. As a result, the sun would not shine, but would merely be a cold ball of inert protons, precluding the possibility of life on earth. If the nuclear force were only a *few percent* stronger…the sun would explode, once again precluding the possibility of life on earth. It is an extraordinary fact that the strength of the nuclear force *just happens* to lie in the narrow range in which neither of these two catastrophes occurs…providing the warmth and light that are vital for life to exist on earth.

Dr. Aviezer's second example is the existence of water and air on earth.[6]

> It was recently discovered that, shortly after they were formed, all three planets (Earth, Venus and Mars) had large amounts of surface water. The deep channels that are observed today on the surface of Mars were carved out long ago by the copious fast-flowing Martian primordial surface waters. Similarly, Venus was once covered by deep oceans that contained the equivalent of a layer of water three kilometers deep over its entire surface. However, in the course of time, all surface waters on Mars and Venus disappeared. How did the Earth escape this catastrophe?
>
> The answer is that the Earth escaped this catastrophe by sheer "accident"! The Earth just happens to be sufficiently distant from the sun that our surface water neither evaporated nor decomposed, as happened on Venus. Moreover, the Earth just happens to be sufficiently close to the sun that the temperature remains high enough to prevent the oceans from freezing permanently, as happened on Mars. Therefore, the Earth alone, among the planets of the solar system, is capable of supporting life.

---

5. Ibid., 24.
6. Ibid., 24-25.

> Similar remarks apply to the atmosphere. Studies have shown that the planetary atmosphere is controlled by a very delicate balance involving the subtle interplay of many factors. This balance is so delicate that if the Earth were only slightly closer to the sun, the surface temperature would be much higher than the boiling point of water, precluding all possibility of a life-sustaining atmosphere.
>
> Similarly, if the Earth were only slightly farther from the sun, the concentration of carbon dioxide in the atmosphere would become so high that 'the atmosphere would not be breathable by human beings.' Fortunately, the Earth's orbit just happens to lie at the crucial distance from the sun that permits the formation of a life-sustaining atmosphere.

Dr. Aviezer concludes with a humorous example: if the same person won the lottery three weeks in a row, a "guiding hand" would immediately be suspected, and the individual would receive a visit from the fraud division of the police![7] Similarly, the string of highly improbable events that made life on Earth possible must be attributed to the guiding hand of the Almighty.[8]

Maimonides writes that an appreciation of nature can draw a person close to Hashem and inspire a person both to love Him *(ahavat Hashem)* and to stand in awe of Him *(yirat Hashem).* [9] In our generation we are given an even greater opportunity to draw close to Hashem due to the magnificent scientific discoveries of the last hundred years. One who contemplates the magnificence even of the tiny bacterium E. Coli or the intricacies of the human anatomy can profoundly enrich his *yirat*

---

7. Ibid., 34.
8. Rav David Fohrman's video presentation entitled *Seeing God in Science* is accessible at https://www.alephbeta.org/course/lecture/vaera-seeing-god-i. Rav Fohrman outlines the role of Hashem in the Big Bang, which was an enormous explosion. He notes that there was an obvious need for a Director to be meticulously coordinating these events so that everything would be calibrated perfectly. Explosions are chaotic events and could have not begun the creation of the world had Hashem not perfectly controlled the impact of the Big Bang.
9. *Hilkhot Yesodei HaTorah,* Chapter 1.

Hashem and *ahavat Hashem*. Science has the potential to inspire a deep admiration of Hashem and the magnificence of His works.[10]

Portal #2: The Tradition: Nahmanides and *The Kuzari*

For Nahmanides[11] and for Rabbi Yehuda HaLevi, author of *The Kuzari* (1:25), the most persuasive argument for faith in Torah is tradition (*mesora*). As noted in *The Kuzari*, the most extraordinary miracles associated with great events in Jewish history – the exodus from Egypt and the giving of the Torah on Mount Sinai – were witnessed by millions of people who passed this information on to their descendants year after year at their Seder table and other venues. This is unlike the miracles claimed by other religions, which allegedly occurred before a very limited number of people. It is important to emphasize that we are the only religion to believe in a mass revelation that has been passed down in an unbroken chain from generation to generation. Indeed, most Jews today are the biological descendants of the people who experienced the mass revelation.

The Jews who accepted the Torah were not a docile and gullible people who accepted everything that Moses told them at face value because of his seductive and persuasive oratory. On the contrary, they constantly bickered with and disobeyed Moses, who was a very poor speaker.[12] Virtually the only time we were unified was at Mount Sinai,[13] because the authenticity of the Sinai experience itself was profoundly compelling and unquestionably persuasive.

Similarly, we find in every generation that observant Jews are not passively trusting people who accept what they are told. Every significant

10. Dr. Harry Lieman, an Orthodox Jew who is a renowned fertility specialist, described in a lecture at Torah Academy of Bergen County the very large number of potential problems a couple might encounter in their quest to have a child. He noted with great wonder that nevertheless, eighty five percent of couples are able to produce a child in a year or less of attempting to do so. He noted this as an example of that which is proclaimed in Psalms 104:24: "O Lord, how manifold are Your works! In wisdom have you made them all."

11. Ex. 13:16.

12. Ex. 4:10, 6:12 and 6:30. *Drashot HaRan* (number 3) explains that Moses' speech impediment makes it clear that we accepted Moses' message due to the substance of his message, not to his eloquence.

13. Rashi on Ex. 19:2.

talmudic and halachic issue is carefully examined by both experts and laymen who rigorously analyze every new and old opinion. Despite these many disputes, observant Jews agree upon core values and beliefs such as the divine authorship of the Torah. Maimonides[14] states that if there is no dispute regarding a particular law, then this law must originate as a tradition from Sinai. Examples of such laws are the halakha that our tefillin must be colored black and that our mezuzot contain only the two sections of "*Shema*" and "*Vehaya im shemoa.*" If such undisputed matters were not of heavenly origin, we would surely be fighting vigorously about these laws in the manner we do about so many other halakhot.[15]

A contentious people that believes in mass revelation

The Israeli novelist Amos Oz noted:[16]

> Judaism and Israel have always cultivated a culture of doubt and argument, an open-ended game of interpretations, counter-interpretations, reinterpretations, opposing interpretations. From the beginning of the existence of Jewish civilization, it was recognized by its argumentativeness.

Shimon Peres, Israel's former president, told an interviewer while still in office that "the greatest Jewish contribution to the world is

14. *Hilkhot Mamrim* 1:3.
15. This might be the reason why the *Sefer HaḤinukh* (Mitzva 21) rules that women are included in the mitzva of recounting the story of our exodus from Egypt *(sippur yetziat mitzrayim),* even though it is a positive and time bound mitzva (from which women are normally excused). The essence of *sippur yetziat mitzrayim* is the transmittal of faith from one generation to another. Women are thus certainly included in this mitzva. This also explains why grandparents play such an important role at the Passover Seder (see *Oznayim LaTorah* on Ex. 10:2). Torah Academy of Bergen County graduate Josh Strobel uses a similar argument to explain Nahmanides' opinion (Kiddushin 34a) that women are obligated to count the *omer,* despite the fact that it is a positive and time bound mitzva. Josh notes that the counting of the *omer* serves as the link between the Exodus story and the Sinai revelation, the two pillars of our *emuna* (see Torah Academy of Bergen County, *Bikkurei Sukka,* Section 60).
16. Quoted in Dan Senor and Saul Singer, *Start-Up Nation: The Story of Israel's Economic Miracle* (Toronto: McClelland & Stewart, 2011), 51.

dissatisfaction," which he said "is bad for the country's leaders, but very good for science and progress."[17] Nearly every page of Gemara is filled with arguments. In the centuries after the finalization of the Talmud, the disputes persist with great vigor. Maimonides' code and the *Shulḥan Arukh* were surrounded by controversy. Excellent lectures and high-level yeshivas are distinguished by intense debate and argument. The Gemara[18] relates how R. Yoḥanan experienced severe depression after the death of Resh Lakish because his students did not challenge him. R. Yoḥanan deeply missed Resh Lakish's persistent questioning, which had helped him to refine his Torah thoughts.

Perhaps it is for this reason Hashem chose the Jewish people – the notoriously stiff-necked nation – to serve as His witnesses.[19] If such an argumentative and contentious people confirm the veracity of the Sinai revelation despite the extensive demands it makes upon its adherents, then it most certainly is true.[20]

In addition, it is inaccurate to state that Orthodox individuals who remain steadfast in their belief in the Sinai revelation are docile and naive personalities. Nothing could be further from the truth. To experience traditional Jewish argumentativeness one must encounter the dizzying array of varieties of Orthodoxy – Sephardic, Yemenite, Ashkenazic, Ḥasidic and Modern Orthodox are only the main groups, within which there exist dozens of sub-groups. Orthodox Jews vehemently debate thousands of halakhic and philosophical issues. Even the supermarket shelves, where some kosher food items bear the certification of four different kashrut agencies, bear witness to the contentious nature of contemporary Orthodox Jewry. Yet all of the myriad subdivisions within

17. Quoted in Seth M. Siegel, *Let There be Water: Israel's Solution for a Water-Starved World* (New York: Thomas Dunne Books, St. Martin's Press, 2015), 235.
18. Bava Metzia 84a.
19. Is. 43:10.
20. This is one meaning of the surprising talmudic statement (Beitza 25b) that the Torah was given to the Jewish people "because they are fierce." The fact that such a fierce people maintain a tradition of mass revelation greatly adds to the credibility of this tradition. Hashem chose to give the Torah to such a fierce people because this quality bolsters their claim of being descendants of the nation that experienced a mass divine revelation. In the section "The Stiff-Necked People," below, we develop this idea at greater length.

Orthodoxy are united by the belief in the Sinai revelation and the other pillars of Orthodox faith.

As a nation, we are an extraordinarily intelligent people who have contributed an unparalleled proportion of Nobel Prize winners. Hashem seems to have chosen the most argumentative and brilliant people to serve as His witnesses because if such a people is convinced of revelation it must be true. The difficulty of many of the Torah's laws, such as circumcision, the sabbatical year, and pilgrimage to Jerusalem at festivals, further clinches this point. A bright and contentious nation could not have been persuaded to accept the many challenging laws of the Torah as the binding command of God had they not been thoroughly aware of its divine origins.

When Orthodox Ashkenazic, Sephardic and Yemenite Jews interact, they find that their prayers and observance of mitzvot are essentially the same; the differences are primarily stylistic. This is because each group of Jews has, incredibly, preserved the tradition with a minimum of variation. We survive as Jews only because we maintain our ancient traditions.

Portal #3: The *Arukh HaShulḥan's* Argument from Jewish History

In 1903 Rabbi Yeḥiel Michel Epstein, known as the *Arukh HaShulḥan,* wrote, "There is no greater sign and proof than our survival of nearly two thousand years of Exile. The only reason for our survival is because of Hashem's providence that is not removed from us even for a moment like a father who watches over his only child and chastises him for the latter's benefit."[21]

Indeed, one who ponders the wonders of Jewish history realizes that logically, we should have disappeared long ago. Our survival – unparalleled by any other culture – attests to the fact that Hashem watches over His special people. Indeed, the stories of the Jewish people's close encounters with extinction in the Tanakh (such as the infertility of Abraham and Sarah as well as Isaac and Rebecca, the exodus from Egypt and the parting of the Red Sea, and the deliverance from Haman) have been repeated in our time.

21. *Arukh HaShulḥan* 1:10.

The Jewish people were considered lost and finished as a nation after World War II. Yet we managed to establish the State of Israel in 1948 despite overwhelming odds. Rabbi Yehuda Amital (the head of of Yeshivat Har Etzion) often commented that future historians will likely cast grave doubts on the authenticity of the story of a downtrodden people who lost a third of their numbers within six years yet managed to reestablish their homeland by winning a war fought on multiple fronts three years later.

Similarly, one who reads Michael Oren's *Six Days of War* can only be amazed at how a desperate situation for the Jewish state turned into a stunning victory for Israel. For example, one is amazed at the irrational behavior of the Egyptians, Jordanians, and Syrians, who prematurely retreated at their respective positions of battle, thereby enabling Israel to take control over so much territory. One can only conclude, as even Moshe Dayan did at the conclusion of this war, that this is another example of Hashem sustaining His people. Similarly, Israel's emergence after the Yom Kippur War was another incredible feat. The Arab armies were primed for battle (unlike 1967), and Israel was dangerously unprepared. Despite this fact and the need to fight on two fronts, Israel emerged badly bruised, but victorious.

Mark Twain's famous words regarding the Jews help clinch the *Aruch Hashulḥan's* argument:

> If the statistics are right, the Jews constitute but one percent of the human race. It suggests a nebulous dim puff of stardust lost in the blaze of the Milky Way. Properly the Jew ought hardly to be heard of, but he is heard of, has always been heard of. He is as prominent on the planet as any other people, and his commercial importance is extravagantly out of proportion to the smallness of his bulk. His contributions to the world's list of great names in literature, science, art, music, finance, medicine, and abstruse learning are also away out of proportion to the weakness of his numbers. He has made a marvelous fight in the world, in all the ages; and has done it with his hands tied behind him. He could be vain of himself, and be excused for it. The Egyptian, the Babylonian, and the Persian rose, filled the planet with sound and splendor, then

> faded to dream-stuff and passed away; the Greek and the Roman followed, and made a vast noise, and they are gone; other peoples have sprung up and held their torch high for a time, but it burned out, and they sit in twilight now, or have vanished. The Jew saw them all, beat them all, and is now what he always was, exhibiting no decadence, no infirmities of age, no weakening of his parts, no slowing of his energies, no dulling of his alert and aggressive mind. All things are mortal, but the Jew; all other forces pass, but he remains. What is the secret of his immortality?[22]

Religious Jews understand very well that divine providence is the secret of our immortality. Indeed, Rav Yaakov Emden said in the introduction to his commentary to the Jewish Prayer book that the greatest miracle is the continued survival of the Jewish people, even greater than the miracle of the splitting of the *Yam Suf*.

Portal #4: Rav Soloveitchik's Argument from Halakha

Rav Soloveitchik writes in his classic essay, *Halakhic Man,* that the halakha is the most compelling proof for the truth of Torah: "We require neither miracles or wonders to prove the existence of God, for the halakhah itself bears witness to its Creator."[23] I understand this to mean that the scholar (or student guided by a fine teacher) who plumbs the depths of the halakhic structure will be overwhelmed with its beauty and intricacy to the point that he is left with no option other than to accept the divine origin of the system. It also might mean that one who spends a lifetime dedicated to abiding by the halakhic system will conclude that it is indeed the finest prescription for a fulfilling and rich life. He will also comprehend the recurring theme in Deuteronomy that the Torah's rules are *letov lakh* (in our best interest). Indeed, the Midrash states that it is better that we not focus our attention on Hashem but rather observe the Torah, for its light will draw people close to Hashem.[24]

---

22. Mark Twain, "Concerning The Jews," *Harper's Magazine*, March 1898, 527-535.
23. Rabbi Joseph B. Soloveitchik, *Halakhic Man* (Philadelphia: Jewish Publication Society, 1983), 85-86.
24. *Petiḥa* to Lamentations Rabba 1:2.

Only Orthodox Judaism withstands the test of time.
Many believe in the divine origin of the Torah but wish to be presented with evidence that Orthodoxy is the proper manner of Torah interpretation and practice. One answer is that truth withstands the test of time while lies do not, as stated in Proverbs: "The lip of truth shall be established forever; but a lying tongue is but for a moment."[25]

The Jewish people as a whole have passed the test of time. As Mark Twain observed, all the great empires and cultures of the past have come and gone, yet only the Jewish people remain as vigorous as they were in ancient times. Similarly, there have been many deviationist sects in Judaism since ancient times, when most of the Jews of the Northern Kingdom of Israel deviated from the Torah. After them came Sadducees, Essenes, Samaritans and Karaites. Many of these groups were powerful, large, and highly influential for very significant periods of time. However, these groups have either ceased to exist or are in their death throes.

The same pattern holds true today for non-Orthodox versions of Judaism. It is well known and documented that non-Orthodox versions of Judaism are in rapid decline (or, in the case of Reconstructionist Judaism, failing to gain significant traction). For example, the commonly-cited 2013 Pew survey of Jews in the United States revealed that among non-Orthodox Jews, the intermarriage rate is 71 percent.[26] Moreover, in a 2011 op-ed entitled "Judaism is More than '*Tikun Olam*,'"[27] Joel Alperson writes:

> Non-Orthodox Judaism is confronted by rising levels of secularism that almost always lead to assimilation – a trend that within a generation or two could render Reform and Conservative Judaism largely irrelevant in North America (and abroad as well). Non-Orthodox Jews' general discontent with and resulting departure from Jewish life, left alone, stands to bring Reform and Conservative Judaism to a state of obsolescence.... This prediction is

25. Prov. 12:19.
26. http://www.pewforum.org/2013/10/01/jewish-american-beliefs-attitudes-culture-survey/.
27. Jewish Telegraphic Agency, July 27, 2011.

> neither original nor new. From studies about very high interfaith marriage rates to growing assimilation percentages, we should know by now that the non-Orthodox way of life is failing by just about every metric we have at our disposal. [28]

By contrast, Orthodox communities are vigorous, vibrant and rapidly expanding. This is entirely counterintuitive! One would think the less demanding versions of Judaism, which are more in harmony with contemporary values, would thrive at the expense of the traditional, less flexible principles of Orthodoxy. Yet it is specifically the *most* demanding and *most* traditional version that is the paradigm of successful Judaism in the twenty-first century. Indeed, the enduring version of Judaism is the authentic form of Judaism. In the 1950's, sociologists in both the U.S. and Israel predicted that Orthodox Judaism would soon disappear. But today there are more than two million Orthodox Jews worldwide. They are the only Jewish religious group that is increasing in numbers.[29]

In Israel the adherents of ideologically motivated secular Zionism made enormous sacrifices and contributions to create a Jewish state. But secular Zionism has been declining for decades. The Zionists who remain steadfast in their devotion to the Jewish state are the religious Zionists. This is evidenced by reports that a disproportionate percentage of combat officers in the Israel Defense Forces are Orthodox religious Zionists, although this group constitutes only about ten percent of the population of Israel.[30] Religious Zionists also serve in

---

28. Joel Alperson is a past national campaign chair for the United Jewish Communities, who states that he is not Orthodox.
29. Rabbi Lawrence Kelemen presents rational arguments for the divine origin of the Oral Law in a video entitled *Rational Approach to the Divinity of the Oral Tradition* (https://www.youtube.com/watch?v=V4OzkVQte6g).
30. Daniel Gordis writes (*Israel: A Concise History of a Nation Reborn*; New York: Harper Collins, 2016, 391): "By 2010, though the national religious community represented no more than 10 percent of Israel's population, they made up some 25 to 30 percent of soldiers in combat units. Similarly, there had been a dramatic increase in the percentage of graduates of the officers' training course who were from the religious community; that rate had risen from a mere 2.5 percent in 1990 to 26 percent in 2008. Israel's military leadership – but also its patriotic passion – was now coming from a very different segment of society."

highly disproportionate number in the elite combat units in the IDF. In recent decades the influence of secular Zionist ideals on Israeli youth has waned steadily, whereas religious Zionist commitment is stronger than ever.

A precedent for every modern phenomenon

Rav Soloveitchik's assertion is also illustrated by the incredible enterprise of applying the ancient halakha to the contemporary situation. In the last hundred years, the world in general and the Jewish people in particular have undergone a dramatic and unprecedented degree of change in all areas ranging from technology to social and political reality. Nonetheless, great halakhic authorities have readily applied the venerated concepts of the Gemara to modern circumstances.

Amazingly, halakhic decisors find a precedent in the Gemara for virtually every new phenomenon that emerges in society. The halakha is a fully functional and sophisticated system of law despite the general inability to create new rules. This is because of the miraculous existence of a model in the Bible or Gemara for every new situation that emerges.[31]

---

31. An example is Rabbi Shlomo Zalman Auerbach's (*Minḥat Shlomo* 1:10) argument for permitting the opening of a refrigerator door on Shabbat even if this causes the motor to go on earlier than it would have had the door not been opened. This widely-accepted ruling is based on the fact that opening the door will not *immediately* cause the motor to turn on. The inevitable time delay between the opening of the door and causing the motor to go on leads Rabbi Auerbach to classify this as an "indirect action (*gerama*)" or a "secondary reaction (*koaḥ sheni*)." He cites as precedent the following case discussed in the Gemara (Sanhedrin 77b): An individual ties up another in front of a powerful stream of water stopped by a dam. He opens the dam and thereby kills the victim. If the water killed the person immediately, then the perpetrator is sentenced to death because he directly (*koach rishon*) killed someone. However, if the water did not kill him immediately (i.e. there was a significant delay between the action of releasing the dam and the rushing waters killing the victim), the perpetrator is not subject to the death penalty because he has killed indirectly (*koach sheni*). Similarly, in the case of the refrigerator, after the door is opened at least a few seconds will elapse before the inflowing warm air affects the motor and causes it to go on. It is astonishing that the Gemara's discussion of such a bizarre scenario can shed light on an analogous situation that is now a routine part of our lives. This is only one example; many such analogies are presented in the four volumes of my *Gray Matter* series reviewing contemporary halakhic disputes.

For example, precedents exist in the Gemara for dealing with electricity,[32] in vitro fertilization,[33] and the situation of Jews who deviate from halakha and are psychologically incapable of grasping their error.[34] A perusal of any issue of the Israeli Torah journal *Teḥumin* and the American-based *Journal of Halacha and Contemporary Society* demonstrates halakha's applicability to the contemporary situation in the Jewish state despite the lapse of two thousand years since we had last enjoyed political independence.[35]

A comparison with the United States Constitution, an extraordinary document created by human hands, is instructive. Undoubtedly, the Constitution has succeeded far beyond the expectations of its authors; however, critics have recently noted that it does not adequately address contemporary technological and social phenomena, which could not have possibly been anticipated by its human authors. The Constitution does allow for amendments, but this is an acknowledgement that America's Founding Fathers could not have foreseen every eventuality. The fact that the Torah contains precedents for every new phenomenon leads us to the conclusion that the Torah is of divine origin and that the Talmud and its commentaries are the result of continued divine assistance. There exists no parallel in any other culture in the world. Natural occurrences as a rule are not singular; they reoccur throughout history. A unique occurrence points to a supernatural wonder.

Rabbi Hershel Schachter once observed that new challenges posed by technology and other novelties have forced talmudic scholars to refine and define areas of Torah that were not addressed in earlier

32. Sanhedrin 77b.

33. Ḥullin 70a.

34. Sanhedrin 26b.

35. It appears providential, that the nineteenth and early twentieth centuries saw the publication of several highly-regarded and authoritative halakhic works, such as the *Mishna Brura, Arukh HaShulḥan, Ben Ish Ḥai* and *Kaf HaḤaim*. These works codified and stabilizied the Halakhic system just as the technological breakthroughs of the modern era were starting. They served as the basis on which the great halakhic decisors applied the Jewish law to the wide variety of new situations brought about by the new age. The twentieth century was also blessed with some of the greatest halakhic minds in Jewish history, such as Rav Moshe Feinstein, Rav Ovadia Yosef, and Rav Shlomo Zalman Auerbach, who brilliantly applied halakha to the new realities.

generations. For example, questions of the precise definition of motherhood and paternity have been formulated, intensely debated and refined by twentieth and twenty-first century decisors due to unprecedented developments in science and technology. The developments and discoveries have enriched the Torah to an extent far beyond any reasonable expectation.

The response to biblical criticism

It is inspiring to study Tanakh using the Tanakh journal *Megadim*[36] and the *Da'at Mikra* commentary. They utilize sophisticated tools of modern literary analysis – the very same devices employed by Bible critics to denigrate Torah – to provide stunning insights into Tanakh and *Ḥazal.* A survey of every issue of *Megadim* contains breathtaking new insights into our holy Torah and *Ḥazal. Da'at Mikra* is a late twentieth-century commentary on the entire Tanakh written by Orthodox scholars who have used the tools of archaeology, geography, and knowledge of ancient Near Eastern languages to add invaluable insights to Torah knowledge. This work also responds to the claims and accusations of biblical criticism in a poignant and effective manner.[37] As Rabbi Mordekhai Breuer observes, just as the pole upon which Haman wished to hang Mordekhai was used to hang Haman, the methods that Bible critics wish to use to disparage the Torah are used to bring glory to Torah and *Ḥazal.*[38]

Rabbi Amnon Bazak wrote a superb response to biblical criticism in his landmark book *Ad HaYom HaZeh (To This Day),* an English translation of which is available online.[39] Rabbi Bazak, who is exceedingly well read both in traditional and academic Tanakh study, presents compelling arguments against the conclusions of biblical criticism. In the following paragraph Rav Bazak sums up the case that he and others have made against the "documentary hypothesis":

36. *Megadim* is published by Herzog College.

37. Many of the insights that appear in these works are repeated in the essays that appear on Rav Menachem Liebtag's website, www.tanach.org.

38. Rabbi Breuer's observation appears in an essay entitled "*Yihudo Shel Nes Purim,*" which is printed in *Esther Hi Hadassa* (Alon Shevut: Herzog College, 1997), 66.

39. The Israel Koschitzky Virtual Beit Midrash, http://etzion.org.il/en/topics/fundamental-issues-study-tanakh

However, beyond these debates, the main difficulty in the documentary hypothesis is the very notion that several sources were brought together to form a single work – not an anthology comprising several sources placed in succession, but a single, continuous text in which the various sources are intertwined so as to preserve continuity of theme, despite the disparate origins of the sources. There is no precedent for such an enormous editorial enterprise and there is no known document from the ancient world that was compiled in such a way. Why would the anonymous redactor decide to take disparate sources and to weave them into a single work? We might also note that no mention is made anywhere of the independent existence of any of these individual documents prior to their combined presence in the Torah, nor has any archaeological discovery ever been made of any of them in pristine individual form.[40]

Portal #5: Fulfilled Prophecies[41]

There are numerous examples of Torah promises that have been fulfilled. The fulfillment of these promises demonstrates that the Torah is the product of a divine author, because these predictions have been realized against all reasonable odds. A human author could never have anticipated that such unlikely situations would materialize thousands of years after they were initially recorded.

---

40. http://etzion.org.il/en/shiur-4d-duplication-and-contradiction-continued. Biblical criticism, on the basis of perceived contradictions between two accounts of the same events in Tanakh, claims that the disparate stories are products of different authors. The responses given by traditional commentators are incisive and rich. Rav Soloveitchik's magisterial work *The Lonely Man of Faith* is an outstanding example. Besides providing insights into the essence of the religious experience and human identity, this book is a cogent rebuttal to the biblical critics' approach to the differences between the Creation story presented in Gen. 1 and Gen. 2. Rav Soloveitchik also offers a brief but resounding rebuttal to the critics' approach to Ex. 3:13 and 6:3 in *The Emergence of Ethical Man* (Jersey City: Ktav Publishing House 2005), 170-171.
41. This section is an expansion of the ideas expressed by Rabbi Motti Berger and Rabbi Asher Resnick in an article entitled *The Seven Wonders of Jewish History* (http://www.aish.com/jl/h/h/48965856.html).

Eternal Israel

Earlier in this chapter, we stressed the miraculous nature of Jewish survival throughout the ages. Tanakh[42] refers to the Jewish people as "Eternal Israel *(Netzaḥ Yisrael).*" Historian Paul Johnson cogently notes in the epilogue to his work *A History of the Jews:*

> If the earliest Jews were able to survey, with us, the history of their progeny, they would find nothing surprising in it. They always knew that Jewish society was appointed to be a pilot-project for the entire human race. That Jewish dilemmas, dramas and catastrophes should be exemplary, larger than life, would seem only natural to them. That they should over the millennia attract such unparalleled, indeed inexplicable, hatred would be regrettable but only to be expected. Above all, that the Jews should still survive, when all those other ancient people were transmuted or vanished into the oubliettes of history,[43] was wholly predictable. How could it be otherwise? Providence decreed it and the Jews obeyed. [44]

---

42. I Sam. 15:29 according to some explanations; see *Da'at Mikra*. Other sources that teach the eternality of the Jewish people include Ex. 31:16, Lev. 26:44, II Sam. I 7:26, Is. 45:17 and Rashi to Gen. 15:10 and Num. 29:11.

43. In December 2014 I took three of my children to the exhibit *Assyria to Iberia at the Dawn of the Classical Age* at Manhattan's Metropolitan Museum of Art. The exhibit featured artifacts from the ancient Near East on loan from great museums throughout the world, such as the British Museum in London and the Israel Museum in Jerusalem. The artifacts were from Jewish/Israelite as well as Assyrian, Philistine, Babylonian and Phoenician cultures. While the pieces were magnificent, the most remarkable phenomenon at the museum was my family. There were no Babylonian, Phoenician or Philistine fathers bringing their children to see the exhibition of ancient artifacts from their cultures. This is because these cultures have long vanished in the sea of history. Yet when my (then) eleven-year-old daughter Atara saw an altar, she immediately identified the horns of the altar mentioned in Tanakh. The only ancient culture whose descendants exist and thrive (and attend the exhibit) are the Jews. Indeed, the Pulitzer Prize-winning author and historian Barbara Tuchman once observed that of all the peoples of the world from three thousand years ago, it is only the Jews who live in the same place, speak the same language and practice the same religion (Barbara Tuchman, "Israel: Land of Unlimited Impossibilites," in *Practicing History* [New York: Ballantine Books, 1981], p.134).

44. Paul Johnson, *A History of the Jews,* New York: Harper Collins, 2009, 629.

However, Paul Johnson concludes:

> The historian may say: there is no such thing as providence. Possibly not. But human confidence is such an historical dynamic, if it is strong and tenacious enough, is a force in itself, which pushes on the hinge of events and moves them. The Jews believed they were a special people with such unanimity and passion, and over so long a span, that they became one. They did indeed have a role because they wrote it for themselves. Therein, perhaps, lays the key to their story. [45]

The problem with saying that the realization of the Torah's predictions result from self-confidence is that it does not account for the fulfillment of the severe punishments set forth in the Torah.[46] Regrettably, we have seen the actualization of these predictions as well.[47] The Jews certainly did not want these horrors to befall them, and yet they did. Confidence cannot account for their fulfillment; only the divine will can explain it.[48]

Exile and Return

The usual course of history is for nations that are exiled from their land to assimilate within a few generations into the larger population of their new land and to lose their original identity. Nonetheless, the Torah

45. Ibid.
46. Lev. 26, Deut. 28.
47. Nahmanides (Deut. 28:42) outlines how these punishments were fulfilled during and after the destructions of the First and Second Temples. Unfortunately, the Holocaust fulfilled these predictions as well.
48. In Dr. Milton Steinberg's *As a Driven Leaf,* the classic talmudic scholar Elisha ben Abuya is portrayed as abandoning his faith largely due to his conclusion that the Jewish people had no chance of surviving the Roman onslaught. Such a conclusion was entirely rational and legitimate given the historical context. The survival of the Jewish people, clearly, is only attributable to supernatural forces. Dr. Steinberg has R. Akiva tell Elisha ben Abuya, "Do you imagine that any earthly power can crush a people that lives to communicate a God-given message of faith, justice and mercy to all men? All the empires of the world united in unholy league have not the might to exterminate us." Milton Steinberg, *As a Driven Leaf* (New York: Behrman House Publishing, 1939), 239.

predicts[49] that we will be exiled from our land and scattered to the four corners of the globe,[50] but will eventually return to our original land.[51] The Torah predicts something that runs counter to human nature, and yet the prediction has been fulfilled.

The Land of Israel is desolate while we are in exile.[52]
Nahmanides, writing in the thirteenth century C.E., notes the fulfillment of the prophecy that, following our expulsion from the Land of Israel, the land would be desolate.[53] This would publicize our punishment – as forewarned by the Torah – for failing to honor our religious and moral obligations. Elsewhere, Nahmanides[54] comments on the Torah's decree that if and when we are exiled, our enemies will fail in the land: "This is a great proof and promise to us, as there is nowhere else in the entire world a land that was beautiful and productive and was inhabited for so long and yet is currently desolate. From the time we were forced out of the land, it has accepted no nation; and they all try to settle it but meet with no success."[55]

In the 1260's, Nahmanides reported: "What shall I tell you concerning the condition of the Land.... She is greatly forsaken and her desolation is great.... That which is of greater holiness is more desolate than that which is of lesser holiness. Jerusalem is most desolate and destroyed."[56]

In 1867 the famous author Mark Twain made a similar observation when he visited the Land of Israel. In *Innocents Abroad* he wrote:

> Of all the lands there are for dismal scenery, I think Palestine must be the prince. The hills are barren, they are dull of color, they are

49. Deut. 4:27
50. Is. 11:12
51. Deut. 30:1-10
52. This section summarizes insights by Rabbi Yaakov Asher Sinclair (http://ohr.edu/this_week/torah_weekly/3513).
53. Lev. 26:32-35, Deut. 29:13.
54. Lev. 26:16.
55. Lev. 26:32.
56. Letter to his son from Jerusalem, 1267. This letter is printed in Rabbi Chaim Dov Chavel's edition of *Kitvei HaRamban* (Jerusalem, Mossad Harav Kook, 1963), 1:368.

> un-picturesque in shape. The valleys are unsightly deserts tinged with a feeble vegetation that has an expression about it of being sorrowful and despondent. The Dead Sea and the Sea of Galilee sleep in the midst of a vast stretch of hill and plain wherein the eye rests upon no pleasant tint, no striking object, no soft picture dreaming in a purple haze or mottled with the shadows of the clouds. Every outline is harsh, every feature is distinct, there is no perspective – distance works no enchantment here. It is a hopeless, dreary, heart-broken land. [57]

Compare this dismal scene with the Torah's grim warning:

> And the alien that shall come from a far land, shall say, when they see the plagues of that land, and the sicknesses which the Lord has laid upon it; and that the whole land is brimstone, and salt, and burning, that it's not sown, nor bears, nor does any grass grow on it…then all the nations shall say, Why has the Lord done thus to this land?[58]

Since the 1880s we have seen the Land of Israel awaken. The land we see today is totally different from the one Nahmanides and Mark Twain experienced. Rabbi Nachum Rabinowitz of OU Kosher writes, "Israel is nothing short of an agrarian miracle…. Often compared to the state of New Jersey due to similar land mass, Israel contains less arable land than the US's fifth smallest state, and has vastly fewer water resources. Nonetheless, Israel dwarfs New Jersey's agriculture output more than fourfold." [59]

The Land of Israel remains faithful to the Jewish people,[60] as it is fruitful for us and desolate for our enemies. The sections of the Gaza Strip inhabited by Jews were so productive that its bounty was sought after throughout the world, even in mainstream supermarkets in the

57. Mark Twain, *The Innocents Abroad* (New York: Oxford University Press, 1996), 485.
58. Deut. 29:21-23.
59. https://oukosher.org/passover/articles/shemittah-diaspora.
60. This phrase was coined by Rav Soloveitchik during a lecture I heard him deliver at Yeshiva University in 1981.

United States; the Hamas-controlled Gaza Strip has emerged as one of the poorest places on earth.

A people that dwells alone

The Torah describes the Jewish people as "dwelling alone."[61] This phrase accurately portrays our destiny as always being somewhat isolated from the rest of humanity. Secular Zionists – brilliant and talented as they were in laying the foundations for a Jewish state – mistakenly thought that the Jewish people would cease dwelling alone once the Jewish state was established. They thought a Jewish state would bring an end to anti-Semitism, which they attributed to our being "different" in not possessing a homeland.

Israeli ambassador Yehuda Avner reports that Israeli Prime Minister Golda Meir remarked how lonely she invariably felt when she attended a session at the United Nations. "We have no family there," she said. "Israel is entirely alone there. But why should that be?"[62] Golda Meir, who was thoroughly secular, did not find an answer to her momentous question.

However, an Israeli leader with a more traditional bias, Menachem Begin, understood fully that this phenomenon is in accordance with the Torah's *prediction*. Prime Minister Begin stated, "One does not have to be a mystic for the imagination to be stirred by such an improbable vision of a nation forever dwelling alone. Is it not a startlingly accurate prophecy of our Jewish people's experience in all of history?"[63]

Refuting the secular Zionists, religious Zionist Jacob Herzog writes:

> The theory of classic Zionism was national normalization. What was wrong with the theory? It was the belief that the idea of a 'people that dwells alone' is an abnormal concept, when actually a "people that dwells alone" is the natural concept of the Jewish

61. Num. 23:9, Deut. 33:28.
62. Yehuda Avner, *The Prime Ministers: An Intimate Narrative of Israeli Leadership* (London: The Toby Press, 2010), 396.
63. Ibid.

> people. That is why this one phrase still describes the totality of the extraordinary phenomenon of Israel's revival. If one asks how the ingathering of the exiles, which no one could have imagined in his wildest dreams, came about, or how the State of Israel could endure such severe security challenges, or how it has built up such a flourishing economy, or how the unity of the Jewish people throughout the Diaspora has been preserved, one must come back to the primary idea that this is "a people that dwells alone." More than that, one must invoke this phrase not only to understand how the Jews have existed for so long; one must invoke it as a testimony to the Jewish right to exist at all in the land of their rebirth.[64]

A tiny nation that brings blessing to the world

Hashem promised Abraham that his descendants would bring blessing to the world.[65] The Jewish people on both national and individual levels have fulfilled this pledge, even though the Torah predicts that our nation will remain small in number during their exile.[66] The basic noble values of Western society, such as kindness to the weakest members of society, honoring parents, and a day of rest, all emanate from the teachings of the Torah.

Paul Johnson expressed the profound impact the Jewish people have had upon the world as follows:

> Certainly, the world without the Jews would have been a radically different place. Humanity might have eventually stumbled upon all the Jewish insights. But we cannot be sure. All the great conceptual discoveries of the human intellect seem obvious and inescapable once they had been revealed, but it requires a special genius to formulate them for the first time. The Jews had this gift. To them we owe the idea of equality before the law, both divine and human; of the sanctity of life and the dignity of human person; of the individual conscience and so a personal redemption; of

64. Jacob David Herzog, *A People that Dwells Alone: Speeches & Writings of Yaacov Herzog* (New York: Sanhedrin Press, 1975), 52.

65. Gen. 12:3.

66. Deut. 4:27.

> collective conscience and so of social responsibility; of peace as an abstract ideal and love as the foundation of justice, and many other items which constitute the basic moral furniture of the human mind. Without Jews it might have been a much emptier place.[67]

The State of Israel, totally out of proportion to its size, brings blessing to the entire world in many ways including water technology,[68] medical breakthroughs and cyber security. Over the years, Israel has led critical humanitarian missions to respond to many natural disasters across the globe, often setting up the first and largest emergency hospitals.

Anti-Semitism

Deuteronomy warns that if we are exiled as a result of sin, "and you will become an astonishment, a proverb, and a byword, among all the nations into which the Lord shall lead you." [69] Despite emerging from diversified countries, cultures, religions, lifestyles, and philosophies, there is one commonality shared by many peoples of the world who have encountered Jews: they all, at one point or another, included individuals – and even large segments of their populations – who did not like Jews. The universality and persistence of anti-Semitism has puzzled many thinking individuals.

---

67. http://www.simpletoremember.com/jewish/blog/paul-johnson-on-the-jews/. Rabbi Ken Spiro authored a book entitled *World Perfect* in which he affirms the cogency of Paul Johnson's assertion. Rabbi Spiro's insights are also available online (http://www.aish.com/sem/wp/).
68. Israel's supporting nations throughout the globe with water technology, dramatically improving the quality of life in more than one hundred less-developed countries (including the poorest of the poor), is documented in Seth Siegel's breathtaking book *"Let There be Water: Israel's Solution for a Water Starved World,"* 208-218.
69. Deut. 28:37. The media's obsession with Israeli and Jewish matters may be seen as a fulfillment of that which is stated in the portion of rebuke (*tokhaḥa*) that we will be a *shnina,* a conversation piece (see Onkelos and Rashi on this verse). Matti Friedman, a reporter for the Associated Press in Israel reports: "When I worked in the AP's Jerusalem bureau, the Israel story was covered by more AP news staff than China, or India, or all of the fifty-odd countries of sub-Saharan Africa combined" (http://honestreporting.com/must-read-matti-friedman-on-the-medias-obsession-with-israel/). Also see Daniel Freedman *The World's Deadly Obsession with Israel, Forbes* (June 24, 2010), http://www.forbes.com/2010/06/23/israel-hamas-middle-east-opinions-columnists-daniel-freedman.html.

Experts struggle to find an explanation, outside of biblical prophecy, to fully account for the ongoing phenomenon of anti-Semitism. Torah prophecy and insight can shed significant light on the true causes.

Conclusion

Only a divinely authored text could accurately anticipate the future destiny of the Jewish people, including predictions that we will live forever, that there will always remain Jews who faithfully adhere to the Torah,[70] that the Land of Israel will remain faithful to the Jewish people, and that the Jews will always be a nation apart from the rest of the family of nations.[71]

Moreover, none of the Torah's prophecies have been contradicted. Some remain unrealized to date – and we eagerly await their fulfillment – but none have been negated. Our great-great-grandparents would have been shocked if told in 5677 (1917) that within a century nearly a majority of the Jewish people would be living in a Jewish state in *Eretz Yisrael,* that Israel would possess one of the world's mightiest armies, that it would be a great center of Torah study, and that it would be called a "start-up nation" due to its incredible development of innovative ideas and products in a stunning variety of areas.[72] But these things happened – and the final redemption will happen too.

---

70. Deut. 31:21 affirms that the Jews will not forget the Torah. Rashi explains, "This is a promise that the Torah will never be entirely forgotten by the Jewish people." The Book of Esther (9:28) states that it will be forever remembered and practiced by the Jewish people. This is a stunning prophecy to be recorded in the Book of Esther, given that the Jews had just narrowly escaped total annihilation by Haman. The Gemara (Megilla 7a) writes that the fulfillment of this passage in the Book of Esther proves that this book was written with divine inspiration.

71. Many Orthodox Jews intuit that the Torah is a divine document because its stories resonate as the stories of *our* lives. For example, tiny Israel standing strong in the face of a vastly larger numbers of enemies makes the stories of the Hasmonean defeat of a much larger Greek army, Ahab's defeat of a vastly larger Aramean army (I Kings chapter 20), Saul and Jonathan's defeat of a dramatically larger Philistine army (I Samuel chapters 13 and 14), and Abraham defeating four mighty Mesopotamian kings with only three hundred and eight soldiers, resonate deeply with us.

72. The Talmud (Megilla 16a) observes that the Jewish people are "compared [in the Book of Genesis] to both dirt (Genesis 28:14) and to stars (Genesis 15:5). When they descend they fall to the lowest depths of dirt but when they rise they rise to the highest realms like the stars." This talmudic passage resonates deeply with the

THE "FRED THEORY" ON THE ORIGINS OF THE TORAH

In a video presentation entitled *A Rational Approach to the Divine Origin of Judaism,*[73] Rabbi Lawrence Kelemen defends the tradition that Jews today are the descendants of the people who experienced a mass divine revelation at Mount Sinai. Like Rabbi Judah HaLevi in *The Kuzari,* Rabbi Kelemen cogently points out that had this event been fabricated, it would have been impossible to convince millions of people that it had occurred. Rabbi Kelemen explains and rejects a number of secular theories regarding the origin of the Sinai story, one of which he calls the "Fred Theory."

Rabbi Kelemen reasons as follows: The claim that three million people heard God speak – a claim found in every complete Torah scroll that has been found – is either true or false. If false, at some point it would have had to be fabricated. It could not have been fabricated close to the alleged time of the event (e.g. by Moses himself), because then everyone would have remembered that no such thing happened. The claim would have had to be made by someone else – say, "Fred" – at a later time. "Fred" would claim that the national prophecy happened in the distant past and had been forgotten, but now he, Fred, was restoring to the people their ancestral traditions. This presumes that at some time there was a long period of amnesia about the national past. But there is no record either of a period of such amnesia, or of a person who brought back the ancient tradition. Such a person would surely have been noted in a history which contains accounts of the doings of many major and minor figures.[74] There are no plausible candidates for the role of "Fred."

Despite the logical reasoning in Rabbi Kelemen's disproof of "Fred Theory," one historical figure is often regarded as a "Fred" – King

Jews of the past decades. We experienced the reality of this insight with the extreme and terrible fall of the Holocaust contrasted with the spectacular turnaround in the Jewish State's stunning military and technological achievements.

73. https://www.youtube.com/watch?v=PEg_Oys4NkA.

74. Rabbi Kelemen notes that, culturally, Jews are obsessive about giving credit to those who contributed to our people. A review of almost any page of the Talmud and a visit to almost any synagogue of any denomination (with their many plaques honoring those who helped the community) confirms this assertion. It is very difficult to imagine that the Jewish people would fail to record the identity of someone who had made such a contribution as reintroducing the Torah.

Josiah. II Kings relates that a Torah scroll was discovered in the Temple, and Josiah spread the word among the people about its appearance.[75] Josiah was the first king in seventy-five years to support Torah observance. This seventy-five-year period is the only possible example of a "national amnesia" that a "Fred" could repair. Before we delve into the explanation of these verses, we must review the basics of Josiah's life story.

Josiah: The Early Years

When Josiah's evil grandfather Menashe died after fifty-five years of rule, his son Amon succeeded him. Amon continued his father's evil practices but ruled for only two years before his assassination. The Book of Kings describes how Josiah succeeded his father Amon at the tender age of eight. As the next in the Davidic line, he was installed as the king, even though he obviously was unfit to rule at that age. The people of Judea, despite their spiritual shortcomings, zealously honored the Davidic tradition even after they had assassinated an unpopular king. Josiah took an interest in the proper Torah way at age sixteen, and he began the process of purifying the Temple at age twenty.[76]

In toto, the Jewish people had experienced seventy-five years – fifty-five of Menashe, two of Amon, and eighteen more until Josiah matured and was fully committed to Hashem – of rule under monarchs who were, to say the least, not dedicated to Torah law.[77] Despite this handicap and the enormity of the challenge, Josiah embarked on his program of national reformation.

In the course of Josiah's efforts to purify the Temple, the High Priest discovered a Torah scroll that was open (as explained by the Midrash[78]) to the *tochaḥa* (reprimand) of Deuteronomy. As explained

75. II Kings 22:8-13.
76. II Chron. 34:3.
77. II Chron. 33:12-18 records that Menashe made a sort of *teshuva* (repentance) in the later years of his reign. Radak (on II Kings 22:8) understands that Menashe's teshuvah occurred late in his life. He cites and disagrees with *Seder Olam,* which states that Menashe repented in the twenty-second year of his reign.
78. This interpretation is supported by Josiah's sharp reaction to his finding of the book. The Book of Deuteronomy has many positive facets. It is difficult to understand why Josiah reacted so strongly if it was not open to the reprimand.

by the Midrash HaGadol[79] and Radak,[80] Josiah correctly saw this as a bad omen and sought the interpretation of a prophet.[81] His messengers went to the prophetess Ḥulda and brought back a crushing reply: as a result of the Jewish people's grievous sins, Hashem had resolved to destroy the Temple. Ḥulda noted, however, that since Josiah had expressed remorse for the evil committed by his predecessors and his people, he would be spared from experiencing this terrible event in his lifetime and would die a peaceful death.

Reaction to Huldah's Prophecy

The Book of Kings records that Josiah did not accept this prophecy with equanimity.[82] Instead, he reacted by embarking on a massive campaign for national, spiritual renaissance. He gathered all of the Jews and demanded that the nation make a solemn commitment to dedicate itself wholeheartedly to the service of Hashem, crystallized by an exhaustive elimination of idol worship from the Land of Israel. He eradicated the idol worship of his grandfather Menashe as well as the misdirected places of worship *(bamot)* of Jeroboam and King Solomon that had stood for hundreds of years, structures that not even Josiah's righteous predecessors (other than Hezekiah) had dared to disturb.

Josiah's Achievements – Passover Sacrifice, Justice, and Expanded Borders

For a period of thirteen years, Josiah enjoyed great success as a ruler. He organized the most widespread observance of the Passover sacrifice since the days of the Book of Judges.[83] Jeremiah describes Josiah's reign as a time when justice prevailed in the Land of Israel.[84]

II Chronicles states that Josiah carried out reforms not only in Judea but throughout the Land of Israel.[85] It is surprising to hear

79. Deut. 27:26.
80. II Kings 22:8
81. II Kings 22:11.
82. II Kings 23:1-24.
83. II Kings 23:22.
84. Jer. 22:15.
85. II Chronicles 34:6-7, 21.

of a Judean king affecting the northern part of the country. This was possible because during Josiah's reign, the Assyrian Empire that had controlled the northern portion of the country since the reign of Hezekiah was collapsing.[86] Josiah appears to have seized the opportunity to expand the borders of his kingdom to include the former Northern kingdom.

II Kings, however, indicates the limitations of Josiah's reform. It states that Josiah succeeded in eliminating the idolatry that "appeared" in Judea.[87] This seems to imply that the idolatry that was not in plain view remained. Shortly thereafter, we are told that there was never a *king* who so sincerely returned to Hashem either before or after Josiah. This, too, seems to imply that only king Josiah had returned, and that the people had *not* wholeheartedly partnered with him in his efforts.

Indeed, Ḥazal relate that during Josiah's time, many Jews covertly worshipped idols,[88] hiding the idols behind their doors in order to escape detection by soldiers enforcing Josiah's rule. It seems that the soldiers were not particularly thorough in their searches, but carried out the royal decree perfunctorily and without enthusiasm. This also explains why the Jews deserved the destruction of the Temple not very long after Josiah's death. Despite Josiah's efforts, the impact was superficial, as evidenced by their removal of only public idolatry. Finally, this also explains why Jeremiah was castigating the Israelites even during Josiah's reformation.[89]

The Tragic Death of Josiah

Thirteen years after he began his reformation in earnest, Josiah was killed at the age of thirty-nine by Pharaoh Necho's Egyptian army. This traumatic episode is described in one cryptic verse.[90] It is almost as if the prophet does not want to record this event and therefore presents the story in the shortest and most obscure manner possible.

86. *Da'at Mikra* on Chronicles, p. 933.

87. II Kings 23:24.

88. Ta'anit 22b; see Rabbi Elazar HaKalir's lament on the untimely death of Josiah (which is included in the Ashkenazic service for the Ninth of Av).

89. Jer. 3:6-10, 25:3.

90. II Kings 23:29.

Assessing the Extent of the Tragedy

Josiah's death was a multidimensional tragedy. It seems that he was motivated to wage war to prevent Pharoah Necho from extending his sphere of influence in the Middle East and thereby impinging on Josiah's control of the northern portion of Israel. Unfortunately, the Book of Kings records that after the death of Josiah, the Egyptians seized control of the Land of Israel and the subsequent Judean "kings" were merely vassals controlled by Egypt. The Babylonians then took over from the Egyptians.[91] Thus the death of Josiah effectively marked the end of Jewish sovereignty in the Land of Israel. Sovereignty was not regained for centuries, until the days of the Hasmoneans.

However, the most profound aspect of this tragedy is the fact that such an incredibly righteous king could die in battle. In fact, one could argue that it is for this reason that the Jewish people ignored Jeremiah's impassioned pleas to repent before the destruction. People most likely felt that serving Hashem was not worthwhile. While Menashe served every sort of idol and reigned peacefully for fifty-five years, Josiah, who destroyed the idols, was killed prematurely in battle at age thirty-nine. Therefore impassioned pleas for repentance fell on deaf ears.

Furthermore, had Josiah lived until the age of sixty-seven (as did Menashe), his reformation could have remained in effect for another twenty-eight years, totaling forty-one years. In that amount of time, a new generation that had not known Menashe could have emerged and been much more committed to Torah life than their parents' generation, and the destruction of the Temple might have been averted.[92]

Josiah as "Fred"

Our brief biography has shown that Josiah was a noble individual whose actions had only minimal impact on the Jewish people during his reign

91. II Kings 24:7.

92. For a similar approach, see Joseph B. Soloveitchik, *The Lord is Righteous in All His Ways: Reflections on the Tish'ah be-Av Kinot* (Jersey City: Ktav Publishing House, 2006), 285-286.

and even less influence after his death. While he tried to impose adherence to the Torah upon all of the Jews, the compliance for the most part was insincere. Although Josiah was very powerful, it seems he lacked the charisma to genuinely influence the wider population. Accordingly, how can anyone reasonably assume that Josiah convinced the Jewish people that their ancestors had received the Torah from Sinai or even that he discovered a long-lost book of the Torah?

The Jewish People are and have always been a contentious people who do not easily accept authority. Thus, many or even most Jews did not accept Josiah's religious reformation despite his legitimate authority as a king. How could anyone reasonably assert that Josiah managed to convince a highly skeptical people that their ancestors experienced a mass revelation at Sinai if he could not even convince them to abandon idolatry?[93]

Understanding the Discovery of the Book of the Torah

Skeptics point to the discovered book of the Torah publicized by Josiah as evidence that Josiah was the one who fraudulently convinced the Jewish people that their ancestors experienced a mass revelation at Sinai. However, the text of Kings does not state that books of Torah were unknown until Josiah introduced the Torah to the Jewish people. Indeed, the traditional understanding is not that Josiah was involved in the discovery of a previously-unknown book. Rather, as explained earlier, Josiah found a *specific* book of Torah that was opened to the reprimand section of Deuteronomy, indicating impending tragedy. The traditional explanation accounts very well for Josiah's terrified reaction to hearing about the book's discovery.[94] This is especially so according to Ḥazal's view that the section to which the Torah scroll was rolled included the verse describing how the Jewish people and the king will be exiled to

93. The same may be said regarding the attribution of the redaction of the Torah to Ezra. As is evident from Nehemiah chapter 13, Ezra failed to convince our people to refrain from intermarriage and public violation of Shabbat.

94. II Kings 22:11.

an unfamiliar land.[95] The skeptical approach does not at all explain why Josiah panicked when he discovered the Torah scroll.

Da'at Mikra, the recently completed commentary of Orthodox academicians, adds an alternative *pshat* (straightforward explanation without the use of Midrash to understand the text) explanation of Josiah's discovery. Based on the parallel account in Chronicles of this incident, which states that Josiah discovered the Torah scroll "*beyad Moshe* (in Moses' hand),"[96] *Da'at Mikra* explains that Josiah encountered a precious artifact – the very Torah scroll that was written by Moses and placed on the side of the Ark to warn us of great punishment if we sin.[97] Josiah did not expect to find this specific artifact, which was thought to be lost. *Da'at Mikra* suggests that the priests hid this Torah during the reign of one of the evil Judean kings such as Aḥaz or Menashe for fear of its desecration.

Skeptical interpretations of the discovery of the Torah scroll, on the other hand, make two unreasonable leaps of faith: the incredible proposition that Josiah fraudulently introduced the Torah (or even a portion of it) to the Jewish people, and that merely encountering a Torah scroll (or the Book of Deuteronomy) would prompt the mighty Josiah to tremble with fear.

Alternatively, some skeptics argue that Josiah fraudulently introduced not the entire Torah but just the Book of Deuteronomy. As "evidence" they cite the absence of any reference at all in Isaiah, Amos, and Hosea to the Book of Deuteronomy. *Da'at Mikra,* however, lists numerous parallels between Deuteronomy and these prophets in its introductions to each of these books.

Finally, the Torah's prediction that it will not be forgotten from the Children of Israel[98] precludes the scenario of a "Fred figure" presenting a divinely authored Torah that had been lost for centuries. Had a Fred figure presented a lost text, it would not be accepted as divinely authored since the text states that it will never be forgotten!

---

95. Deut. 28:36.
96. II Chron. 34:14.
97. Deut. 31: 24-26
98. Deut. 31:21

Conclusion

As we have noted, there is cogent evidence to support the belief in the mass divine revelation at Mount Sinai. The doubter must make tortuous interpretations of the texts regarding Josiah and assume that the Jewish people accepted the fraudulent claims of a king with minimal charismatic influence. It is unreasonable to believe that Josiah managed to perpetrate the greatest fraud ever to occur in Jewish history. Moreover, the secular approach does not account for Josiah's deeply pained reaction to the news of the discovery of the Torah scroll. It also requires belief that the Jewish nation, a most argumentative and contentious people, were fraudulently persuaded that their ancestors experienced a mass revelation. Finally, the Torah's prediction that it will never be forgotten precludes the possibility of its fraudulent introduction as a lost document. On the other hand, belief in the Sinai experience is the far more reasonable and sensible approach in general, and specifically to Josiah's publicizing the discovery of the Torah scroll.[99]

Postscript

Rabbi Yoel Bin-Nun, an Israeli Orthodox Tanakh expert, relates an incident that highlights the absurdity of the skeptical approach to Josiah's discovery. A student of Rabbi Bin-Nun delivered a lecture at a Bible conference (which included both secular and Orthodox scholars) on the parallels between Deuteronomy and Isaiah. A secular scholar, upon hearing the lecture, noted the cogency of the parallels but asked how they were possible if the Book of Deuteronomy was written only in Josiah's time, since Isaiah prophesied decades before Josiah's birth. Rabbi Bin-Nun's student humorously responded, "Don't you know that Isaiah was a prophet?"

99. Y.M. Grintz (*Iyunim BeSefer Melachim*, Kiryat Sefer: *HaHevra L'Ḥeker HaMikra*, 1985, 349-370, cited in footnote 9 by *Da'at Mikra* in its discussion of II Kings 22:8) presents multiple proofs that the secular theory of Josiah fraudulently introducing the Book of Deuteronomy or all of the Pentateuch is false. Rabbi Amnon Bazak also presents cogent reasons for rejecting the secular approach to Josiah and the Torah (http://etzion.org.il/en/shiur-4b-duplication-and-contradiction-continued).

THE STIFF-NECKED PEOPLE: THE PERFECT NATION TO RECEIVE THE TORAH

Throughout our history[100] the Jews have received many appellations. Among the more famous – and positive – are "The Chosen People," "People of the Book," "Eternal People," and "Light unto the Nations." Exodus chapter 32 finds our ancestors receiving yet another tag – one that evokes mixed feelings, yet in whose depth may lie the secret of our eternity.

The source of the appellation is Hashem himself, who says the following to Moses in the terrible aftermath of the Golden Calf: "I have seen [observed] this people, and behold they are a stiff-necked people. Now leave Me alone and My wrath will blaze against them and destroy them. I will then make you into a great nation."[101] Rashi explains that the Jews are "so called because they turn their stiff necks towards those who reprimand them and refuse to listen."

One chapter later, Hashem informs Moses that He will be now be sending a proxy, an angel, to watch over Israelites instead of leading them directly. In explaining why, Hashem invokes this notion twice again:

> and I will send an angel before thee; and I will drive out the Kena'ani... into a land flowing with milk and honey: for I will not go up in the midst of thee; for thou art a stiffnecked people: lest I consume thee on the way. [102].... Say to the children of Yisra'el, You are a stiffnecked people: I will come up into the midst of you for a moment and consume you.[103]

Given this context, one can reasonably assume that "stiff-necked people" is a pejorative label, connoting a noxious combination of impudence and stubbornness.

---

100. I thank Rav Asher Brander for allowing me to adapt and expand his article on this topic, "Supremely Stubborn," published in his work *Teachings: In-Depth Reflections on the Parshah* (Jerusalem: Mosaica Press, 2011), 284-289.
101. Ex. 32:9-10.
102. Ex. 33:3.
103. Ex. 33:5.

The Problem

Here's the problem: In defending the people Israel, Moses uses the very same notion as the essential rationale for our salvation:

> And Moshe made haste, and bowed his head toward the earth.... And he said, If now I have found favour in Your sight, O Lord, let my Lord, I pray You, go among us; for it is a stiffnecked people; and pardon our iniquity and our sin, and take us for Your inheritance.[104]

In this case, Moses employs the term "stiff-necked" as a reason to receive God's mercy. How could Moses be using this term to win Hashem's favor?

Four Classic Solutions: Ibn Janach, Ibn Ezra, Zohar Ḥadash, and Midrash

Ibn Ezra presents two possible solutions to the problem. First, he cites the opinion of Rabbi Mereinos (Rabbi Yonah Ibn Janach) who explains that the word *ki* in our context ("*ki* it is a stiff-necked people") should be rendered as *even though* it is a stiff-necked people, for the word *ki* can also mean "even though."[105] Thus Moses is asking Hashem to find the Israelites deserving of mercy *despite* their stubbornness.

Opting for the standard usage of the word *ki* as a causative, Ibn Ezra offers a different approach. He explains that what Moses means is "*because (I admit)* that we have sinned, that we are a stiff-necked nation, therefore you should forgive." Hashem, we don't attempt to redefine truth in light of our behavior, nor do we make a theology of our weaknesses – a tendency from which frail man often suffers.

In a third interpretation Moses turns to God and says: "Hashem, Your people do not want an agent. We want the Divine Manager!" Why? The words of the *Zohar Ḥadash* explain: "For it is a stiff-necked people and You shall forgive," as meaning, "The Jews are obstinate and wearying

104. Ex. 34:9.

105. Ibn Ezra (Ex. 13:17) cites Rabbi Moshe Ibn Gikatilla, who interprets the word *ki* in this verse to mean "even though." In Josh. 17:18 and Ps. 41:5 the word *ki* can also be reasonably understood as meaning "even though."

and when they sin, the angel can only do judgment and not forgiveness, but You are merciful and gracious."[106] An angel is constricted; he has no access to divine mercy and understanding. Therefore, when we sin the angel must punish us. But You, Hashem, can fathom us in great depth and can find in our being stubborn the very building blocks of forgiveness.

A fourth approach is suggested by the Midrash:

> R. Yakim said: Three are the undaunted: among beasts, it is the dog; among birds, it is the cock; and among the nations, it is Israel. R. Isaac ben Redifa said in the name of R. Ammi: You think that this is said disparagingly, but it is really in their praise. R. Abin said: To this very day Israelites in the Diaspora are called the stiff-necked people.[107]

The Stiff-Necked People: The Perfect Nation to Receive the Torah

Taking up the theme of the Midrash, Rabbi Samson Raphael Hirsch writes: "The natural innate obstinacy of the race... made Israel the most suitable for the revelation of the Divinity of His Torah." [108]

"Stiff-necked" is thus not necessarily pejorative. Stiff-neckedness is a character trait, and character traits are good or bad depending on how they are expressed. The Kotzker Rebbe once taught that every emotion and thought has value in the appropriate measure at the appropriate time. A Ḥasid once asked: "Rebbe, of what value is heresy or doubt?" The Kotzker thought for a moment and responded: "When a beggar knocks on your door, don't believe that God will provide. Take out your wallet and give him money."

Indeed, our stiff-neckedness has served us well. Does anyone really doubt that by all standards of natural history, we ought to have been a relic of the past, an academic fascination for aspiring PhDs? Instead, thanks to our stiff-neckedness, writers from such as Rabbi

106. *Lekh Lekha* 41b.

107. Exodus Rabba 42:9.

108. Ex. 34:9.

Yaakov Emden to Mark Twain have pointed to the immortality of the Jew as one of the great enigmas and miracles of human civilization.

Dr. Yaffa Eliach relates a story that illustrates how our stubbornness translates into our immortality:

> A Jewish labor battalion, slaving under brutal Nazi control, refused to eat on Yom Kippur despite threat of execution for failure to comply. After the fast was completed, the Nazi commander approached the group and said:
>
> "I know that you fasted today, but I am not going to invoke the death penalty you deserve according to the law. Instead you are going to climb that mountain and slide down on your stomachs. Those among you who would like to repent may say they were wrong to disobey army regulations and fast today. Those who wish to do so may raise their hands."
>
> Not a single hand went up. And so, the tired, soaked, starving, emaciated Jews climbed the wet, slippery mountain. When they reached the top, they were ordered to slide down on their stomachs. When they reached the bottom, they were ordered to line up again. They were asked if there were individuals who wished to repent and be spared the ordeal. Mud-covered figures with feverish eyes looked at the clean shaven German officer in silent defiance. And so ten times they repeated the humiliating performance, each time with more determination, each time with more strength, climbing and sliding from an unknown Polish mountain which on that soggy Yom Kippur night became a symbol of Jewish courage. After the ordeal was over, "a young German officer of low rank walked over to the group and said, 'I don't know who will win this war, but one thing I am sure of – people like you, a nation like yours, will never be defeated, never.'"[109]

Our stubborn nature has enabled us to persist and survive the most extreme challenges imposed upon us, from the brutal atheistic rule of

109. Yaffa Eliach, *Hasidic Tales of the Holocaust* (New York: Oxford University Press, 1982), 101-105.

the Soviet Union to the challenge of observing Shabbat in the United States in the first six decades of the twentieth century despite the great fear of losing one's job.[110] Our "stiff-necked" tradition has suited us well over the past thousands of years and will, with Hashem's help, continue to pave the way for our successes in the future.

We may add that the stubborn nature of the Jewish people adds credibility to our belief that our ancestors received the Torah from God at Sinai. The fact that a most contentious, argumentative, and highly intelligent people accepted the divine origin of the Torah testifies to the veracity of this claim! We can now understand that Moses was arguing that Hashem should forgive us, because precisely the fact that we are the stiff-necked people proves the truth of Hashem and the Torah!

Conclusion

Mark Twain wondered about the secret of the Jews' immortality. Part of the answer is our natural inclination to be the stiff-necked people. This stubborn nature has allowed us to persevere in our staunch commitment to Torah observance despite enormous challenges in each and every generation throughout the millennia. Thoughtful individuals recognize that we are indeed the stiff-necked people and that this very trait constitutes yet another reason to acknowledge the divine origin of the Torah.

THE MANNA TEST[111]

The giving of the Torah was not the only miraculous event witnessed by three million people. Also miraculous – and repeated once daily for forty years – was the fall of the manna.

110. I stand in awe of my grandfather (and namesake), Chaim Adler zt"l, who stood firm and was fired week after week for refusing to work on Shabbat, in grand "stiff-necked people" tradition. It took great courage and steadfast determination for my grandfather to do this in the 1920's, when his wife and five small children depended on him for sustenance, and when government welfare was not extended even to those in the direst of circumstances.

111. This chapter is an expansion of the section of Rabbi Shmuel Goldin's *Unlocking the Torah Text: Shemot* (New York: Gefen Publishing House, 2010) found on pp. 117-120. Thank you to Rabbi Goldin for granting permission to reproduce and expand his discussion.

Responding to the complaints of the hungry Israelites in the desert, Hashem introduces the miraculous fare that will sustain the nation during their travels: "Behold, I will rain bread from heaven for you; and the people shall go out and gather a certain portion every day, that I may test them, whether they will follow my Torah, or no."[112]

This "test" is recapitulated in the Book of Deuteronomy:

> And you shall remember all the way which the Lord your God led you these forty years in the wilderness, to humble you, and to prove you, to know what was in your heart, whether you would keep His commandments, or no. And He humbled you, and suffered you to hunger, and fed you with manna...that He might make you know that man does not live by bread only, but by every word that proceeds out of the mouth of the Lord does man live....
>
> Who fed you in the wilderness with manna...that He might afflict you, and that He might prove you, to do you good at the latter end.[113]

Abarbanel's Question

Why does Hashem associate the miracle of the manna with testing? As the Abarbanel asks, "What was the nature of the test administered by God through the bestowal of daily sustenance?...This was a kindness, not a test!"[114]

Four classic approaches

Rashi argues that the test does not lie within the manna itself.[115] Rather, he contends, the trial actually emerges from an ancillary source. Hashem grants miraculous sustenance to our people and simultaneously tests them by determining "whether they will observe the commandments associated [with that sustenance]." These commandments included the instruction to collect each day only the amount of manna necessary for

112. Ex. 16:4.
113. Deut. 8:2-3, 16.
114. Ex. 16:4.
115. Ex. 16:4.

that day, the prohibition of collection on the Shabbat, and the directive to collect a double portion on Friday in order to properly prepare for Shabbat.

Many other commentaries, however, do not accept Rashi's solution to the mysterious "test" of the manna. Nahmanides, for example, emphatically declares, "But this [Rashi's explanation] is not correct.... [The manna itself] was a trial to them."[116] While the text supports the position that the manna itself was a trial, the question remains: what, specifically, was the test embodied by this miraculous food?

The commentaries offer, with subtle variations, three global approaches. Each approach carries overarching lessons that move well beyond the specific phenomenon of the manna.

According to the first approach, Hashem tested and developed the faith of the Israelites by depriving them of the usual forms of sustenance and survival. Nahmanides, among others, champions this position in his commentaries on Exodus and in Deuteronomy:

> [Hashem] could easily have led them through the surrounding cities. He led them, instead, through a wilderness of snakes, fiery serpents and scorpions, where the only bread fell from the heaven each day.
>
> This was a serious trial for them: to have no other option, to enter a great wilderness...to have no sustenance other than the manna which fell on a daily basis and which melted when the sun waxed hot.... Nevertheless, they did all this in obedience to God's command.... From this [God] would know that they would obey His commandments forever.[117]

With this approach, Nahmanides remains true to his general position concerning divine tests:[118] God tests man in order to actualize his inherent potential. Through the trial of the manna, by severely ration-

116. Ex. 16:4.

117. Deut. 8:2.

118. Gen. 22:1

ing and circumscribing the sustenance of the Israelites, God solidifies their internal potential for faith. This faith, once realized, will sustain them not only in the wilderness but also through their turbulent journey across the face of history.

The second approach contends that by providing us with the manna, Hashem confronts our fledgling nation with the plethora of challenges that emerge from a life of ease. Far from a test of deprivation, the manna actually constitutes a *nisayon ha'osher,* a trial of wealth and plenty. The *Or HaḤayim* notes, for example, that the manna provides the Israelites with the unfamiliar phenomenon of leisure time. Hashem wonders: Will they walk in My ways? Will they maximize their newly available time productively in the pursuit of Torah study and observance?[119] Sforno, for his part, suggests that Hashem wanted to determine whether the Israelites will follow His dictates when "they are sustained without any pain."[120] People often turn to God in times of need but ignore Him in times of comfort. Through the manna Hashem challenged our ancestors to turn to Him even when our sustenance was attained with ease.

According to the third and perhaps most cogent interpretation, the manna is meant to sensitize the Israelites to their dependence upon Hashem as they journey toward national independence. This interpretation is reflected in the following talmudic conversation:

> The students of R. Shimon bar Yoḥai asked: "Why did the manna not descend for Israel once annually?" He answered: "[In order that each Israelite] would worry – perhaps no manna will descend tomorrow.... Thus they all turned their hearts to their Father in Heaven."[121]

Centuries later Rashi's grandson, Rabbi Samuel ben Meir (often referred to as the "Rashbam"), mirroring the positions of numerous other

119. Ex. 16:4.
120. Ex. 16:4.
121. Yoma 76a.

commentaries, elaborates upon the statement of R. Shimon bar Yoḥai: "Since each and every day their eyes will turn to Me for their sustenance, they will come to believe in Me and walk in the ways of My Torah."[122]

A New Approach Based on the Kuzari

We suggest a new approach based on a classic approach of Rav Judah Halevi in the first section of *The Kuzari*. As is well known, *The Kuzari* proves the authenticity of our unparalleled claim of being descendents of the (approximately) three million individuals who witnessed the divine revelation at Mount Sinai. He bolsters this proof by noting that the entire nation also witnessed the manna miracle every day – except for Shabbat – for forty years.

The Torah states that our eyes became completely opened to the undeniable truth of Hashem and the Torah only after having experienced the daily arrival of the manna for forty years.[123] An avowed skeptic could imagine that Moses somehow managed to fool our ancestors at Sinai by staging a false revelation experience. However, no reasonable individual could argue that Moses could stage the presentation of magic food for an entire nation, in a barren desert, over a forty-year period, on a daily basis, and in many different locations.

Thus the manna is, in the words of *The Kuzari*, "evidence of the truth of the Torah that cannot be denied." Accordingly, one may interpret the manna as a test to Jews of all generations "whether we shall observe the Torah."[124] The manna was not only a test for the generation that received it, but remains a relevant trial for all generations. We pass this test when we recognize the magnitude of the miracle of the manna and allow it to compel us to live a life of Torah observance, fully convinced of its truth.

Conclusion: A Reflection on the Observance of Sukkot

On Sukkot, when Jews sit in the Sukkah and relive the experience of our ancestors residing in the Sinai desert, we can think not only of

122. Ex. 16:4.
123. Deut. 29:3-5.
124. *The Kuzari*, 1:86.

the Sukkot in which we lived but also of other aspects of the Midbar experience. We have the opportunity to contemplate the miracle of the manna, conveying a lesson that, to this day, we forget at our own peril: Whether we are wandering in the wilderness or living in a highly urbanized society, we are dependent upon God for our sustenance each and every day.

SKEPTICISM AND THE WAR ON AMALEK

A gentleman who taught for decades at various public schools before teaching at a yeshiva high school was amazed how the yeshiva students constantly challenged the points he raised in class. A student who transferred from public school to a yeshiva high school commented that he was shocked by this same propensity, but what perplexed him further was how his rabbis seemed to revel in the difficult questions posed by the students. Such behavior is not atypical among our people, as we have noted earlier. Indeed, it seems that Moses had to struggle with our skeptical and contentious nature from the first. This, according to some commentators, is the significance of the strange way in which the war against Amalek in Ex. 17:8-16[125] was carried on.

Strange Way of Waging the Amalekite War

The *Be'er Yosef*[126] identifies five very odd aspects of the Amalekite war. First, why does Moses ask Joshua to lead this battle? Moses led us in battle against Siḥon and Og,[127] so why not do so against Amalek? It is most strange that in our first battle Moses leaves the military leadership to his student instead of managing the battle himself.

Moreover, why does Moses disengage from the battle and ascend a nearby hill instead of involving himself from the sidelines? To draw an analogy from sports, it is as if the head coach of a football team took a vacation while his team was playing its first game! Although Nahmanides[128] explains that Moses retreats to engage in prayer, we may ask why

125. This is the portion that is read on Purim morning.

126. *Parashat Beshalaḥ.*

127. Num. 21:34, Deut. 1:4.

128. Ex. 17:9.

Moses does not do so during the battles against Siḥon and Og. Clearly, this behavior is specific to the war waged against Amalek.

A third atypical facet of this war is that Moses takes the "rod of God" (the staff he used in connection with many of the plagues in Egypt) to the hill and then never uses it! Sforno[129] explains that Moses used it to indicate when he was praying for our victory, in order that the Israelites might join their hearts to him and pray with him. Sforno believes this is analogous to the cloths that used to be waved in the vast synagogue in Alexandria, Egypt in order to indicate the time to answer Amen.[130] Although Sforno's approach is most interesting, there is no explicit evidence in the Pentateuch for his assertion, and thus there is room for an alternative explanation.

A fourth unusual feature of this war is that it is the only battle recorded in the Pentateuch in which the results waver so frequently, as the Israelites are successful when Moses holds his hands high and lose momentum when his hands are down.

A fifth odd aspect is that it is the only time in the Pentateuch where Moses exhibits physical frailty, needing Aharon and Ḥur to support his arms. This is most unusual considering that Moses is described as maintaining his vigor even on the day of his death.[131]

Our Skepticism Prior to the Amalekite War

The *Be'er Yosef* argues that the key to this solution lies in understanding our national attitude at the onset of this war. The verse immediately preceding the account of the war with Amalek states that we doubted whether Hashem was among us.[132] Our doubt is quite perplexing, considering that we had very recently witnessed the ten plagues in Egypt, the splitting of the Yam Suf, and the delivery of the manna. What additional evidence did we need?

The *Be'er Yosef* explains that we entertained the possibility that Moses, not Hashem, was responsible for the great miracles we had

129. Ex. 17:9.
130. Sukka 51b.
131. Deut. 34:7.
132. Ex. 17:7.

witnessed. We considered that perhaps Moses was a master manipulator of nature and was somehow able to bring about the plagues, the splitting of the sea, and the daily portions of manna. Evidence for the *Be'er Yosef's* position may be drawn from two sources. In Ex. 16, we said to Moses and Aaron that "you" took us out of Egypt.[133] We also demanded from Moses that *he* give us water in the desert instead of asking him to ask Hashem for water.[134]

The Amalekite War as a Response to Skepticism

According to the *Be'er Yosef's* view, Moses arranged for the war against Amalek to be waged in a manner that would dispel any of our lingering doubts. Moses sought to make it absolutely clear that it is Hashem *exclusively* who brought – and continues to bring – every miracle. With this insight we can explain the five oddities we identified earlier.

Moses completely withdraws from his battle in order to make it crystal clear that neither he nor Aaron were responsible for the astonishing miracles against Amalek. Moses stands on the top of the hill to make obvious his minimal involvement in the incredible win. Similarly, the rod is conspicuously withdrawn from use in order to undermine assumptions that their success was a result of any special powers associated with that staff. Likewise, it is most appropriate that on this occasion Moses publicly exhibit an episode of physical frailty. Finally, the battle wavers, explain Ḥazal, depending on whether we subordinate our hearts to Hashem.[135] Thus, each Jew *experienced* that his trust and faith in Hashem brought the victory, and that lack of *emuna* and *bitaḥon* (trust) spells failure. All the Israelites were thus given the opportunity to experience and fully understand that Hashem is responsible for the great miracles and not Moses, Aaron, or the rod.

However, perhaps the fact that we succeeded only when Moses's hands were raised would seem to imply just the opposite – that Moses *was* responsible for the miracle. Ḥazal[136] explain that it was not Moses'

133. Ex. 16:3.
134. Ex. 17:2.
135. Rosh HaShana 29a.
136. Ibid.

hands that brought about the victory; rather, Moses was simply pointing to the heavens to remind us that success is all from Hashem. Ḥazal's insight is most convincing considering that the Amalekite war is the only occasion where we find Moses displaying physical vulnerability. If Moses's raised hands were somehow responsible for the victory, then these extraordinary hands wouldn't become weak and require support by Aaron and Ḥur.

Thus we emerged from the war of Amalek with a renewed sense of faith, spiritually and mentally primed to accept the Torah at Sinai. Interestingly, the *Be'er Yosef's* insight helps explain the surprising opinion of R. Yehoshua[137] that Jethro was motivated to join our people not only after hearing about the splitting of the sea but also by hearing of the war against Amalek. Commentaries have noted that it is readily understandable that Jethro would be inspired by the splitting of the sea, but have wondered why the war against Amalek would motivate him to join us. Based on *Be'er Yosef's* approach, we suggest that the manner in which the war against Amalek was waged clarified that the splitting of the sea was an authentic miracle.

Conclusion: A Skeptical People

The *Be'er Yosef's* insight helps explain the phenomenon mentioned above, namely, the skeptical and contentious nature of our people, a trait that extends to the early beginnings of our nation. Already in the Sinai desert, although we had witnessed a series of astounding miracles, we remained unconvinced!

As mentioned earlier, the Gemara notes that Hashem specifically chose to give the Torah to us, the most *az* of all nations.[138] One could translate *az* as "fierce," but I suggest it be translated as "brazen" in the sense that we are strong minded and not easily swayed.[139] As stated earlier, Hashem chose the Jewish nation – the most brazen of people – to receive the Torah, because we are the most suited to serve as His

137. Zvaḥim 116a.
138. Beitza 25b.
139. Such as *"az kenamer"* (brazen like a leopard), Avot 5:20.

witnesses[140] that this revelation indeed occurred. If such an argumentative and contentious people confirm the veracity of the Sinai revelation despite the extensive demands it makes upon its adherents, then it most certainly is true.

Postscript

Benjamin Franklin is reported to have rejected belief in the Sinaitic revelation because he thought God would have revealed himself to the entire world.[141] Our discussion provides one response to this position. God specifically chose a most argumentative and contentious people to confirm the veracity of the Sinaitic revelation.

A "NATURAL" EXPLANATION OF THE TEN PLAGUES

The Ten Plagues served to demonstrate Hashem's existence and continued control of the world, as is stressed many times in the Book of Exodus.[142] We know that they occurred because our ancestors witnessed these events as a nation[143] and have recounted these events every year from parent to child.

Some skeptics, though, have questioned whether the Ten Plagues were indeed supernatural occurrences. During the past sixty years some have studied meteorological patterns in Egypt and neighboring areas and have offered "natural explanations" for the Ten Plagues. We argue that even if one were to accept these theories as correct, they do not undermine the Torah assertion that the Ten Plagues were results of divine intervention.

In fact, Maimonides already acknowledges that a skeptic *could* doubt the supernatural nature of the Ten Plagues, but does not consider this a crucial question. He writes:

> The Jews did not believe in Moses, our teacher, because of the wonders that he performed.... What is the source of our belief in him? The [revelation] at Mount Sinai. Our eyes saw, and not

---

140. Isaiah 43:10.
141. H.W. Brands, *The First American: The Life and Times of Benjamin Franklin* (New York: Random House, 2000), 94.
142. Ex. 8:18, 9:14-16 and 10:1-2.
143. Deut. 4:34-35.

> a stranger's. Our ears heard, and not another's.... He entered the thick clouds; the Voice spoke to him and we heard, 'Moses, Moses, go tell them the following:....' All Israel were witnesses to [the appointment of] Moses, our teacher, at [the revelation at] Mount Sinai, and it was unnecessary for him to perform any further wonders for them.... How is it known that the [revelation] at Mount Sinai alone is proof of the truth of Moses' prophecy that leaves no shortcoming? [Exodus 19:9] states: 'Behold, I will come to you in a thick cloud, so that the people will hear Me speaking to you, [so that] they will believe in you forever.' It appears that before this happened, they did not believe in him with a faith that would last forever, but rather with a faith that allowed for suspicions and doubts.[144]

It is possible that Hashem brought about the Ten Plagues in a manner that leaves room for a skeptic to question their supernatural nature. This conforms to Maimonides's view that *only* the Sinai revelation was presented in a manner that obliterated any doubt. There is, nonetheless, much opportunity to refute the skeptic, as we shall see.

A Sample Theory

A naturalistic approach to the Ten Plagues was first articulated by Greta Hort in 1958,[145] and others have since articulated similar approaches with variations.

The basic theory may be summarized as follows:[146]

> Plague 1 (the water turned to blood and the fish died): Unusually intense floods in the southern parts of the Nile Valley caused unusually large amounts of the red soil in that area to be

144. *Hilkhot Yesodei HaTorah* 8:1-2 (translation from http://www.chabad.org/library/article_cdo/aid/904992/jewish/Yesodei-haTorah-Chapter-Eight.htm).
145. "The Plagues of Egypt," *Zeitschrift fur die Altestestamentliche Wissenschaft* 70 (1958), 48–59.
146. See Nachum Sarna, *Exploring Exodus* (New York: Schocken Books, 1987), 70-73.

introduced into the Nile. The flood could have produced large quantities of toxins that would kill fish.

Plague 2 (frogs): The dead fish sickened the frogs and forcing them to the land.

Plagues 3 and 4 (infestations of biting insects and flies[147]): The lack of frogs in the river would have let insect populations, normally kept in check by the frogs, increase massively. The rotting corpses of fish would have attracted significantly more insects to the areas near the Nile.

Plagues 5 and 6 (livestock disease and boils): There are biting flies in the region that transmit livestock diseases; a sudden increase in their number could spark epidemics. Biting flies increased dramatically in the decaying plants left by the heavy flooding, then carried the skin disease from dead cattle to the live cattle and humans, causing the plague of "boils."

Plague 7 (fiery hail): The severe weather that had caused the unusual torrent, then brought hail.

Plague 8 (locusts): The weight of hail would destroy most crops, leaving several insects and other animals without a normal food source. The remaining crops therefore would be destroyed by swarms of locusts.

Plague 9 (darkness): The excessive load of mud from the high Nile flood dried into an unusually heavy covering of powdered silt. A violent dust storm lofted the silt into the air, and the cumulatively devasting effects of the earlier plagues on the soil meant that the matter released into the atmosphere would have been extraordinarily dense and abundant, blocking out the sun.

Plague 10 (death of the firstborn): The last plague affected the firstborn due to food poisoned by locusts. When people emerged after the darkness, the firstborn would be given priority,

147. According to R. Neḥemiah (Exodus Rabba 11:3), the plague of *arov* (the fourth plague) involved biting insects such as hornets and mosquitoes. The Midrash, however, favors the opinion that *arov* refers to a mixture of wild animals.

> as was customary in Egypt, and would consequently be more likely to be affected by disease carried by the food.

Nahmanides writes that Hashem made a fierce east wind blow the entire night to give the Egyptians the opportunity to think the Red Sea was split by natural causes and not by Hashem.[148] He clarifies, however, that the Egyptians had ample opportunity to recognize Hashem's involvement, such as the fact that the Red Sea was split into sections.[149] Unfortunately for the Egyptians, they did not exercise their common sense and recognize Hashem's presence.[150] Whatever prevented the ancient Egyptians from engaging in clear and rational thought at the Red Sea, their misjudgment sheds great light on non-believers today. They are misled by the superficial, secular, surface of the world behind which Hashem hides and ignore the abundant evidence of divine involvement in the world due to personal agendas or biases.

Similarly, one only needs to exercise common sense to recognize that the hand of Hashem orchestrated these incredible episodes. We shall present three counter-arguments to the skeptic's theory of the Ten Plagues.

Responses to the Challenge

Natural events repeat themselves

A strong proof that Hashem brought about the Ten Plagues is the fact that natural events repeat themselves. A series of events even remotely similar to the Ten Plagues has not occurred since the Jewish Exodus from Egypt approximately 3,300 years ago. If the Ten Plagues were natural events that were not coordinated by Hashem, they should have reoccurred at some point in the past three thousand years.

---

148. Ex. 14:21.

149. Ps. 136:13.

150. Nahmanides explains (Ex. 14:21) that the Egyptians' fierce hatred of the Jews skewed their judgment and led them to ignore the ample evidence of divine intervention on behalf of the Israelites. Torah Academy of Bergen County student Yaakov Miller suggests two alternative possibilities: that the inflated egos of the Egyptians led them to ignore the clear evidence, or that the bias towards a natural interpretation of the world misled them.

Timing

Furthermore, the timing of the events clearly illuminates Hashem's involvement. Moses announced the plagues in advance and sometimes even declared in advance their time of termination. The most striking example is the conclusion of the second plague (frogs). Moses approaches Pharaoh and asks him when he would like to end this plague. Pharaoh surprisingly responds, "Tomorrow," to which Moses happily responds that he will honor this request in order to prove "that there is none like Hashem."[151]

Ibn Ezra[152] explains that Pharaoh did not ask for the immediate end of the frog plague because he suspected that these plagues were brought about by natural means regarding which Moses had greater knowledge than he and his learned advisors. Pharaoh thought that Moses expected him to request the immediate cessation of the plague and made the offer because he knew the plague was ending. Pharaoh thought to thwart this strategy by surprising Moses with a request to end the plague the next day. Moses, in turn, was pleased to have the opportunity to prove that the plagues were conducted by Hashem's design, and not the automatic working of nature. Thus, it could be that Hashem brought about the plagues in a natural manner, but the timing makes it abundantly clear that He was controlling the situation.

Interestingly, this may explain how Pharaoh hardened his heart during the first five plagues.[153] He may have convinced himself that the Ten Plagues were a natural event, despite the clear evidence to the contrary. This is not unlike contemporary skeptics who, due to personal agendas and/or psychological barriers, ignore Hashem's existence and/or the divine authorship of the Torah. Indeed, the skeptics' arguments require a far greater "leap of faith" than does the Orthodox Jewish view.

A miracle within the Ten Plagues

Finally, there were significant indications within the plagues that demonstrate they were of a divine nature. The most conspicuous example

151. Ex. 8:5-6.
152. Ex. 8:6.
153. Ex. 7:3.

is the fire that was within the hail,[154] an overt miracle witnessed by an entire nation, whose members have passed this fact down to their descendants, generation after generation, in an unbroken chain that lasts even until today. Rashi refers to this phenomenon "as a miracle within a miracle."[155] The naturalistic theory for the plague of fiery hail does not account for this specific phenomenon. Hashem may have introduced the fire in the hail specifically to dispel any doubt as to the divine character of the Ten Plagues.

Conclusion

Hashem prefers to act in a way that cooperates with nature.[156] Historically, times when Hashem explicitly manipulated nature to orchestrate outlandish miracles did not elicit a more sincere commitment from those who witnessed them. On the contrary, we responded more authentically to miracles that occurred subtly, without major disruption to our environment. However, there have been occasions when Hashem deemed it necessary to jolt us spiritually by performing an awe-inspiring, supernatural, and (otherwise) inexplicable miracle. The specific examples of the plagues serve to deepen our *emuna* either way we wish to interpret them. By no means should we feel obliged to adopt the natural theories about the Ten Plagues as correct. However, we have demonstrated that even *if* the natural theories were true, they are not incompatible with Torah belief. In some ways, they might even enhance our understanding and appreciation of Torah.

154. Ex. 9:24.
155. Ex. 9:24.
156. Nahmanides (Gen. 6:19) and Rashbam (Ex. 14:21) explain that even when Hashem makes a miracle, He seeks to minimize the miracle and present it in the most natural manner possible. In fact, Rabbi Joseph B. Soloveitchik (*Emergence of Ethical Man*, 187-188) specifically embraces the natural explanation of the Ten Plagues: "Behind the passages in the Bible we may discern a distinct intention to describe the plagues as naturally as possible."

Chapter 3

Belief in the 21st Century

BRIDGING THE GAP BETWEEN TORAH AND SCIENCE

Since the time of Aristotle, educated Jews have grappled with apparent contradictions between the divinely authored Torah and information yielded from the world created by Hashem. Maimonides, who grapples with such issues at length in his *Guide to the Perplexed,* is one of the many who have worked to resolve these challenges.

One major issue in Maimonides' time was the scientific community's acceptance of Aristotle's assertion that the world is eternal and thus was never created. In *Guide to the Perplexed,* Maimonides concludes that Aristotle's arguments for this assertion were reasonable but not conclusive.[1] Maimonides surprisingly states that had Aristotle definitively proven that the universe was eternal, he would have reinterpreted Genesis 1 – the story of the creation of the world – to fit with proven fact.

By saying this, Maimonides establishes an important rule: the Torah never contradicts an established fact. Thus, when faced with a contradiction between Torah and assertions made by scientists, we have two fundamental options: either the scientists are incorrect or the manner in which we interpret the Torah is incorrect (or both).

1. *Guide to the Perplexed,* 2:25.

Maimonides stopped short of reinterpreting Genesis 1 because he was not fully convinced of Aristotle's arguments. This issue remained unresolved until the mid-1960's, when two scientists – Arno Penzias and Robert Wilson – scanned the heavens with a special antenna and detected a weak radiation filling all of space. Working with P.J.E. Peebles at Princeton University, they identified this ubiquitous radiation – now known as the cosmic microwave radiation background – as the residual energy of the Big Bang. Penzias and Wilson were awarded the Nobel Prize for their breakthrough. Their discovery changed humanity's understanding of our universe to include a definitive beginning to our world, in accordance with the Torah's view.

Thus, the believing Jews from Aristotle's time (the fourth century BCE) until the 1960's, who stubbornly clung to the belief that the world was created in spite of the overwhelming scientific consensus, were validated after all.[2]

This is an example that should be borne in mind whenever one seeks to resolve seeming contradictions between Torah and science.

Different Approaches to Resolving Conflicts

There is a wide variety of approaches to resolving apparent conflicts between Torah and science.

In light of the experience with Aristotle's disproven theory of the world's eternity, one could simply conclude that the exercise of harmonizing Torah and science is unnecessary. The Torah contains divinely revealed truths; by contrast, scientific belief is constantly changing. A friend of mine related that at his graduation ceremony from Harvard

2. Dr. Nathan Aviezer wrote the following note to this author (on September 16, 2016) regarding some recent theories of physics that assume the existence of multiple universes and multiple Big Bangs: "These theories are still speculative, but let us assume that these theories eventually become confirmed. What are the implications of these theories for the Torah creation narrative? It is important to realize that the Torah is not a science textbook. The Torah only includes information that is relevant to us, that is, to contemporary human beings. Therefore, it follows that the Torah is describing our universe and our Big Bang. The Torah word "creation" thus means the creation of our universe. Previous Big Bangs and other universes which have no connection with us would not be included in the Torah."

University Medical School, the dean of the medical school declared, "Much of what we taught you is incorrect!" The dean was in the process of urging the graduates to continue pursuing their medical education; however, one could (as many believing Jews do) reasonably refrain from trying to resolve Torah with conclusions made by scientists that might be proven incorrect millennia, centuries, years, or even days later. One could argue that the "Big Bang" theory rendered Maimonides' grappling with Aristotle's theory of eternity pointless, and we therefore need not repeat Maimonides' efforts to reconcile Torah and science.

This approach is advocated by Rabbi Moshe Meiselman in an extensive and rich work entitled *Torah, Chazal and Science*.[3] Rabbi Meiselman is a Torah scholar of the first rank and also earned a doctorate in mathematics from the Massachusetts Institute of Technology in 1967.

Rabbi Meiselman vigorously argues for the position, which he cites in the name of Rav Joseph B. Soloveitchik, that inquiry regarding the origin of the universe (cosmology) is beyond the legitimate sphere of science.[4] Rav Meiselman forcefully asserts that all statements of the talmudic sages were divinely inspired and are therefore immutable. A major theme of the book is that modern science is transitory and unreliable compared to the divine wisdom of Ḥazal. Rabbi Meiselman argues extensively against accommodating religion to science either by rejecting traditional texts or giving them a revisionist reading.

We should note that Rabbi Menachem Mendel Schneerson, the renowned Lubavitcher Rebbe, adopts a similar approach.[5] In any area of conflict, he argues that the simple meaning of the Torah takes absolute primacy over science. He writes that "science formulates and deals with theories and hypotheses, while the Torah deals with absolute truths. These are two different disciplines, where 'reconciliation' is entirely out of place." It is important to note that not only was the Lubavitcher Rebbe a major Torah authority, but he also devoted significant time to studying

3. Rabbi Moshe Meiselman, *Torah, Chazal and Science* (Lakewood: Israel Bookshop Publications, 2013), 263-272.
4. Ibid., 693-721.
5. Rabbi Menachem M. Schneerson, "A Letter on Science and Judaism," printed in *Challenge: Torah Views on Science and Its Problems* (Jerusalem: Association of Orthodox Jewish Scientists 1978), 142-149.

mathematics and science at two world-class higher institutions of learning, the University of Berlin and the Sorbonne in Paris.

Rabbi Meiselman does not completely dismiss science. For instance, in chapter 22, Rabbi Meiselman presents a very thorough explanation of the Talmud passage (Shabbat 107b) where Ḥazal seem to espouse a belief in spontaneous generation, which the scientific community has unanimously rejected since the late nineteenth century. Here, Rabbi Meiselman accepts the scientific position and argues for an interpretation of Ḥazal's position that does not conflict with accepted scientific fact.[6]

Rabbi Meiselman argues for the exercise of caution in regard to scientific theory and against what he calls "cavalier allegorization" of Torah and Ḥazal. He marshals enormous resources of learning to show that ultimately, however the challenges are resolved, not a single scientific fact disproves either the Bible or the Talmud.

Two important caveats should be made in regard to Rav Meiselman's monumental work.

First, as regards Rav Soloveitchik's views on evolution, a different approach than that presented in *Torah, Chazal and Science* appears in *The Emergence of Ethical Man*,[7] a work based on Rav Soloveitchik's original lecture notes edited with the guidance of his son-in-law and leading student Rav Aharon Lichtenstein. There, Rav Soloveitchik states that reconciliation is possible between the Torah's account of creation and the theory of evolution. (It is not surprising to discover discrepancies in Rav Soloveitchik's thinking; he was an exceedingly fluid thinker who would constantly revise his ideas.)

The other caveat is in regard to Rav Meiselman's utter rejection of the position of Rabbi Abraham ben Moses ben Maimon, the son of Maimonides, who famously asserts that Ḥazal occasionally relied on

6. He understands the Talmud to be saying that the relationship between lice eggs and their progenitors is not visible to the naked eye. Halakha does not take cognizance of that which is not visible without the aid of an instrument (*Arukh HaShulhan*, Yore De'a 84:36 and Rabbi Moshe Feinstein, *Igrot Moshe*, Yore De'a 3:120:5).
7. Rabbi Joseph B. Soloveitchik, *The Emergence of Ethical Man* (Jersey City: Ktav Publishing House, 2005), 5.

contemporary scientific understanding, which was sometimes flawed.[8] This approach is cited as valid by such contemporary mainstream figures as Rabbi Ḥaim David Halevy,[9] Rabbi Shaul Yisraeli,[10] Rabbi Aharon Lichtenstein,[11] and Rav Hershel Schachter.[12] In a position between that of Rabbi Meiselman and Rav Lichtenstein, Rav Ovadia Yosef[13] holds that although the majority of authorities do not adopt the approach of Rabbi Abraham ben Moses ben Maimon, one who espouses this view should not be dismissed as a heretic.

A very different approach seeks to avoid conflict between science and Torah by asserting that they are simply not talking about the same things. Thus Rabbi Natan Slifkin, in *The Challenge of Creation*,[14] argues that in Genesis 1 Hashem teaches eternal values on how to conduct one's life, but does not intend to impart scientific information. Thus it is not necessary either to take Biblical cosmology literally or to insist that Ḥazal

---

8. Rabbi Abraham ben Moses ben Maimon's position is expressed in a letter which is published in the introductory section of the *Ein Ya'akov.*
9. *Teshuvot Aseh Lekha Rav,* 5:49
10. Rabbi Shaul Yisraeli, *Perakim Bemaḥshevet Yisrael* (Pardes Hanah: Midrashit Noam, 1964), 304-308.
11. Rabbi Michael Taubes relates that Rav Aharon Lichtenstein told a gathering of Yeshivat Har Etzion students that there is nothing objectionable about saying that Ḥazal based their medical/scientific rulings on the best information available at the time. Here, Rav Lichtenstein follows the approach of Rabbi Abraham ben Moses ben Maimon. This author similarly heard Rav Lichtenstein say that it is best to avoid killing lice on Shabbat and Yom Tov in light of modern science's rejection of spontaneous generation. The debate surrounding Rabbi Abraham's assertion might hinge on two approaches presented by Nahmanides (Deut. 17:11) regarding the famous teaching (cited by Rashi ad. loc.) that we must follow Ḥazal "even if they say that right is left or left is right." Nahmanides first explains that this principle is intended to avoid a chaotic situation if the central authority is not accepted. See, for example, the dramatic story of R. Yehoshua's argument that Rabban Gamliel erred regarding the date he established Rosh Ḥodesh (Rosh Hashana 25a). However, Nahmanides then articulates a second approach: that Hashem intervenes and prevents Ḥazal from making errors.
12. Rabbi Hershel Schachter "Science and the Sages," *Jewish Action* (New York: Orthodox Union, Winter 2014) 50-55, available online at https://www.ou.org/jewish_action/12/2014/science-sages/.
13. *Yabia Omer*, vol. 10, Yoreh De'ah, no. 24.
14. Rabbi Natan Slifkin, *The Challenge of Creation* (Brooklyn: Yashar Books, 2006).

were always correct in describing the physical world. "Genesis," Rabbi Slifkin writes, "is best understood not as a scientific account but rather as a theological cosmology. As such, it presents a powerful worldview that has accomplished amazing objectives with mankind."[15]

A primary source for this approach is Maimonides' bold assertion, mentioned earlier, that had Aristotle proven that the world is eternal, Maimonides would have interpreted the Torah allegorically since it is impossible for the Torah to contradict reality. Accordingly, our literal interpretation of the Torah would need to be altered if it does not correspond with demonstrable fact.[16] Likewise, Maimonides insists repeatedly in his *Guide to the Perplexed*[17] that Torah passages that suggest the corporeality of Hashem must be interpreted allegorically since the corporeality of God contradicts fundamental logic (an infinite God cannot be restricted to a body). Rabbi Abraham Isaac HaKohen Kook applies the abovementioned statement by Maimonides and writes that if the theory of evolution is proven, he himself would consider reinterpreting Genesis 1.[18]

It is important to also recognize the different roles of Torah and science. Torah teaches values, the meaning and significance of life and how to live a spiritual and moral life. It comes to address the issues that science does not address. An extended treatment of this delineation of roles is provided by Rabbi Jonathan Sacks in *The Great Partnership: Science,*

15. Ibid., 344.
16. A precedent for Maimonides' position may be found in R. Yaakov's reinterpretation (Kiddushin 39b) of Ex. 20:12 and Deut. 22:7 in light of the terrible incident of a boy who fell to his death after climbing a tree at his father's request to shoo away the mother bird before taking the eggs. The boy died from an injury sustained while fulfilling two commandments for which the reward is long life. This incident caused Elisha ben Abuya to lose his faith; his grandson, R. Yaakov, reinterpreted the promise of long life to refer not to this world but the next. The Gemara concludes that had Elisha ben Abuyah interpreted the verse in this manner, he would not have abandoned his faith. Maimonides may have concluded from this Gemara that where there appears to be a contradiction between Torah and reality, we must reinterpret the Torah.
17. Section one, chapters 1-30.
18. Letter #91.

Religion, and the Search for Meaning[19]. Rabbi Sacks presents the primary thesis of this book in his successful debate against outspoken atheist Richard Dawkins.[20]

This approach has been highly controversial, and the controversy is nothing new. After Maimonides interpreted Genesis 18:1 allegorically,[21] saying that the three angels must have appeared to Abraham in a vision because angels do not eat human food, Nahmanides rejected this approach in the strongest of terms due to its incompatibility with the Torah's text,[22] stating that "these words which contradict the Torah are forbidden to be heard much less to be believed." Nahmanides' fierce repudiation of Maimonides' allegorical interpretation is still invoked to temper the position that contemporary science has proven the need to reinterpret the Torah in a non-literal manner. (And after all, history shows that Maimonides' hesitation in regard to the eternality of the world was validated, in stark contradiction to scientists who believed the world was eternal from the time of Aristotle until the 1960's.)

So far we have looked at several basic approaches to the problem of reconciling Torah and science. Maimonides was willing to reinterpret Torah passages in an allegorical sense if they conflicted with scientific fact, though in the case of the eternity of the universe he hesitated to do so and his hesitation turned out to be well-founded. Rabbi Abraham ben Moshe ben Maimon regarded Ḥazal's statements about the natural world as based on the best information available at the time, and

19. Jonathan.Sacks, *The Great Partnership: Science, Religion, and the Search for Meaning* (London: Hodder & Stoughton, 2011).

20. https://www.youtube.com/results?search_query=rabbi+sachs+vs.+richard+dawkins. A briefer but compelling video presentation of this point by Rav David Fohrman entitled "Why Aren't Dinosaurs in the Torah" may be accessed at https://www.alephbeta.org/course/lecture/noach-where-did-the

21. *Guide to the Perplexed*, 2:42.

22. Nahmanides notes that according to Maimonides the angels' visit to Lot (Gen. 19) and the subsequent rescue of Lot from the destruction of Sodom was only a vision. Such an approach, argues Nahmanides, does violence to the text of the Torah and thus the alleogorization is entirely invalid. Nahmanides (Gen. 9:12) does, however, interpret the rainbow covenant made by Hashem after the flood in accordance with science. In this instance, interpreting the Torah in harmony with scientific fact does not violate the text.

thus subject to revision. Rabbi Meiselman utterly rejects any attempt to reinterpret the Torah in light of scientific theory, such as in regard to the age of the universe. Rabbi Slifkin holds that the Torah is basically a guide for human conduct and does not need to be reconciled with scientific findings at all.

Another very different approach to the Torah-science dichotomy holds that Torah and modern science can indeed be reconciled without compromising the integrity of either discipline. This approach is represented by Orthodox scientists such as Dr. Nathan Aviezer and Dr. Gerald Schroeder, who argue that Genesis 1 is in complete harmony with modern science.[23] We will examine their positions in some depth.

RESOLUTIONS TO APPARENT CONTRADICTIONS

We shall look at Dr. Aviezer's and Dr. Schroeder's responses to four major challenges posed by science in our time. First is the contradiction between traditional Torah belief that the world is less than 6000 years old and the scientific assertion that the universe is many billions of years old. The second issue is the question of the compatibility of the Big Bang Theory and the Torah's account of creation in Genesis chapter one. A third major issue is the scientific claim, supported by archaeological evidence, that man is millions of years old rather than less than

23. Dr. Aviezer's works include *In the Beginning: Biblical Science and Creation* (Hoboken: Ktav Publishing House, 1990) and *Fossils and Faith: Understanding Torah and Faith* (Hoboken: Ktav Publishing House, 2001). Dr. Schroeder's views are available at length in his books *Genesis and the Big Bang* (New York and Toronto: Bantam Books, 1992) and *The Science of God: The Convergence of Scientific and Biblical Wisdom* (New York: Broadway Books, 1998), and are summarized on the Internet as well (www.geraldschroeder.com). Dr. Aviezer earned his doctorate in physics at the University of Chicago and served as the chairman of the physics department at Bar Ilan University. Dr. Schroeder earned his doctoral degree at the Massachusetts Institute of Technology and then spent five years on the staff of the MIT physics department prior to immigrating to Israel, where he joined the Weizmann Institute of Science and then the Volcani Research Institute, while maintaining a laboratory at the Hebrew University. His doctorate spans two fields: earth sciences and physics.

A number of other Orthodox physicists have addressed these issues, including Dr. Herman Branover and Dr. Cyril Domb, who edited, along with Rabbi Aryeh Carmell, the classic work *Challenge: Torah Views on Science and Its Problems* (Jerusalem: Association of Orthodox Jewish Scientists, 1978).

6000 years old as stated in the Torah.[24] The fourth issue is the use of the theory of evolution to assert that the world as we know it came about without a Director (i.e. Hashem).

The Age of the Universe

While the contemporary scientific community accepts that the universe is fourteen billion years old, the Torah records that the world was created in six days less than 6000 years ago. A variety of solutions have been proposed to resolve this issue.

Traditionalists such as the Lubavitcher Rebbe and Rav Meiselman insist that the world was created less than 6000 years ago with no need to reinterpret or otherwise revise this traditional belief in light of modern science, as we explained earlier.

Rabbi Yisrael Lipshitz (1782–1860), the author of the renowned *Tiferet Yisrael* commentary to the Mishna, addressed the issue of the dinosaur remains that were discovered in the nineteenth century in an essay entitled "*Drush Or Haḥayim*" (published in many editions of the Mishna after tractate Sanhedrin). He resolves the contradiction to the Torah by citing Midrash Genesis Rabba 3:7, which states that there were worlds prior to this one. Rabbi Naftali Tzvi Yehuda Berlin (1816-1893),[25] however, rejects this approach citing Midrash Exodus Rabba 1:2, which states that these worlds were reduced by Hashem to *tohu vavohu,* utter oblivion.

A third approach that has been presented by a variety of Orthodox scientists during the past half-century[26] argues that the six days of Creation should be interpreted metaphorically. Indeed, the term *yom* (day) does refer in the Tanakh to an era, such as Malachi 3:23 which describes the messianic era as the *yom Hashem,* the day of God. This

24. Dr. Schroeder (*Genesis and the Big Bang,* 30-33) dismisses the suggestion that the great flood in Noah's time distorted the fossil record, making the fossils appear much older than they truly are. He argues that the compatibility of the archaeological record of the Early Bronze Age and the biblical record of the development of bronze metal in the time of the prediluvian Jubal (Gen. 4:22) proves that the Flood did not alter the fossil record.

25. *Ha'amek Davar,* Gen. 7:3.

26. One example is Professor Aron Vecht's essay "Genesis and Geology," in Domb and Carmel, *Challenge: Torah Views on Science and Its Problems,* 176-187.

approach is bolstered by Genesis (1:14-19) recording that the the sun was created only on the fourth day of Creation, leaving much flexibility regarding the length of the first three days of Creation. Dr. Aviezer[27] embraces this approach.

Dr. Schroeder, however, rejects the argument that the six days of Creation are not meant to be understood literally,[28] since the Talmud (Hagigah 12a), Rashi (s.v. *Middat Yom*), and Nahmanides (Gen. 1:3) all tell us that the word "day" in the context of each of the six days of Creation means 24 hours. Dr. Schroeder argues that the Torah's assertion of Creation in six days and the scientific conclusion that the world is nearly fourteen billion years old are entirely compatible:

> Today, we look back in time and we see approximately 14 billion years of history. But how would they be perceived from the Bible's perspective of time? Looking forward from when the universe is very small – billions of times smaller – the Bible teaches that six days passed. In truth, they both are correct. What's exciting about the last few years is we now have quantified the data to know the relationship of the perception of time from the beginning of stable matter, the threshold energy of protons (their nucleosynthesis) looking forward and our measure of the history of the universe. It's not science fiction any longer. A dozen physics textbooks all bring the same generalized number. The general relationship of the stretching of space between the era of proton anti-proton formation, the time near the beginning at the threshold energy of protons when the first stable matter formed, and time today is a million million. That's a 1 with 12 zeros after it. So when a view from the beginning [of the universe] looking forward says "I'm sending you a pulse every second," would we see a pulse every second? No. We'd see one every million million seconds. That's

27. Aviezer, *Fossils and Faith*, 12-13.

28. Rabbi Simon Schwab (1908-1995) in "How Old is the Universe" (*Challenge: Torah Views on Science and Its Problems*, 164-174) also rejects the non-literal interpretation of the six days of creation since it "violates the literal meaning of the divine text and robs the seventh day of its sacred significance."

> the stretching effect of the expansion of the universe on the perception of time.
>
> The biblical text shows us (and the Talmud[29] confirms) that the soul of Adam was created five and a half days after the Big Bang creation. That is a half day before the termination of the sixth day. At that moment the cosmic calendar ceases and an earth based calendar starts. How would we see those days stretched by a million million? Five and a half days times a million million, gives us five and a half million million days. Dividing that by 365 days in a year, comes out to be 15 billion years. NASA gives a value of about 14 billion years. Considering the many approximations, and that the Bible works with only six periods of time, the agreement to within a few percent is extraordinary. The universe is billions of years old but from the biblical perspective those billions of years compress into five and a half, 24 hour days.[30]

In a talk at Torah Academy of Bergen County, Dr. Schroeder offered as proof for his method of reconciliation the fact that Genesis 1's description of the days of creation (at least until man is created) is written from the *perspective* of the beginning of Creation. Dr. Schroeder noted that the days of Creation are described as the second, third, fourth, fifth, sixth and seventh days, but the first day is described[31] as *yom echad* (day one), not *yom rishon* (the first day).

Nahmanides[32] explains that since there was not yet a second day, the Torah cannot describe the first day of Creation as *yom rishon.* Only after the second day is complete may one describe the days in relative terms such as the second and third day. However, day one must be presented using an absolute term. This is similar to the fact that only after World War II was the Great War referred to as World War I. Before the

29. Sanhedrin 38b.
30. http://geraldschroeder.com/wordpress/?page_id=53 and *Genesis and the Big Bang*, 33-55.
31. Gen. 1:5.
32. Gen. 1:5.

Second World War occurred, the relative term of the First World War would not have made sense.

Accordingly, since we live many years after day one of Creation, why does the Torah not use the relative term of *yom rishon,* since many days have passed since day one until now? The answer is that the days of Creation are not written in terms of our *current* perception of time, but rather the perception of time at Creation. It is logical to use the term "day one," since day two, from the perspective of Creation, had not yet occurred. Thus, we see that the days of Creation are terms utilizing the perspective of the beginning of Creation and not our current retrospective, "earth-based" vantage point.

Dr. Aviezer, however, rejects Dr. Schroeder's approach and cites prominent Orthodox Jewish physicist Dr. Barry Simon of the California Institute of Technology as also rejecting Dr. Schroeder's thesis.[33] Dr. Jeremy England, an Orthodox physics professor at MIT, also expressed significant reservations about Dr. Schroeder's approach in a communication to this author dated December 14, 2016.[34] Dr. Aviezer favors a nonliteral interpretation of the word "day" that appears in Genesis chapter one.

The "Big Bang" Theory and Belief in Hashem

Dr. Aviezer and Dr. Schroeder agree that the "Big Bang" theory is an argument in favor of belief in Hashem. They argue that through their respective resolutions of the discrepancy between the age of the universe as taught in the Torah and the age ascribed to the universe by the proponents of the "Big Bang" theory, they have eliminated one impediment to believers embracing the "Big Bang" theory, which is supportive of Creation and a Creator. For, as common sense as well as Maimonides teaches, if the world was created in time, it most certainly had a Creator who created it in time.[35] If there was a Big Bang, it follows that there was

33. Aviezer, *Fossils and Faith,* 12-13.

34. Rabbi Schwab presents (*Challenge: Torah Views on Science and Its Problems,* 165-174) a similar but far less ambitious approach to argue that Creation took both six days and billions of years. Rabbi Schwab utilizes the idea of relativity and time dilation to support his argument, without quantifying the equivalence of the two time-spans with the equation utilized by Dr. Schroeder.

35. *Guide to the Perplexed,* 1:71.

a "Big Banger," as argued by Dr. Peter Kreeft, professor of philosophy at Boston College in a brief but compelling video presentation.[36]

In addition, it is worth noting that in *Genesis and the Big Bang,* Dr. Schroeder explains that the energy released in the first moments of the Big Bang radiated at such high frequencies that it would have been invisible to the naked eye, and that only later did it cool sufficiently to produce visible light.[37] According to Dr. Schroeder, Genesis 1:3-4, which records that Hashem said, *"Let there be light, and light came into existence… and Hashem separated between the light and the darkness,"* might refer to this cooling process. "The parallel between the opinion of present-day cosmological theory and the biblical tradition that predates it," writes Dr. Schroeder, "is striking and almost unnerving." Dr. Schroeder explains:[38]

> As the thermal energy of the photons fell to 3000K, thus allowing electrons to bind in stable orbits around hydrogen and helium nuclei, not only did the photons break free from the matter of the universe ('separated' in the language of the Torah), but they became visible as well. Light was now light and darkness dark, both theologically and scientifically.

Accordingly, Dr. Schroeder argues that, far from being a threat to Torah belief, the "Big Bang" theory actually supports it. In Dr. Schroeder's words, "the Big Bang Theory is the best thing that has happened to religion since Moses brought the Torah down from Sinai."[39] What remains to be seen in the coming years and generations is whether scientists will sustain or discard the Big Bang Theory.

---

36. Dr. Peter Kreeft, *God vs. Atheism: Which is More Rational?* https://www.youtube.com/watch?v=4T_P14JjMcM. Dr. Kreeft forcefully argues that "Belief in God is far more rational than atheism."
37. Gerald Schroeder, *Genesis and the Big Bang: The Discovery of Harmony between Modern Science and the Bible* (New York: Bantam Books, 1992), 67.
38. Schroeder, *Genesis and the Big Bang,* 89. Dr. Aviezer adopts a similar approach in *In the Beginning,* 14.
39. Dr. Gerald Schroeder, *Creation in 6 Days or 15 Billion Years?* https://www.youtube.com/watch?v=XGH6ey6c2rQ&t=3s.

Dr. Aviezer notes[40] that the Big Bang Theory actually solves the problem posed by the creation of the celestial luminaries only on the fourth day of Creation, after light was created on the first. If we understand the "Let there be light" of the first day of Creation as referring to the Big Bang which preceded the creation of the sun, moon and stars, this apparent contradiction is resolved. In fact, the Zohar[41] many centuries before 1965 notes that "And God said let there be light" is the first act of creation.[42]

Interestingly, Nahmanides[43] teaches

> At the briefest instant following creation all the matter of the universe was concentrated in a very small place, no larger than a grain of mustard.[44] The matter at this time was so thin, so intangible, that it did not have real substance. It did have, however, potential to gain substance and form and to become tangible matter. From the initial concentration of this intangible substance in its minute location, the substance expanded, expanding the universe as it did so.[45]

Dr. Schroeder comments on this: "Ancient biblical scholars did not have the aid of radioastronomy or spectroscopy. So how did they have the insight, a thousand years ago,[46] to form an account of the Big Bang so strikingly similar to our modern theories?"[47] Dr. Schroeder argues that the divine origin of the Torah is the source of the knowledge.[48]

---

40. Nathan Aviezer, *In the Beginning: Biblical Science and Creation* (Hoboken: Ktav Publishing House, 1990), 7-17.
41. Zohar, introduction, paragraph beginning *Vayomer Elokim yehi or*. The Zohar's explanation of Genesis 1:3 might be compatible with the Big Bang Theory.
42. Genesis 1:3 is the first time the Torah records a pronouncement from God. The Zohar explains the first two verses of the Torah as a general introduction to the Creation story, so that verse three begins the specific description of Creation.
43. Gen. 1:1
44. A grain of mustard in rabbinic parlance refers to the tiniest possible speck (see, for example, Berakhot 31a).
45. Quoted in Schroeder, *Genesis and the Big Bang*, 65.
46. Nahmanides lived from 1194-1270.
47. Schroeder, *Genesis and the Big Bang*, 67
48. Similar to their arguing for the compatibility of the Big Bang Theory and Torah, Dr. Aviezer and Dr. Schroeder both argue for the compatibility between quantum

Age of Man

A third discrepancy between the Torah and science is the age of man. *Scientific American*'s April 2012 edition, for example, includes a cover article reporting the discovery of human fossils which scientists claim date back two million years old. Dr. Schroeder presents a bold approach: "Adam was the first human, the first Homo sapiens with the soul of a human, the *neshama*. That is the creation listed in Genesis 1:27. Adam was not the first Homo sapiens."[49] Dr. Aviezer develops a similar approach based on Sforno's comment on Genesis 1:26.[50]

Dr. Schroeder finds support for this assertion in three classic Torah sources. Maimonides' *Guide to the Perplexed*[51] speaks of "animals co-existing with Adam that were identical to humans in shape and intelligence, but because they lacked the *neshama*, they were animals."[52] Dr. Schroeder explains a Mishna[53] that "discusses 'masters of the field' *(adanei hasadeh)* that were animals but so identical to humans that when they died one could not tell them apart from a dead human. Masters of the field implies farming – a skill that predates Adam by at least 2000 years, according to pollen studies in the border area between Israel and Syria." Dr Schroeder also cites Nahmanides, who "details the flow of life that led to the Adam, the first human. Nahmanides closes his comments there with the statement that when this spirituality was infused into the living being, that being changed to another kind of man. Not changed to man but another kind of man, a homo sapiens/hominid became spiritually human."[54]

One may ask, however: for what purpose would Hashem create a human being without a *neshama*? Tosefot Yom Tov provides a possible

---

mechanics and Torah. In the nineteenth century some philosophers denied the possibility of free will based on Newtonian or classical mechanics. The discovery of quantum mechanics in the twentieth century updated classical mechanics and makes it easier to explain the existence of free will, according to Dr. Aviezer (*Fossils and Faith*, chapter 7) and Dr. Schroeder (*The Science of God*, chapter 10).

49. Schroeder, *Genesis and the Big Bang*, 149-152.
50. Aviezer, *Fossils and Faith*, 39-52.
51. *Guide to the Perplexed* 1:7.
52. http://geraldschroeder.com/wordpress/?page_id=79.
53. Kilayim 8:5.
54. Gen. 2:7.

answer.[55] He argues that although all human beings are created *betzelem Elokim* (in the image of Hashem), this refers to divine potential. However, those people who do not observe the seven Noahide laws requiring basic decency such as refraining from murder, theft, and adultery, are not considered to be created in the image of Hashem.

Accordingly, we argue that Hashem might have at first created human beings without a *neshama* to serve as a warning that human beings have the potential to regress to a being without a soul. Indeed, "monsters" such as Hitler and Stalin *(yimmaḥ shmam)* may be described as human beings without a soul. According to this approach, one may describe a human being's soul as "use it or lose it." One who does not respect and express the basic spiritual drives of one's *neshama* loses his *neshama* and regresses to a type of human that existed prior to the creation of Adam.

Dr. Aviezer and Dr. Schroeder's suggestion that human beings without a soul could have existed two million years before the creation of Adam, dovetails with their acceptance of the view that the world is billions of years old. However, those who adopt a more traditional worldview (such as the Lubavitcher Rebbe and Rav Meiselman who insist that the world is less than 6000 years old) would not subscribe to Dr. Aviezer's and Dr. Schroeder's approach.

Rejecting Random Evolution

Many in the Orthodox community summarily reject evolution as incompatible with Torah belief. Thus, they argue that the theory of evolution is incorrect. A primary advocate of this approach is the Lubavitcher Rebbe who writes that the theory of evolution

> has not a shred of evidence to support it. On the contrary, during the years of research and investigation since the theory was first advanced, it has been possible to observe certain spieces of animal and plant life of a short life-span over thousands of generations yet it has never been possible to establish a transmutation from one species into another, much less to turn a plant into an

55. Avot 3:14.

> animal. Hence such a theory can have no place in the arsenal of empirical science.[56]

Dr. Aviezer and Dr. Schroeder, on the other hand, do not necessarily reject evolution as an explanation of how the world developed. They simply argue that there must have been a director to evolution, namely Hashem. Dr. Schroeder argues that advances in complexity do not happen spontaneously. He explains that it is terribly flawed to believe "that randomness can produce meaningful stable complexity. This impossibility of randomness producing order is not different from the attempt to produce Shakespeare or any meaningful string of letters more than a few words in length by a random letter generator. Gibberish is always the result."[57]

Dr. Schroeder concludes, "Neo-Darwinian evolutionary theory calls out for randomness to set the course of life's development. Evolution, Bible style, also sees life develop from the simple (day three and day five) to the highly complex (humanity on day six), but realizes that in this world, random reactions are simply not up to accomplishing that task. Random reactions alone simply do not and can not produce stable order. That is the lesson of the laws of thermodynamics."[58]

Dr. Schroeder added in a communication to this author (dated November 16, 2016):

> Simon Conway Morris,[59] one of the world's leading living paleontologists, in his book, "Life's Solution: Inevitable Humans in a Lonely Universe," avers that there must be some metaphysical force allowing life to find the few viable mutations among the huge, even vast, number of deadly mutations. If the mutations were indifferent, then the likelihood of success becomes highly questionable. Just think, from the initial burst of energy

56. Domb and Carmel, *Challenge: Torah Views on Science and Its Problems,* 148.
57. http://www.geraldschroeder.com/EvolutionBibleStyle.aspx.
58. Ibid.
59. Dr. Conway Morris has held the Chair of Evolutionary Palaeobiology in the Earth Sciences Department at Cambridge University since 1995, is a major exponent of the compatibility of God and evolution, and is a strong critic of militant atheists.

> that marked the Big Bang creation of our universe, that energy has been able to morph and morph again and again and finally develop consciousness, joy; from where does a beam of energy have the ḥutzpah to feel love? But it is accepted that the energy of the Big Bang became alive and self-aware and filled with the most extraordinary potential blessing of all, love.

We noted earlier that Rabbi Kook[60] did not believe it was necessary for an Orthodox Jew to reject the theory of evolution. Thus, we find today Orthodox Jews who utterly reject evolution and other Orthodox Jews who argue that evolution is compatible with Torah provided one accepts Hashem as the director of evolution, tilting events in the direction of the divine plan for the world.[61]

A Fresh Approach: Dr. Jeremy England

A fresh approach to tensions between Torah and science has been articulated by a young Orthodox professor of physics at MIT, Dr. Jeremy England. Dr. England happens to be at the forefront of research into the origin of life and is regarded by some as "the next Darwin." Dr. England states in a video presentation:

> I do not think there is any problem with being both a scientist while also having a commitment to *HaKadosh Baruch Hu* (Hashem) and Torah. I would almost go so far to say that those who see a strong tension there either need to have a subtler understanding of Torah or what science is, or both.[62]

---

60. Letter #91.

61. In a press release dated December 27, 2005 (and archived at http://www.rabbis.org/news/article.cfm?id=100635) the (Orthodox) Rabbinical Council of America stated "that significant Jewish authorities have maintained that evolutionary theory, properly understood, is not incompatible with belief in a Divine Creator, nor with the first 2 chapters of Genesis." It concluded that Orthodox "beliefs do not rest on the purported weaknesses of Evolutionary Theory, and cannot be undermined by the elimination of gaps in scientific knowledge."

62. *"Orthodox Jewish All Star, Dr. Jeremy England, 'The Next Darwin,'"* https://www.youtube.com/watch?v=crJ7cPFN5ug.

Dr. England does not subscribe to Dr. Aviezer and Dr. Schroeder's efforts to harmonize contemporary science with the text of Genesis 1. Dr. England likens this endeavor to be "a kind of forbidden mixture of meat and milk that isn't the mission of an *oved Hashem* (servant of God)."[63]

Dr. England believes the resolution of the tension lies in the use of language. He is quoted[64] as explaining:

> When it says God said let there be light, the point is that the light by which we see the world comes from the way we talk about it. And we have choices to make about how to talk about the world. A second and related point is that when you look at the Tower of Babel, God doesn't want us to only talk about the world one way.
>
> You start with a tower and one language, and at the end of the day it doesn't stay that way and that's because God doesn't want it to be that way. From the standpoint of Tanakh it is a sort of inevitability of social physics that when you start with one language you end up with many languages, and the reason is because the world is too complicated to capture with one. And there's something missing from your account of it once you are limiting your description in that way.

Dr. England explains in further detail in an essay entitled "The Partly Predictable World," published in the December 2015 issue of *Commentary* (pages 27-33). He explains that just as biologists and physicists describe the same phenomenon using different terminology or language, so do Torah and science describe Creation using different "languages." Creation, Dr. England explains, is presented in the Torah using language that is suited to the goal of preparing its readers to serve Hashem following a specific code of law.[65]

---

63. E-mail to this author dated December 14, 2016.
64. Simona Weinglass, "Meet the Orthodox Jewish physicist rethinking the origins of life," *The Times of Israel*, October 29, 2015. This article is archived at http://www.timesofisrael.com/meet-the-orthodox-jewish-physicist-rethinking-the-origins-of-life/.
65. Dr. England presents Rashi on Gen. 1:1 as support for this idea. Rashi states that the Creation story is included in the Torah to teach that since God created the world

Dr. England further clarified his approach,[66] noting:

> We live in a time and a place where everyone around us talks about the models natural scientists have made of the world as though this is what actually is, as though the job of a scientist is just to turn over rocks and discover things that are intrinsically true about the world. In fact what scientists do is make persuasive cases for models that they themselves concoct. This doesn't mean these models are lies, but it does mean that there are multiple compelling ways of characterizing the same world that need not be mutually translatable in a precise sense, and the question of what accounts we need most urgently in order to accomplish *avodat Hashem* (service of God) is presumably the one the Torah is concerned with.

Mr. Shmuel Rosenblatt, a young instructor at Torah Academy of Bergen County with a strong background in both philosophy and science, explained in a lecture that the Creation account in Genesis imparts lessons necessary for *avodat Hashem* (the service of God). Chapter One describes man as part of nature, part of the evolutionary chain of development, if you will. Chapter Two, on the other hand, describes man as distinct from nature and as the recipient of a command from God. Man's challenge (and the essence of *avodat Hashem*) is to transcend his biology, the Chapter One side of his personality, and emerge as the spiritual man of Chapter Two.[67]

Conclusion

A person of faith in the early twenty-first century is not forced to choose between belief in Hashem and Torah and scientific and academic studies,

He enjoys the right to assign the Land of Israel to the nation He deems most fit to control this special land.

66. In an e-mail addressed to this author on December 25, 2016.

67. Lecture given at Torah Academy of Bergen County. Mr. Rosenblatt noted that his approach follows in the footsteps set by his great-grandfather Rabbi Joseph B. Soloveitchik in his monumental works, *The Lonely Man of Faith* and *The Emergence of Ethical Man*.

because a wide variety of approaches have been presented to resolve the tensions between Torah and science.

Thus, while one may have a preference for one of the many approaches we outlined, he should not unnecessarily rule out the others. When presenting this issue to students, whether adults or youngsters, I present the full range of approaches, as we cannot be certain which of these approaches is correct. Moreover, one may find it very worthwhile to adopt a combination of each of these approaches. Whatever one's perspective on this issue, it is undoubtedly in the best interest of lovers of Torah and science to be familiar with each of these views.

Postscript: Ḥazal ahead of their time

As a postscript, it may be worthwhile to note that Ḥazal are not always in conflict with modern science! On the contrary, on a number of matters they were ahead of their time.

In his book, Rabbi Meiselman notes that Ḥazal[68] were aware that *pi* is an irrational number (an irrational number is one that can be expressed neither as an integer nor as a proper fraction of two integers). This was not known beyond Ḥazal until the eleventh century.[69]

Rabbi Meiselman also notes that Ḥazal insist that only five grains are capable of becoming leavened *(ḥametz)*.[70] These are wheat, barley, oats, rye and spelt. Rav Meiselman notes: "To this day no additional gluten-containing species (a grain can rise only if it contains gluten) have been found."[71]

He also adds that Ḥazal were ahead of their time in recognizing that hemophilia is hereditary and specifically passed on through the mother.[72]

Similarly, he writes that Ḥazal were the first to recognize that the liver can regenerate itself.[73]

---

68. See Maimonides, *Perush HaMishnayot,* Eruvin 1:5 and Tosafot HaRosh on Eruvin 14a.
69. Meiselman, *Torah, Chazal, and* Science, 153-155.
70. Pesaḥim 35a.
71. Meiselman, *Torah, Chazal, and Science,* 155-157.
72. Yevamot 64b.
73. Hullin 3:2.

Rabbi Meiselman presents these examples to demonstrate that Ḥazal did not merely arrive at their conclusions based on the available knowledge of the time. Rather, Rabbi Meiselman cites Rabbi Judah HaLevi, who writes that Ḥazal reached these deductions due to *hashgaḥa* (subtle intervention and support from Hashem).[74]

Most remarkable, though, is Ḥazal's statement regarding the dimensions of Noah's ark. Rabbi Meiselman cites Genesis Rabba, which teaches: "The length of the ark should be three hundred cubits, fifty cubits wide and thirty cubits high (Gen. 6:15). Bar Ḥitya said.... The Torah has taught us the way of the world – if one wishes to build a boat that will stand off shore, one should make its width one-sixth of its length and its height one-tenth of its length."[75]

Rabbi Meiselman cites contemporary studies that verify that a barge with the Ark's dimensions would have optimal stability. He also notes that Ḥazal drew only one practical inference from the Ark, despite the many technical considerations that must have gone into the making and operating of the Ark. Moreover, Rav Meiselman notes that in the Babylonian flood story, the Ark constructed by the hero is described as a cube, a totally unseaworthy structure.[76]

This fascinating information constitutes an important addition to the many layers of evidence of the divine authorship of the Torah that we have outlined. It also corroborates Rabbi Judah HaLevi's assertion that the Talmud and other classic rabbinic writings were written with divine assistance and support.[77]

---

74. *The Kuzari*, 2:64, 3:41 and 4:23.
75. Genesis Rabba 31:10.
76. This contrast is an important addition to the many differences between the Torah and ancient Near Eastern literature compiled in Rabbi Amnon Bazak's *Ad HaYom Hazeh*, which is available in English at Yeshivat Har Etzion's Virtual Beit Midrash (http://etzion.org.il/en/teacher/8095) *Shiurim* (lessons) numbers 08a, 08b and 08c.
77. Dr. Kenneth Prager of Columbia Presbyterian Medical Center in New York City has written and lectured extensively about the potency and cogency of the *asher yatzar* blessing, which Jews recite after using the bathroom (http://www.daat.ac.il/daat/kitveyet/assia_english/prager.htm). In a lecture on this topic at Torah Academy of Bergen County, Dr. Prager noted that a majority of illnesses are the result of the obstruction or rupture of bodily structures such as blood vessels or other channels as described in the *asher yatzar* blessing. For example, blockage of the coronary

AN INTRODUCTION TO ARCHAEOLOGY AND TANAKH

There have been extensive archaeological excavations conducted in the Middle East during the past two hundred years. There are some who seek to marshal evidence from these discoveries to disprove the authenticity of the Tanakh. Orthodox scholars, such as Rabbi Amnon Bazak, have presented a cogent response to such criticism.

Many of the stunning discoveries made in that time corroborate the narrative of the Tanakh, such as the discovery of the tunnel dug by Hezekiah to bring water to Jerusalem,[78] which is now an enormously popular site visited each year by thousands.

Another example is the Sennacherib Prism displayed at the British Museum. It is a chronicle of many of Sennacherib's military victories, including his campaign in Judea, as is recorded in Kings.[79] Interestingly, Sennacherib boasts only that he set siege to Jerusalem and that he trapped Hezekiah "like a bird in a cage."[80] In this case – unlike other recordings of his military campaigns – Sennacherib does not specifically mention that he conquered Jerusalem. This fits with the Tanakh record of Sennacherib setting siege to Jerusalem, but failing to conquer it.[81] Sennarcherib's failure to record the miracle of the great plague in which 185,000 Assyrian soldiers were smitten by an angel – which is recorded in Tanakh[82] – is not surprising since in the ancient world, it was unusual for kings to record their defeats and failures. Sennacherib, following this pattern, would record only that he surrounded Jerusalem, but would not record his miraculous defeat.[83]

---

artery leads to a heart attack; blockage of a blood vessel in the brain leads to a stroke; blockage of a bronchial tube leads to pneumonia. Not infrequently such blockage or rupture leads to death. How were Ḥazal aware of this fact 1600 years ago? The divine influence on the talmudic process might be the only reasonable conclusion.

78. II Kings 20:20.
79. II Kings 18:13.
80. The discovery of Sennacherib's words sheds light on Isaiah's words, "As birds hovering, so will the Lord of Hosts defend Yerushalayim; He will defend it and deliver it; He will pass over it and spare it." (Is. 31:5).
81. II Kings 19.
82. II Kings 19:35.
83. Also on display at the British Museum are very large bas-reliefs of Sennacherib's conquest of Lakhish found on a palace wall of Sennacherib (Sennacherib's conquest

Excavations of Tanakh sites in Israel are an exciting and ongoing enterprise. For example, in the summer of 2015, an archaeological team from Bar Ilan University discovered the enormous gate to the city of Gath.[84] In the fall of 2015, a team from the Hebrew University of Jerusalem unearthed the seal of King Hezekiah,[85] in 2016 an artifact was unearthed which corroborates the biblical account[86] of King Hezekiah's campaign to eliminate idolatry,[87] and a 3,000-year-old King David era seal was discovered by the Temple Mount Sifting Project.[88]

Critics, however, draw conclusions negating the veracity of the Tanakh text based on the *lack* of archaeological evidence for certain events. A first response to such assertions is to note the highly precarious approach of drawing conclusions from absence of evidence. This is particularly true in archaeology where little from the ancient world has been preserved and precious little of what has been preserved has been excavated.

Many situations validate the peril of drawing conclusions from the absence of archaeological evidence. The December 2010 issue of *National Geographic* magazine featured an article entitled "Kings of Controversy" by Richard Draper noting that until the 1993 discovery of an ancient stele[89] inscribed with "House of David," there was no

---

of Lakhish is mentioned in II Kings 18:13-14). The fact that Sennacherib set up an eight foot by eighty foot depiction of his conquest of Lakhish and did not set up a mural of a conquest of Jerusalem, the capital city of Judea and seat of the Jewish Temple, also indicates that he did not conquer Jerusalem.

84. http://www.timesofisrael.com/archaeologists-unearth-the-gate-to-goliaths-hometown/. This report also mentions that evidence was found of a massive earthquake in the eighth century B.C.E, which might be the earthquake described in Amos 1:1.
85. http://www.cnn.com/2015/12/03/middleeast/king-hezekiah-royal-seal/.
86. Kings II 18:3-4.
87. http://www.timesofisrael.com/iron-age-toilet-is-evidence-judean-king-dumped-on-the-gods/.
88. http://www.jpost.com/Israel-News/Rare-3000-year-old-King-David-era-seal-discovered-by-Temple-Mount-Sifting-Project-419024.
89. A stele is an ancient monument; this stele is commonly referred to as the Tel Dan Stele. This artifact of monumental importance is displayed at the Israel Museum in Jerusalem. There is a possible contradiction, though, between the Tel Dan Stele and the Tanakh. The Stele indicates that the Aramean king killed both the Israelite king Jehoram son of Ahab and the Judean king, Ahaziah son of Jehoram. II Kings 9:14-27 records that the Aramean king only wounded Jehoram and that Jehu subsequently killed Jehoram and

non-biblical evidence that David actually existed. Similarly, the Temple Mount Sifting Project has revealed evidence of a time period whose "historical credibility" archaeologists had questioned for years. With these findings, however, "the existence of the House of David came to be accepted as historical fact by the vast majority of scholars."[90] Rabbi Amnon Bazak cites Ben Gurion University archaeologist Dr. Zipora Talshir who describes the intellectually dishonest reaction of militant secularists to the discovered evidence of King David's existence:

> The appearance of the House of David as a consolidated political concept represented a real problem for deniers of Ancient Israel. They went to great lengths to try to rid themselves of this most inconvenient evidence. Davis proposed impossible alternative readings, which no self-respecting scholar would dare to mention; Lemke, despairing of any other solution, decided that the inscription was a forgery. No other scholar in the academic world has cast the slightest doubt on the reliability of the inscription, the circumstances of its discovery, or its epigraphic identity. There is nothing problematic about this inscription, other than the fact that it deals a mortal blow to a priori claims against the history of the House of David.[91]

Another instance of a faulty conclusion that "undermined" the authenticity of the Torah was made regarding the domestication of camels in the ancient Near East. Militantly secular archaeologists had argued that the absence of evidence of domesticated camels in the Near East prior to the twelfth century BCE "proved" the inaccuracy of the Book of Genesis, which describes the use of camels during the time of the Patriarchs (approximately seventeenth century BCE). However, later archaeological findings demonstrate that camels were domesticated as early as the end of the third millennium B.C.E., but that widespread domestication did not occur until the twelfth century B.C.E. Rabbi Bazak writes:

Ahaziah. However, one could explain that since the wounding of Jehoram by the king of Aram drew Ahaziah to visit him (II Kings 8:29), creating the opportunity for Jehu to kill both Jehoram and Ahaziah, the king of Aram took the credit for killing them.

90. http://etzion.org.il/en/shiur-6b-tanakh-and-archaeology.

91. Ibid.

> This finding sits well with the biblical account, in which camels did not play a central role, and their numbers were relatively small, until the time of the Judges. In the story of Avraham's servant and Rivka, the Torah mentions 'ten of his master's camels' (Bereishit 24:10); in the gifts that Yaakov offers Esav, we find 'thirty milk camels with their young' (ibid. 32:16); and in the account of the sale of Yosef we find a "caravan of Yishme'elim came from the Gil'ad, with their camels carrying gum balm and ladanum" (ibid. 37:25). We may therefore conclude that camels were not common, and were used mainly to carry expensive merchandise. The camels that Avraham's servant brought with him apparently represented a factor in the estimation of the avaricious Lavan (ibid. 30-31). In other narratives in the Torah, camels are absent: in the descent of Yosef's brothers to Egypt we find only donkeys (ibid. 42:26-27, and elsewhere); in the spoils seized from Midian we find 'sixty-one thousand asses' (Bamidbar 31:34), but no mention of any camels. In contrast, from the period of the Judges onwards we find a great many camels. In the war of the children of Gad and the children of Reuven against the Hagri'im, we find: 'And they captured their cattle, [and] of their camels fifty thousand' (Divrei Ha-yamim I, 21). Iyov, at the end of his life, had six thousand camels (Iyov 42:12).[92]

Thus, findings that seemed at first to conflict with the Tanakh account end by confirming it.

Rabbi Amnon Bazak offers a fairly comprehensive review of the archaeological record in regard to Tanakh.[93] He states that there is no

---

92. http://etzion.org.il/en/shiur-6c-tanakh-and-archaeology. In the same lecture, Rabbi Bazak further notes that the militant secularists of the "minimalist school" of archaeology continued to write that the reference to camels in Genesis is anachronistic. In response he cites Kenneth Kitchen, a well-respected scholar of biblical archaeology and Professor Emeritus at Liverpool University, to the effect that "camels are not anachronistic in the early second millennium (Middle Bronze Age)."
93. *Shiurim* 6a through 6i on Yeshivat Har Etzion's virtual Beit Midrash (www.etzion.org/vbm).

archaeological evidence that contradicts the Torah.[94] In turn, he writes there are "many findings that do conform to the biblical narratives from the time of the *Avot* (forefathers), and indicate that these narratives were indeed written with a profound familiarity with the period." He notes the same regarding the era of enslavement and subsequent exodus from Egypt.[95]

In regard to excavations that appear, on a superficial level, to contradict Tanakh texts, the conflicts emerge from either insufficient or inaccurate archaeology or from a flawed understanding of Tanakh. An example of the first variety of error is the conclusion of some archaeologists that the battle of Ai described in the Book of Joshua did not occur, a conclusion based on excavations at Ai showing that the city was not inhabited at the time of Joshua's entry into the land of Yisrael.[96] Others, however, argue that the wrong area had been excavated. They claim to have found the correct location of Ai, which, when subsequently excavated, yielded evidence that it was in fact inhabited during the time of Yehoshua's conquest.[97]

Rabbi Bazak deals persuasively with the sensitive issues regarding the periods of Joshua, the Judges, King David and King Solomon. He combines his trademark, superior analysis of Tanakh with extensive knowledge of archaeology to provide an extraordinary treatment of the conflict. Rabbi Bazak concludes his discussions by noting:

> Our review has also revealed the transience of some central theories in the world of archaeology. The Merneptah Stele is a proof of utmost significance as to the existence at that time of an entity

---

94. Regarding geological evidence for the Flood, Dr. Gerald Schroeder (*Genesis and the Big Bang* 28) writes: "Any 'proof' for or against the occurrence of the biblical Flood of Noah's time is weak. In Genesis we are told that the downpour lasted only forty days and the resulting flood persisted for only 150 days. Sediments from so brief a period would probably not be extensive and, therefore, firm archaeological evidence may never be found."
95. *Shiurim* 6d and 6e on Yeshivat Har Etzion's virtual Beit Midrash (www.etzion.org/vbm).
96. Encyclopedia Judaica II, 471-472.
97. For further discussion of Ai and the archaeological record see Rabbi Amnon Bazak's *Ad HaYom haZeh*, available in English at http://etzion.org.il/en/shiur-6ftanakh-and-archaeology-continued-%D6%Aoyehoshua-and-conquest-land.

known as 'Israel,' and had it not been discovered, quite coincidentally, the research on this subject would be in a completely different situation to what it is today.[98]

Had the Dan Stele inscription not been discovered some twenty years ago, many scholars today would probably still deny the existence of David and Shlomo, arguing that "no findings to concretely confirm their existence have yet been discovered." The amount of material that has been excavated and studied is extremely small, relative to what remains, and we must also take into consideration the fact that in the most important regions, such as the City of David and the Temple Mount, excavations are highly problematic if not altogether impossible.

However, archaeology has contributed, and will continue to contribute greatly to our understanding and appreciation of Tanakh. A walk through the sites where the stories of the Tanakh took place, or standing before archaeological findings from that period, is a powerful and moving experience. Archaeological research also influences and deepens our understanding of different parts of Tanakh. Without the discoveries on the ground, it is doubtful whether we would make the proper differentiation, for instance, between the descriptions of settlement in *Sefer* Yehoshua and those in *Sefer* Shoftim. In addition, archaeological findings have shed light on the events described in the text, such as the campaign of Shishak and the war against Mesha, king of Moab. It seems reasonable to assume that further discoveries with ramifications for this sphere of research still await us, and will continue to interest all those who hold the Tanakh dear.[99]

SHISHAK'S ATTACK ON THE NORTHERN KINGDOM OF ISRAEL: A CASE IN POINT

As an example of how apparent contradictions between Tanakh and archaeological evidence can be resolved, we will examine in detail the

98. This quote is from J. Hoffman, "Historia, Mythos v'Politika," in Y.L. Levine and A. Mazar, *HaPulmus al HaEmet veHistoria BeMikra,* Jerusalem, 5761, 31-32.
99. http://etzion.org.il/vbm/english/archive/tanakh/06i-tanakh.htm.

relation between Tanakh's account of King Shishak's campaign and the war against Mesha, and the archaeological discoveries bearing on these events.

On the southern wall of the Temple of Amon in Karnak, Egypt, is an inscription about the military conquests of King Shishak, a Pharaoh who ruled between 935-914 BCE. The inscription describes a heavy military blow dealt to tens of cities both in the Southern and Northern Kingdoms of Israel, ruled at that point by Rehoboam, the son of King Solomon, and Jeroboam, respectively. This gives a picture of events that seems different from the account in Tanakh. According to I Kings 11:40, Shishak had sheltered Jeroboam during his years of exile, which seems inconsistent with Shishak's attacking the cities of Jeroboam's northern Israelite kingdom. And indeed, I Kings 14:26-28 records only Shishak's attack on the Southern Kingdom and not his attacks on the Northern Kingdom.

Rejection of Potential Solutions

Contradictions between Tanakh and archaeological evidence can sometimes be resolved by questioning the validity of archaeological evidence, as we have mentioned. Ancient kings recorded their own version of their achievements and were hardly objective historians. They were loath to record their failings and sometimes exaggerated their victories. Thus one could, in theory, argue that Shishak inflated his exploits in the land of Israel and recorded that he invaded northern Israel when in fact he did not. This, however, is not a viable approach, since part of a stele celebrating Shishak's victory in northern Israel was discovered in Megiddo, a strategically-located fortress in Israel's Jezreel Valley.

Another approach can be based on the fact that Tanakh, simply put, is not a history textbook. The Book of Kings, for example, often refers to the Chronicles of the Kings of Judea or the Chronicles of the Kings of Israel for a full description of the lives of the various kings it discusses.[100] Thus one could argue that the Tanakh does not record Shishak's invasion of northern Israel simply because it does not seek

100. These lost sources should not be confused with the Book of Chronicles in Tanakh, which was written during the Second Temple period.

to present a full description of all the events that occurred during the reign of Jeroboam. This approach is also unsound because our problem is not simply the Tanakh's *omission* of Shishak's invasion of Northern Israel. Our fundamental problem is that Tanakh presents Shishak as a *friend* of Jeroboam, but the inscription on the Karnak temple presents Shishak as his enemy.

The Solution of Professor Yehuda Elitzur

Professor Yehuda Elitzur, a highly respected Orthodox Jewish Bible scholar, presents an interesting theory to resolve this problem.[101] He suggests that Shishak anticipated that Jeroboam would ally himself with him in his attack on Rehoboam's Judea after Jeroboam led the secession of the ten northern tribes from Rehoboam's kingdom.[102] The plan was orchestrated as a joint military campaign.

However, Rehoboam resisted avenging Jeroboam's rebellion and acquiesced to the split of his kingdom.[103] After Rehoboam's lack of hostility, Jeroboam could hardly muster popular support for an attack on Judea. He had no reason or motive to attack; he was ironically beholden to Rehoboam for his kingdom.

Moreover, Jeroboam understood very well that he should not force his subjects to fight an unpopular war. Jeroboam knew that the northern tribes' secession derived from King Solomon's overburdening the people with unpopular building projects. Thus he could not afford to ignore public sentiment, since that was the very force that had swept him into office in the first place.[104] Hence, Professor Elitzur suggests that Jeroboam failed to uphold his agreement with Shishak, abandoning their collective plan to decimate Judea. In response, Shishak attacked Judea (and plundered the wealth accumulated by King Solomon, as recorded in the Book of Kings), harming the Southern Kingdom but not destroying it.

---

101. http://www.daat.ac.il/elitzur/maamarim/plishat.asp.
102. I Kings 12.
103. I Kings 12:22-24.
104. Torah Academy of Bergen County alumnus Jeremy Doberman adds that new regimes, as opposed to well-established dynasties, must be particularly sensitive to public sentiment.

His real fury was channeled against Jeroboam, who betrayed him by backtracking on previous plans.

This explains some of the politics. Still, it leaves us with a further question: Why does the Tanakh fail to mention the attack on Jeroboam's kingdom? The depiction in the Book of Kings is ahistorical, as if it deliberately omits the great military events and puts the entire emphasis upon the Temple. The most reasonable explanation for its focus is that the purpose of the transmission of the story is not to report historical events, however important they may be, but to teach spiritual lessons. It would appear that the Tanakh presents historical events within the context of the concept of reward and punishment. Shishak's attack on Jerusalem is described because it punishes the people of Judea for their idolatry.[105]

A variation of this approach is that Tanakh records Shishak's attack on Jerusalem not only to record the punishment for Judea's idolatry, but also to celebrate Rehoboam's wise and righteous decisions in heeding the advice of the prophet Shemaiah, avoiding a civil war with Jeroboam and yielding to Shishak's power. By doing so, Rehoboam avoided the premature destruction of the Temple. This contrasts sharply with later kings of Judea such as Josiah, Jehoiakim, and Zedekiah who paid dearly, eventually losing the Temple, for their failure to obey the directives of Isaiah[106] and Jeremiah[107] to avoid confrontation with a superpower.

Moreover, it teaches that King Solomon's ill-advised alliance with Pharaoh led to the near-destruction of the Temple and to the loss of much of his accumulated wealth. Shishak, the founder of a new Egyptian dynasty,[108] viewed Solomon as an enemy, since Solomon was a friend of his enemy, the previous Pharaoh.

However, Shishak's invasion of the Northern Kingdom only damaged, rather than destroyed, Jeroboam's kingdom. Since Jeroboam is portrayed as a wicked man of the highest order, perhaps the Book of Kings did not mention Shishak's damage to northern Israel because this did not represent adequate punishment for Jeroboam's misdeeds, whereas

105. I Kings 14:22-26.
106. Is. 30:2 and 31:1.
107. Jer. 2:18 and Ta'anit 22b.
108. See Radak and *Da'at Mikra* on I Kings 11:40.

Shishak's damaging of Judea is recorded since it represented adequate punishment for their idolatry.[109] I Kings does record the destruction of all of the males of Jeroboam's family, since this was a just consequence of his evil actions.[110]

An Alternative to Professor Elitzur's Approach

I suggest an alternative to Professor Elitzur's reconstruction of the relationship between Shishak and Jeroboam. One should hardly be shocked at a king attacking a former ally. Many have observed that "nations have no permanent allies, only permanent interests." A well-known demonstration of this principle is Hitler's alliance with Stalin to jointly invade Poland in 1939, followed by Hitler's invasion of the Soviet Union in 1941. Hitler allied with Stalin when he felt it was in his interest to do so and then attacked Stalin when he felt similarly.

The same may have occurred with Shishak and Jeroboam. I suggest that Shishak wished to plunder the wealth accumulated by King Solomon that was stored in Jerusalem. Shishak, however, feared attacking a united and mighty Israel. He felt his only hope of taking the gold lay in weakening Israel by supporting Jeroboam, who was determined to split Israel into two kingdoms. Thus, Shishak sheltered Jeroboam when the latter escaped from King Solomon, because Jeroboam's revolt would facilitate the achievement of Shishak's goals in the south (divide and conquer).

However, once Shishak had plundered the gold of the Southern Kingdom, his alliance with Jeroboam became irrelevant since Jeroboam was no longer useful to Shishak. Instead, Shishak set his sight on the Jezreel Valley, which was in Jeroboam's kingdom, because the international trade route between Egypt and Mesopotamia ran through this valley. One who controlled the trade route had the ability to increase his wealth, and this seems to have been Shishak's goal. With the once

109. Torah Academy of Bergen County alumnus Jared Mayer adds that this phenomenon is somewhat similar to the halakhic principle of *kam lei biderabbah mine* (if one performed two sins simultaneously, Beit Din administers only the harsher punishment). Similarly, Tanakh records only the harsher punishment meted out by Hashem to Jeroboam.

110. I Kings 15:29.

united and mighty Israelite nation, split and weakened, Shishak was easily able to defeat Jeroboam's kingdom and assume control of the international trade route. Indeed, the inscription on the Karnak Temple mentions many key Jezreel Valley locations attacked by Shishak, such as Megiddo and Beit She'an.

Conclusion

Understood properly, the archaeological record regarding Shishak hardly undermines the Tanakh. Instead, it specifically augments our understanding of the events described in I Kings, and enriches our appreciation of the goals of the text when we learn of the events Hashem chose not to include in its composition. This is yet another example of the principle that there cannot be a contradiction between external sources and Torah. Either we do not properly understand or interpret the external sources or the Torah, or perhaps both! A sophisticated and thorough understanding of Torah and the pertinent external material resolves possible contradictions, since the Torah constitutes absolute truth as the revealed wisdom of Hashem. If one's generation is unable to resolve the difficulty, we can be confident that insight and/or information gleaned and developed in future generations will pave a path towards a solution.

II KINGS 3 IN LIGHT OF THE MESHA STELE

Sometimes an archaeological find can shed light on an episode in Tanakh that appears mysterious without the find. The Mesha Stele is an example of this.

II Kings 3 relates that in response to Moab's rebellion against the Israelite kingdom, the Israelite king Jehoram, the son of Ahab, formed a coalition with the kingdom of Judea, led by the righteous King Jehoshafat, and the king of Edom. En route to the battle, this triple alliance ran out of water. Jehoram called upon the prophet Elisha, who had joined the troops going to the battle, to miraculously provide water and rescue the three armies. Elisha spoke harshly to Jehoram, but kindly about his partner Jehoshafat. After miraculously providing water, Elisha instructed the alliance to smite Moab and engage in General Sherman-like warfare against Moab, destroying all in their path including the fruit trees. After the army had successfully executed Elisha's plan and wreaked havoc upon Moab, the war ended inconclusively, with the alliance dissolving in a last-minute debacle.[111] Moab was left in shambles, though Jehoram's goal of restoring his control over Moab was not achieved.

The thoughtful reader is left with many questions regarding this episode. First, why did the righteous king Jehoshafat join this battle? Perhaps it is because his son married Ahab's daughter Athaliah (sister of Jehoram). Indeed, Jehoshafat allied himself with Ahab in his war against Aram (I Kings 22). However, Jehoshafat narrowly escaped death in that war and thus refused to ally himself with Ahab's son Ahaziah in his quest for gold, recorded in I Kings 22:49-50. Why, then, did Jehoshafat join Jehoram son of Ahab in his quest to regain control over Moab? Moreover, why was Elisha clearly pleased with Jehoshafat's participation in this war?[112]

The second question is: why did Elisha call for such an aggressive campaign against Moab? Furthermore, what was the justification of his order to cut down fruit trees, which violates an explicit Torah prohibition?[113] In his introduction to the Mishna, Maimonides explains that this was a *hora'at sha'a,* a temporary suspension of a Torah law, which an established prophet is permitted to do in case of great need.[114] Maimonides does not clarify, however, the great need that called for a suspension of the Torah prohibition to cut down fruit trees.

A third question is why Elisha, a prolific miracle worker, made a miracle to save the "triple entente" from dying of thirst but did not make a miracle to ensure a complete victory over Moab. Shouldn't Elisha's presence have ensured an unadulterated defeat of Moab? We are left wondering why Hashem apparently did not want the coalition to achieve such a triumph.

---

111. See Ralbag (II Kings 3:27) and Malbim (ibid.) for an explanation of the obscure final verse of Chapter 3, which presents the reason for the dissolution of the alliance.
112. Similarly, Ḥazal *(Avot DeRabbi Natan* 9:4) strongly criticize Jehoshafat for partnering with Ahab but do not criticize Jehoshafat for joining Jehoram's war against Moab.
113. Deut. 20:19-20.
114. A classic *hora'at sha'a* is Elijah's offering a sacrifice on Har Carmel, as recorded in I Kings 18. Elijah did this despite the prohibition against offering a sacrifice outside the Temple (Lev. 17:1-4), due to the extraordinary need to draw the Jews of the Northern Kingdom back to the Torah.

One could answer that, since Jehoram was wicked, he was undeserving of a miracle. If so, then why did the coalition merit obtaining water in a miraculous fashion? Why were the allied armies so successful in their effort to wreak havoc upon Moab? II Kings 3 and its traditional commentaries do not provide clear answers to these three major problems.

The Mesha Stele – A Source for the Answers

With the discovery of the Mesha Stele in the late nineteenth century, the answers to these questions became apparent. Rabbi Bazak writes the following about the Mesha Stele:

In *Sefer* Melakhim we read:

> And Mesha, king of Moab, was a sheepmaster, and he delivered to the king of Israel a hundred thousand lambs, and a hundred thousand rams, with the wool. But it was, when Achav died, that the king of Moab rebelled against the king of Israel... (Melakhim II 3:4-5)
>
> In 1868, a stele (inscribed stone) dating to the 9th century B.C.E. was discovered in what is now Jordan. Its inscription shows that it was established by this same Mesha, king of Moab. It opens with the words, 'I am Mesha, son of Kemosh,[115] king of Moab.' Mesha records that the people of Moab were subservient to Omri, king of Israel, for a long time ['Omri, king of Israel, and they afflicted Moab for many days'] and describes at length how he prevailed against Omri's son, until Israel was annihilated. The Mesha Stele, then, is the earliest external evidence of Moab's battle against Israel, as recorded in the text, and of the existence of the House of Omri.[116]

Mesha ascribes his defeat of the Israelite king as a victory of his god Kemosh as stated in the Stele, "Omri was king of Israel, and oppressed

115. Kemosh is well known in the Tanakh as the god of Moab. For example: "Woe to you, Moab! You are undone, O people of Kemosh!" (Num. 21:29); "Then Solomon built a high place for Kemosh, the abomination of Mo'av... ." (I Kings 11:7).

116. http://www.etzion.org.il/en/shiur-6b-tanakh-and-archaeology.

Moab during many days, and Kemosh was angry with his aggressions." Mesha even presents his success as the subservience of Hashem to Kemosh (heaven forfend) by stating, "I took from it the vessels of J-h-v-h, and offered them before Kemosh."

After his successful rebellion against Jehoram, Mesha erects the Mesha Stele to celebrate his victory, to elevate the Moabite god Kemosh and denigrate Hashem in the most public manner possible. One may hypothesize that Mesha erected numerous such steles in his territory.

The Mesha Stele undoubtedly is describing the initial Moabite rebellion against Jehoram and not the battle between Moab and the "triple entente" which is described in II Kings 3. The stele mentions only that Mesha fought against a descendent of Omri (i.e. Jehoram); it makes no mention of Jehoshafat and Edom.

Armed with this information, we may proceed to answer our three questions. Our answers are a variation of Rabbi Elḥanan Samet's approach presented in his monumental work *Pirkei Elisha*[117]. The modifications emerge from the sharp questioning of Torah Academy of Bergen County students, to whom I presented Rabbi Samet's approach.

Based the Mesha Stele, it is readily understood why the righteous Jehoshafat joined the battle against Moab. Jehoshafat came to correct the terrible *ḥillul Hashem* (desecration of the Divine Name) created by the Moabite king Mesha, something which Elisha wholeheartedly endorsed. Despite the near disaster that occurred in his previous alliance with the Northern Kingdom, Jehoshafat was willing to take the risk in order to counter the terrible disgrace of Hashem's name.

Similarly, Elisha orders the utter devastation of Moab to demonstrate the sheer impotence of the Moabites' false god Kemosh and to reverse the awful *ḥillul Hashem* created by the Mesha Stele. This goal clearly justifies the temporary suspension of the prohibition against cutting down fruit trees. Elisha was hostile to Jehoram due to the latter's indifference to the *ḥillul Hashem* created by the Mesha Stele. Jehoram ben Achav assembled a coalition and waged war against Moab simply to regain control of Moab, but his ambitions were thwarted by a shocking and successful move made in desperation by the Moabite king at the

117. Rabbi Elḥanan Samet, *Pirkei Elisha* (Jerusalem: Makhon Ma'ali'ot, 2007), 85-118.

end of the battle. Therefore, although the *ḥillul Hashem* was corrected, Jehoram's goals remained unmet.[118] Both the reversal of the *ḥillul Hashem* and Jehoram's failure to accomplish his objective are most appropriate and consistent with Torah values.

Why the Book of Kings Does Not Mention the Mesha Stele

Torah Academy of Bergen County students have asked why the Book of Kings does not present the information contained in the Mesha Stele. In response, I cite Nahmanides' assertion that the Torah does not present the story of Abraham's miraculous survival of Nimrod's fiery furnace so as not to publicize the idolatrous beliefs of Nimrod.[119] Similarly, the Tanakh chooses not to publicize the *ḥillul Hashem* created by the Mesha Stele.

This is analogous to the approach adopted by the authors of the *Da'at Mikra* Tanakh commentary. The authors, Orthodox Tanakh scholars who are thoroughly familiar with both the Orthodox and secular approaches to Tanakh, do not mention Bible critics' interpretations of various Tanakh passages. However, the commentary does include an Orthodox response to the criticism. Thus, for those familiar with the arguments of the Bible critics, reading the *Da'at Mikra* commentary provides a response, while those who are unaware of the secular critics' claims will also find the *Da'at Mikra* meaningful and enriching even though they will not grasp the full extent of the commentary's goals. The authors of the *Da'at Mikra* series thus achieve their goals of writing a significant commentary to Tanakh and responding to biblical criticism, without needlessly publicizing anti-religious views.[120]

118. The Mesha Stele also explains why Edom allied with the Jewish kings, a singular event in all of Tanakh. The stele records that Moab had captured territory from the Edomites. This makes clear that the Edomites were motivated by a desire to recover territory.
119. Gen. 11:28.
120. Rabbi Amnon Bazak, authoring *Ad HaYom HaZeh* more than a decade after the completion of the *Da'at Mikra* commentary, presents a frontal response to biblical criticism. He fully presents the views of Bible critics and offers highly persuasive responses to their views. We live in an age of great access to information (the Mesha stele, for example, is prominently displayed in the Louvre in Paris), and it is therefore important for Rabbi Bazak to demonstrate the inadequacies of biblical criticism.

Similarly, one who is not familiar with the Mesha Stele will find II Kings 3 meaningful, but cannot fully appreciate its significance. Far from contradicting Tanakh, the Mesha Stele actually enriches our understanding of Tanakh.

A Final Thought about the Mesha Stele

The ultimate response to the Mesha's bold declaration that Israel is crushed forever is the fact that Moab and Kemosh have vanished and the Jewish people continue to live on. Rabbi Bazak notes "the considerable historical irony in the fact that the two most ancient archaeological proofs concerning the existence of Am Yisrael—the Merneptah Stele and the Mesha Stele both describe the annihilation of Israel: 'Israel is laid waste and his seed is not,' says the former, while the latter asserts, 'Israel has perished; it has perished forever!'"[121] In fact, the only people with widespread knowledge of Moab and Kemosh are the Jews whom Mesha so brashly proclaimed were defeated forever. Israel's survival is the greatest testament to God's continued management of the world. As stated in the Gemara (Yoma 69b), "if not for the fear of the Almighty how could one nation survive among so many [hostile] nations." The continued existence and vibrancy of our people indeed constitutes a great *kiddush Hashem* (sanctification of the Name).

121. http://etzion.org.il/en/shiur-6g-tanakh-and-archaeology-continued-%D6%A0-era-settlement#_ftn6

Chapter 4

Discovering Hashem in Today's World

While Tanakh records many overtly miraculous events, to many people it seems that there are no miracles in our time, and this perception causes them to doubt the occurrence of the Tanakhic miracles. However, this perception overlooks the fact that there is more than one kind of miracle.

The nineteenth-century halakhic authority Rav Yeḥiel Mikhel Epstein distinguishes between three types of divine intervention and the corresponding expressions of gratitude we owe Hashem for each.[1] Miracles that contravene the laws of nature, such as those involved with our exodus from Egypt, demand the recital of the blessing *she'asa nes* (who has made a miracle).[2] In the *Modim* blessing of the *Amida* (the centerpiece of Jewish prayer), we thank Hashem for the "routine" miracles

1. Rav Yeḥiel Mikhel Epstein, *Arukh HaShulḥan, Oraḥ Ḥayim* 219:2-4.
2. Rabbi Hershel Schachter ruled that a congregant at Congregation Shaarei Orah, the Sephardic Congregation of Teaneck, who inexplicably survived a very severe automobile accident, should recite this blessing when passing the accident site.

such as earning a livelihood[3] and everyday survival. *Birkat Hagomel,* the blessing for deliverance from danger recited in the synagogue, is reserved for those occurrences that fall between these two extremes. It is recited when one is saved without a violation of the laws of nature, but the circumstances "somewhat deviate from the boundaries of naturally occurring events into the realm of a miraculous nature."

When we carefully examine the history of our own time, and especially the history of the State of Israel, we see many events that can only be understood as miracles, even when there is no overt violation of the laws of nature. We shall look at some of these events and then return to the question why there seem to be no overt miracles in this time.

THE PURIM DELIVERANCE AS MODEL FOR HIDDEN MIRACLES

The absence of overt miracles is nothing new in Jewish history. Already the Book of Esther, which deals with the Persian period, addresses this situation. As an introduction to our discussion of recent miracles, we will analyze the pivotal episode in the Book of Esther, which is the standard source for an approach to understanding Hashem's involvement in the world in the post-prophetic age. The Book of Esther teaches how to perceive God's involvement even when violations of the laws of nature do not occur. It teaches how to detect the hand of God exquisitely operating behind the scenes alongside calculated and dedicated human activities.

In the Book of Esther, a plot to annihilate the Jews is foiled in part through a brilliant and flawlessly-executed strategy on the part of Esther. Yet it is clear that the strategy would not have succeeded without Hashem's subtle manipulation of events.

Esther's Strategy

As related in the *Megilla* (the Book of Esther), Esther finally acquiesces to Mordekhai's order that she appear before Ahasuerus to plead on

3. Many friends with whom I confide share my experience that Hashem is clearly involved with our efforts to support our families. This idea is expressed by Ḥazal in the saying, "Earning one's sustenance is as difficult as the splitting of the Red Sea (Pesaḥim 118a)."

behalf of her people. After three days of fasting and preparing, Esther appears before the king and invites him and Haman to a party. Why did Esther not do as she was told and plead on behalf of the Jews? Why did she make a party? Moreover, when Ahasuerus asks her what she wants, Esther responds that she wants a second party. Esther's behavior seems inexplicable. Was she simply beset by fear and delaying the inevitable?

Esther was definitely not scared. Indeed, if we read the verses carefully, we notice that the party was prepared prior to her appearance before the king.[4] Clearly, Esther had a plan. Part of the plan was inviting Ahasuerus to the party. In this way she assumes control of the situation and brings Ahasuerus to her turf. She also may be subtly habituating Ahasuerus to doing her bidding. Most intriguing, though, is her request to invite Haman to this party. If she wished to make a request of her husband, why did she invite Haman? After all, two is company; three is a crowd.

Why Does Esther Invite Haman?

The Gemara[5] offers *twelve* solutions to this problem – we shall present five of them – and concludes by saying that the prophet Elijah was asked by Rabba bar Avuha which explanation is correct. He responded that each suggestion is valid. In other words, Esther's inviting Haman had many varied objectives.

Esther had five targets in mind when she invited Haman – Hashem, the Jewish people, Ahasuerus, the ministers other than Haman, and Haman. The invitation was a plea to Hashem to make a miracle to save her people. The fact that she was forced to ingratiate herself with the despicable Haman was intended to dramatize the utter desperation of the situation.[6]

The signal to the Jewish people was that they must intensify their prayers. Despite the dreadful decree, we were not desperately disturbed since we thought that our well-connected "sister" in the palace would

4. Esther 5:4.
5. Megilla 15b.
6. Rashi to Megilla 15b s.v. *yargish*.

manage to save the day. When we became aware that Esther had invited Haman to her party, we thought that Esther became an ally of Haman and abandoned her Jewish identity to spare herself from the decree. This left us with the attitude that only Hashem could save us from annihilation, which in turn led us to intensify our prayers, a method which proved to be quite effective. Indeed, the finest prayer is when we recognize our total dependence on Hashem, such as when we state "*va'anaḥnu lo neda mah na'ase ki elekha einenu* (we do not know what to do because our eyes are turned to you)."[7]

Esther also targeted Ahasuerus in her plan. Her goal was to plant feelings of jealousy and suspicion of Haman in Ahasuerus. It could be that at the party Esther deliberately lavished attention on Haman in order to make Ahasuerus think that she was interested in Haman. It is evident from the *Megilla* that Ahasuerus was a very insecure, suspicious individual, and indeed the Bigtan and Teresh conspiracy shows that he had good reason to be paranoid.[8]

This is especially compelling if we accept the *Da'at Mikra's* identification of Ahasuerus with Xerxes who, in the seventh year of his kingdom, had just suffered a crushing defeat at the hands of the Greeks. If so, many were angry at Ahasuerus, and he had to zealously guard against rebellions since the time for one was ripe.

Esther sought to make Ahasuerus think that Haman was plotting against him and that Esther was a partner in his scheme. Of course, Esther was playing an exceedingly dangerous game and placing her life at great risk, as Ahasuerus would likely kill Esther along with Haman if he became thoroughly convinced. This is an example of the sacrifices that Esther was willing to make for the Jewish people.

In addition, Esther understood that Ahasuerus was fickle and impulsive. She invited Haman so that if she succeeded in convincing Ahasuerus to kill Haman, he would be available for immediate execution before Ahasuerus could change his mind. She also wanted Haman to be available for immediate execution so that he would not have an opportunity to organize a rebellion.

7. This verse is recited in the daily morning prayers.
8. Esther 2:21-23.

Another dimension of Esther's strategy was to inflate Haman's ego. Proverbs[9] teaches that haughtiness precedes one's downfall, because when people become overconfident they let their guard down and become vulnerable to a big fall. Esther sought to do this by inviting him to the exclusion of the other royal advisors. Serving a meal to an enemy is a shrewd tactic to build the enemy's trust, which can later be exploited to his disadvantage. It is evident from the Megilla that Haman's ego was quite delicate and easily bruised (by Mordekhai not bowing to him) or inflated (by Esther's invitation). Thus, his emotions could be readily manipulated.

Finally, Esther sought to incite jealousy of Haman among the other advisors, as they would be upset that only Haman was invited to the party. Ahasuerus' court – like many other royal courts throughout history – was filled with intrigue, suspicion, and envy because the advisors struggled to advance themselves at the expense of others. Esther deftly played on this atmosphere of court intrigue.

Hashem Executes the Plan

We may ask, though, why Esther invited Ahasuerus to a second party instead of simply making her plea at the first party. The answer is that Esther was planting seeds of redemption with the first invitation. Ibn Ezra explains that the seeds had not yet blossomed at that point so she needed to wait and continue with her scheme by inviting Ahasuerus to a second party.[10]

The prayers were obviously effective as Hashem enabled Esther's plan to proceed exactly as designed. Ahasuerus became quite jealous and suspicious, as evidenced by his inability to sleep.[11] He wondered why no one emerged to warn him of the impending plot and he searched his records to see if, in the past, someone had foiled a plot and had not been rewarded, thereby discouraging individuals from coming forward and sounding a warning. When Ahasuerus discovered that Mordekhai had not been rewarded for saving him from Bigthan and Teresh, Ahasuerus began to think of an appropriate reward.

---

9. Prov. 16:18.
10. Esther 5:8.
11. Esther 6:1.

Haman was elated at his exclusive invitation, and this flattery led him to become vulnerable.[12] He carelessly visited Ahasuerus's palace at night, deepening Ahasuerus's suspicion; Ahasuerus thought Haman might be lurking in his courtyard at night in order to kill him.[13] Haman did not exercise caution when Ahasuerus tested him by asking him how he should pay tribute to one he wished to honor. Haman's response that he should dress him in the king's clothes, have him ride the king's horse and the crown be placed on his head, portrayed his ambitions to become the king and confirmed Ahasuerus' suspicion.

The Second Party

All was now in place for Esther's opportunity to make the plea for her people. Ahasuerus was mistrustful, while Haman's ego was inflated and subsequently dealt a severe blow by having to honor Mordekhai in a very public manner[14] and by his wife's painfully discouraging words.[15] Esther made her appeal, exposed Haman, and labeled him an evil man.[16] Ahasuerus stepped outside for a moment and returned just as Haman fell on Esther's bed, deepening Ahasuerus' suspicion of Haman.[17]

Finally, a minister named Harbona, motivated by eagerness to advance his standing in the court and jealousy of Haman, showed Ahasuerus the pole upon which Haman wished to hang Mordekhai,[18] clinching the decision to execute Haman. He was readily available for immediate hanging before Ahasuerus changed his mind and before Haman had an opportunity to organize a rebellion.[19]

---

12. Esther 5:12.
13. Esther 6:4.
14. Esther 6:11.
15. Esther 6:13.
16. Esther 7:4-6.
17. Esther 7:8.
18. Esther 7:9.
19. Ahasuerus does not kill Haman out of the love for the Jews or even for Esther. Indeed, he had not cancelled the decree to slaughter the Jews at this point. Rather, he acts out of pure self-interest, as he perceives Haman as an imminent threat who must be eliminated with haste (Megilla 16a).

Conclusion

The Purim miracle is a prime example of the delicate interplay between human effort *(hishtadlut)* and divine intervention *(hashgaḥah pratit)*. Esther's inviting Haman to the parties was a stroke of genius that set the stage for our deliverance from the evil decree. Yet without *hashgaḥah pratit* facilitating Esther's rise to queen, Mordekhai's saving Ahasuerus from Bigtan and Teresh, Haman's entering the courtyard to ask permission to hang Mordekhai just at the time that Ahasuerus was reminded of Mordekhai foiling the plot, and Haman falling on Esther's bed just as Ahasuerus reentered the palace, the Jews would not have been saved.

Despite Esther's talent and dedication to ensure her brilliant plan's seamless execution, the strategy could not have worked without Hashem tilting these events. Many circumstances had to align harmoniously in order for our fate to be reversed. The discerning reader of the Book of Esther readily recognizes Hashem's involvement and recites the blessing of *she'asa nissim la'avoteinu* (Who made miracles for our ancestors) intently before he reads the Megilla on Purim.

In the following sections, we will similarly demonstrate that in addition to the shrewd efforts of those involved, Israel's establishment – and survival – required too many perfectly-coordinated factors to be purely the result of human effort. Thus it is eminently reasonable to declare, as Rav Soloveitchik did, that Hashem's subtle hand was very much involved in Israel's establishment.

HIDDEN MIRACLES AND THE ESTABLISHMENT OF THE STATE OF ISRAEL

We seek to demonstrate that the United Nations vote which led to the founding of the State of Israel was an event similar to the foiling of Haman's genocidal plan against the Jewish People. Just as Esther's strategy and execution of that plan represented political genius but yet would have been insufficient without God's intervention, the same may be said about the UN vote to partition Palestine into separate Jewish and Arab states. On November 29, 1947, the United Nations voted to establish a Jewish State in part of Eretz Yisrael. The United Nations General Assembly voted 33 to 13, with 10 abstentions, in favor of the Partition Plan. Amazingly, both the United States and the Soviet Union supported the resolution, at the height of the Cold War. Passage of the resolution required a two-thirds majority of valid votes (not counting abstaining and absent members).

In the days prior to the final vote, when countries indicated their voting intentions, it was evident that the required majority was not available. Diplomatic efforts, which continued to the moments immediately before the vote, focused on changing the minds of many of the negative United Nations member states, and in the end the two-thirds majority was attained. In his documentary entitled *Israel: A Nation is Born,*[20] Abba Eban notes that the United Nations partition vote was of profound significance for the Jewish People. He asserts that had the UN declined to establish a Jewish state at that point it was very unlikely to materialize in the future. A negative vote would have proven catastrophic for the Jews.

Believing Jews argue that this vote was a result of divine intervention.[21] Absent a miracle, the United Nations – renowned for its fierce and consistent hostility to Israel – never would have voted to establish a Jewish state in any part of the Holy Land. Rabbi Eliezer Waldenburg, for example, writes that God "placed in the hearts of the United Nations, like Koresh (Cyrus) in his time, to restore to us a portion of our land which was stolen from us."[22] Rav Joseph B. Soloveitchik also holds that the vote to establish a Jewish state was an absolute political miracle, followed by the military miracle of vastly outnumbered and outgunned Israelis managing to overcome six Arab armies invading from three directions.[23]

Some challenge this view, arguing that devoted and intelligent lobbying by Zionist activists brought about this surprising result.[24] While it is indisputable that the Zionist effort to secure this vote was

20. Part One 35:10 to 35:20.

21. Ezra (1:1) states that Hashem motivated Cyrus to make the decision to permit the Jews to return to Zion. Incredibly, Ramban (on Shir HaShirim 8:13) and Radak (on Tehillim 146:3) predict that the nations of the world will permit the Jewish People to return to the Land of Israel.

22. *Tzitz Eliezer* 7:48:12.

23. Joseph B. Soloveitchik, *Fate and Destiny: From the Holocaust to the State of Israel* (Hoboken: Ktav Publishing House, 2000), 26-27.

24. A video of eyewitnesses describing the Jewish efforts and success in obtaining the required votes is available at www.toldotyisrael.com. *November 29, 1947: The Story of a Vote.*

effective and indispensable, we can argue that the UN would never have voted to establish a Jewish state absent divine intervention. Although there were clearly brilliant and brave actions which helped make the State of Israel a political and military reality, these factors alone represent an inadequate explanation for the creation of the State of Israel against overwhelming odds.

One of the key figures in the UN vote and the founding of the State of Israel was the then President of the United States, Harry S. Truman.

The Miracle of Harry S. Truman

Harry S. Truman, the thirty-third President of the United States, is viewed as a modern-day hero and crucial player in the establishment of the State of Israel. This is due to his decision to support the United Nations' establishment of a Jewish state in Palestine in November 1947 and to recognize the State of Israel only eleven minutes after it declared independence in May 1948.

Hashem's hand is readily apparent to any individual who ponders Truman's remarkable ascent to power in 1945 and support for a Jewish state in 1947-1948, both highly improbable events, as we shall discuss. We will base most of our understanding of Harry Truman's life on David McCullough's comprehensive Pulitzer Prize-winning biography.[25]

Truman's unlikely support for a Jewish state

We must begin by noting, first and foremost, that had Truman not instructed the United States ambassador to the United Nations to support the partition of Palestine into a Jewish state and an Arab state, the Jewish state never would have materialized. As the leader of the free world, Truman exercised influence by encouraging other countries to support the partition plan.[26] His recognition of the nascent State of Israel in May 1948 was critical to Israel's emergence as a nation, especially at a time when there was strong support for rescinding the November 1947

25. David McCullough, *Truman* (New York: Simon and Schuster, 1992).

26. Ibid., 601.

partition plan in the wake of intense Arab violence that began the day after the UN vote.

Truman's support was highly unlikely from many perspectives. On a personal level, Truman was raised in rural Missouri, where he was not conditioned to be fond of Jews. In fact, on his first visit to New York, before he was sent to fight in France during World War I, he expressed his dislike of the city because of the many Jews who lived there. He even used a highly derogatory term to describe New York due to its many Jewish residents.[27] It is recounted that Bess Truman (the president's beloved wife who had a great influence upon him) was anti-Semitic to the extent that she would not permit a Jew to enter her house.[28]

Moreover, Truman's venerated secretary of state General George Marshall (the architect of the famed Marshall Plan) urged Truman in the strongest terms against supporting Israel, warning the president that if he supported the Jewish state he would not vote for him in the next election.[29] Truman's spurning of Marshall's advice is astonishing,[30] given the immense respect Truman accorded to Marshall. Truman once remarked that there was not a military decoration big enough for General Marshall.[31]

Marshall's opposition was not at all rooted in anti-Semitism. It emerged from a sober political calculation that the United States could ill afford to antagonize the entire Arab and Muslim world by recognizing and voting for a tiny country that seemed most likely to be destroyed by Arab armies that vastly outnumbered the Jewish defenders. Moreover,

27. Ibid., 110, 286.
28. When talk show host David Susskind asked the ex-president, in 1953, why he had never been invited to the Truman home despite their many interviews, Truman replied: "You're a Jew, David, and no Jew has ever been in the house. Bess runs it, and there's never been a Jew inside the house in her or her mother's lifetime." (Merle Miller, *Plain Speaking: An Oral Biography of Harry S. Truman*, New York: G.P: Putnam's Sons, 1974, 90-91; James Humes, Confessions of a White House Ghostwriter, Chicago: Regnery, 1997, 35).
29. McCullough, *Truman*, 616.
30. Truman's support for partition is even more astonishing in light of the fact that a day before the United Nations vote, a secret CIA report urged President Truman not to lend his support (Daniel Gordis, *Israel: A Concise History of a Nation Reborn*, New York: Harper Collins, 2016, 147).
31. McCullough, *Truman*, 472.

the Arab countries possessed vast weaponry as well as petroleum resources, which were feared to be necessary to power United States military vehicles during what seemed then an inevitable military clash with the Soviet Union led by Joseph Stalin. The communist takeover of Czechoslovakia in early 1948 led many prudent politicians and diplomats to fear that many other countries would be vulnerable to a communist takeover. It was feared that United States' recognition of Israel would antagonize Arab countries and push them to ally themselves with Stalin against the United States and the democratic world.

Truman's rise to the presidency against all odds

Only a decent man of extraordinary character with common sense and religious devotion would have spurned geopolitical considerations in favor of ethical values, such as compassion for the Jewish refugees and recognition of the morality of the Jewish right to establish a state in part of Palestine. Both Truman's predecessor, Franklin Delano Roosevelt,[32] and his successor, Dwight Eisenhower, were not supporters of a Jewish state and would have been highly unlikely to recognize the State of Israel. It is improbable that either of these two tough-minded politicians would have favored basic morality over geopolitical considerations.

Hashem's guiding hand in bringing Truman to power follows the Megilla's pattern, with a series of highly improbable events coordinating seamlessly in our favor. Truman was an unsuccessful farmer and clothing-store owner when chosen in the early 1920's to serve as a county judge in western Missouri's Jackson County. He subsequently made a most unlikely leap from county judge to United States Senator in 1934. He was given almost no chance of reelection in 1940 after a relatively lackluster performance in the Senate during his first term in office.[33] Four years after his remarkable reelection, he was chosen by the Democratic Party to serve as Roosevelt's running mate in the 1944 presidential election. This was yet another astonishing development in light of the fact that Truman did not make an effort to secure this position. In fact, he supported another Democrat, to the extent

32. Ibid., 596.
33. Ibid., 241.

that he even prepared a nomination speech for the man he felt best suited for the position.[34]

In addition, Hashem's hand is evident in that the decision whether to recognize the nascent Jewish state had to be taken in an American election year (1948), when Truman needed to gain the Jewish vote, especially in key "battleground states." Courting the Jewish vote was a significant factor in Truman's deliberations about the issue of the Jewish state.

Cyrus as a hero to Truman

At a young age, Truman, who had developed a love of the Bible[35] and passion for history, counted the ancient Persian Emperor Cyrus (*Koresh*) as one of his heroes.[36] Cyrus was the Persian emperor who permitted Jews to return from exile and build the Second Temple.[37] Much later in life, after being introduced to a Jewish group in 1953 as the one who contributed to the establishment of the State of Israel, Truman protested that he did not merely *assist* in its creation, but rather he felt truly responsible for the Jewish State. "I am Cyrus, I am Cyrus," he proclaimed. How fortunate, or rather providential, it was that Cyrus was one of Truman's idols from a young age!

Clark Clifford

One of President Truman's aides, Clark Clifford, countered General George Marshall's opposition to the establishment of the State of Israel. McCullough[38] describes Clifford's presence on Truman's staff as "almost chance." That Truman followed the young Clifford (whose arguments for recognizing the Jewish State included citations from Deuteronomy)[39] over the highly-experienced Marshall is remarkable, seeing that his very presence in the White House was highly unlikely.

---

34. Ibid., 292-313.
35. McCullough, *Truman*, 989.
36. Ibid., 58.
37. Ezra 1.
38. Ibid., 502.
39. Ibid., 615-616.

Eddie Jacobson

The most extraordinary figure of our discussion is Truman's Jewish friend Eddie Jacobson. Truman remarked to a visiting Israeli diplomat many years later[40] that Jacobson "was the best friend anyone could ever have." That someone with strong anti-Semitic leanings would develop such a strong friendship with a Jew is simply astonishing.

Truman met Jacobson during stateside training for World War I. Together they administered the camp's canteen,[41] and upon returning from the war they decided to become business partners. They opened a men's clothing store, which failed after a few years. It took both men many years to pay off the large debt accumulated while running this establishment. Remarkably, Truman and Jacobson remained very close friends despite this painful experience.

Eddie Jacobson played a decisive role in convincing President Truman to recognize the State of Israel. Zealous advocates for Israel, such as Reform Rabbi Abba Hillel Silver, who pounded on the president's desk and even yelled at the president demanding Truman's support for a Jewish state, had only succeeded in souring Truman on Zionism.[42] When the legendary Chaim Weizmann traveled to America to make the case for supporting a Jewish state, Truman initially refused to meet with him. It was Eddie Jacobson who managed to convince Truman to meet with Weizmann, whose considerable charm and powers of persuasion strongly affected the President. When Jacobson was at first rebuffed by Truman, he somehow (we see it as Hashem's influence) was inspired to compare Weizmann with one of Truman's heroes, Andrew Jackson. The mostly-inapt analogy somehow managed to change Truman's mind, eventually leading to Truman's ultimate decision to support the Jewish State.[43]

40. Yehuda Avner, *The Prime Ministers: An Intimate Narrative of Israeli Leadership* (London: The Toby Press, 2010).
41. McCullough, *Truman*, 107.
42. Ibid., 598-599.
43. Ibid., 606-607.

Rabbi Herzog and President Truman

After the establishment of the State of Israel, Rabbi Yitzḥak Herzog, the Ashkenazic Chief Rabbi, visited President Truman to offer his thanks. Present at the meeting was a secular Jew who served as Truman's advisor for minority relations. Rabbi Herzog told Truman that God placed him in his mother's womb in order to be the first world leader in more than two thousand years to establish a Jewish state in Palestine. The Jewish advisor, who viewed Rabbi Herzog's words as hyperbole, was astonished to see tears streaming down President Truman's face.[44] Truman, described by McCullough as a spiritual man who lived to a great extent by the Bible, deeply appreciated Rabbi Herzog's insight.

Thus we already see that the involvement of President Truman, which was only one factor in the establishment of the Jewish State, required a combination of many unlikely events. As in the Book of Esther, we recognize Hashem's subtle hand in the workings of the world. As stated in Song of Songs: "Behold, he stands behind our wall…he peers through the lattice."[45] The Book of Esther should inspire us to seek Hashem hiding behind the "latticework," as we have sought to do in the case of President Harry S. Truman's most improbable support for the establishment of the State of Israel. Even when reading a book of history, one can encounter the Divine.

A Closer Look at the United Nations' Vote: Paul Johnson and Rav Soloveitchik

In 1998 the renowned British historian Paul Johnson wrote an essay in *Commentary* to commemorate Israel's birthday.[46] He noted: "In the last half-century, over 100 completely new independent states have come into existence. Israel is the only one whose creation can fairly be called a miracle."

As Rav Joseph B. Soloveitchik writes in his classic essay *Kol Dodi Dofeik*,[47] "No one can deny that from the standpoint of international

44. McCullough, *Truman*, 620.

45. Song 2:9.

46. "Israel: The Miracle'," *Commentary*, May 1998, re-published online in 2011 (www.jewishideasdaily.com/878/features/israel-the-miracle/).

47. Soloveitchik, *Fate and Destiny*, 26-27.

relations, the establishment of the State of Israel, in a political sense, was an almost supernatural occurrence." The Rav expounds:

> Both Russia and the Western countries jointly supported the idea of the establishment of the [Jewish] State. This was perhaps the only proposal where east and west were united. I am inclined to believe that the entire United Nations organization was created specifically for this purpose – in order to carry out the mission which the divine providence had set for it. It seems to me that one cannot point to any other concrete achievement on the part of the U.N. Our sages, of blessed memory, already expressed the view that at times, "rain" descends for a single person, or for a single blade of grass. I do not know whom the journalists, with their eyes of flesh and blood, saw sitting in the chairman's seat during that fateful session when the General Assembly decided in favor of the establishment of the state. However, someone at the time who observed matters with his spiritual eye could have sensed the presence of the true chairman Who presided over the session, i.e. the Beloved (Hashem)! It was He who knocked with His gavel on the podium. Do we not interpret the verse "That night sleep from the king fled" (Esther 6:1) as referring to the sleep of the King of the Universe (Megillah 15b). Were it Achashveirosh alone who could not sleep, it would have been of no consequence, and the salvation of Israel would not have blossomed forth on that night. However, if it is the King of the Universe Who, as it were, does not slumber then the redemption will be born. If it had been John Doe who called the session of the United Nations to order, then the State of Israel would not have come into being – but if the Beloved knocked on the chairman's podium, then the miracle occurred.

Incredible Timing

In Esther's story, we can identify three "fingerprints" as proof of Hashem's subtle manipulation of events on our behalf. These include incredible timing, the phenomenon of our enemies acting inexplicably foolishly, and the unfolding of many improbable events, against all expectations. We can detect each of these divine "fingerprints" on the events leading to the 1947 United Nations vote to establish a Jewish state. Paul Johnson[48] notes the incredible timing involved in this momentous UN vote:

> Another paradoxical aspect of the Zionist miracle, which we certainly did not grasp at the time and which is insufficiently understood even now, is that among the founding fathers of Israel was Joseph Stalin. Stalin had no love for Jews; quite the contrary, he murdered them whenever it suited his purposes. In his last phase, indeed, he was becoming increasingly paranoid; had he lived, he might well have carried out an extermination program rivaling Hitler's. Moreover, like Lenin before him, Stalin had always opposed Zionism. He did so not only as a Great Russian imperialist but as a Marxist, and he was consistent on the matter up to the end of World War II and again from 1950 to his death in 1953. But during the crucial years 1947-48, he was guided by temporary considerations of Realpolitik, and specifically by what he saw as the threat of British imperialism.
>
> Stalin ignorantly supposed that the way to undermine Britain's position in the Middle East was to support the Jews, not the Arabs, and he backed Zionism[49] in order to break the 'British stranglehold.' Not only did he extend diplomatic recognition to Israel but, in order to intensify the fighting and the consequent chaos, he instructed the Czech government to sell it arms. The Czechs turned over an entire military airfield to shuttle weaponry to Tel Aviv; the Messerschmitt aircraft they supplied were of particular importance. Then, in mid-August 1948, Stalin decided

48. "Israel: The Miracle," published in *Commentary*, May 1998, 27-33.

49. In regard to the UN Partition Vote, Benny Morris writes, "Soviet Deputy Foreign Minister Andrei Gromyko's speech of May 14, 1947 at the United Nations General Assembly supporting the establishment of a Jewish state stunned Western and Zionist observers. Hitherto, Soviet policy on Palestine had been anti-British and pro-Arab... Moscow had announced a pro-Zionist tack – and sent UNSCOP off to the Middle East with a clear message." Benny Morris, *1948: The First Arab-Israeli War* (New Haven: Yale University Press, 2008), 40-41. Abba Eban reports that before Gromyko's speech not one member nation of the United Nations had explicitly stated its support for partition (*Israel: A Nation is Born* - video presentation Part 1 29:07-29:20).

> he had made a huge error in judgment, and the obedient Czech government ordered a halt to the airlift within 48 hours. But by then the war had effectively been won.
>
> The fledgling Israeli state was equally fortunate when it came to America, benefiting from a phase of benevolence that once again might not have lasted. President Truman[50] was pro-Zionist, and he needed the Jewish vote in the 1948 election. It was his decision to push the partition scheme through the UN in November 1947 and to recognize the new Israeli state (de facto, not de jure) when it was declared in May 1948. But the contrary pressure he had to face, both from the State Department under George C. Marshall and from his Defense Secretary, James V. Forrestal, was immense.[51] If the crisis had come a year later, after the cold war started to dominate the thinking of the West to the exclusion of almost everything else, it is likely that the anti-Zionist forces would have proved too strong for Truman. As it was, American backing for Israel in 1947-48 was the last idealistic luxury the Americans permitted themselves before the realities of global confrontation descended.
>
> Thus, in terms of both Soviet and American policy, Israel slipped into existence through a window that briefly opened, and just as suddenly closed. Once again, timing – or, if one likes, providence – was of the essence.

Soviet and American support for the establishment of a Jewish state affected other countries' votes as well. The East European communist bloc – Czechoslovakia, Poland, Ukraine and Byelorussian SSR along with the Soviet Union – all voted for a Jewish state. Had it not been for Soviet influence, it is extremely unlikely that Poland and Ukraine,

---

50. Paul Johnson notes what he regards as the possibly providential death of President Roosevelt, who turned anti-Zionist towards the end of his life, on the heels of his conference with Saudi Arabian King Ibn Saud. Johnson quotes presidential assistant David Niles as saying, "There are serious doubts in my mind that Israel would have come into being if Roosevelt had lived." *A History of the Jews* (New York: Harper & Row Publishers, 1987), 524.
51. Daniel Gordis, *Israel: A Concise History of a Nation Reborn* (New York: Harper Collins, 2016), 147.

with their long and deep history of anti-Semitism, would have voted for the establishment of Israel. Benny Morris notes the direct impact the United States had on the yea votes from Haiti, the Philippines and many Latin American countries that otherwise planned to vote against the establishment of a Jewish state.[52]

One is not, as Paul Johnson assumes, required to choose between timing and providence. As we noted, providence *expresses* itself through incredible timing.[53] The fact that the UN vote on the partition of Palestine came to the fore during the "window that briefly was opened" in 1947-1948, in terms of both American and Soviet culture, makes God's involvement in 1947 readily apparent to any thinking and informed individual.

One last point of critical timing was involved in the UN vote. In May 1947, the UN formed a Special Committee (UNSCOP) to prepare a report on recommendations for Palestine. In July 1947 the UNSCOP committee members arrived in *Eretz Yisrael* as part of their international investigation. On July 12, 1947, the Haganah-owned ship "Exodus 1947" set sail to Palestine. Benny Morris writes that "the Haganah-Mossad dispatched the Exodus in mid-July for tactical and operational reasons, not out of a political desire to splice the journey with the work of UNSCOP."[54] Zionist leaders brought the UNSCOP members to witness British treatment of the Jewish immigrants from the post-World War II displaced persons' camps. Morris notes the strong impression this dramatic moment had upon the UNSCOP members, with the Yugoslav leader of his mission remarking, "It is the best possible evidence [of the need for a Jewish state] we have."[55]

Our Enemies' Foolish Mistakes

Another way we can detect Hashem's delicate involvement is when our enemies act in a curiously foolish manner. Arab behavior in regard to the

52. Morris, *1948: The First Arab-Israeli War*, 60-61. This book is regarded as the definitive work on the political and military creation of the State of Israel. Chapter Two of this work presents a detailed and extensive account of the United Nations decision to partition Palestine into Jewish and Arab states.
53. This is readily apparent from the Book of Esther.
54. Morris, *1948: The First Arab-Israeli War*, 43.
55. Ibid., 44.

UN partition vote undoubtedly satisfies this description. Benny Morris[56] writes that Arab leaders "came to the [United Nations] assembly cocky and disorganized and remained so until the bitter end." Morris further states:

> Overall, the Arab leadership acted in an astonishingly foolish manner that served only to strengthen the case for the creation of a Jewish state in part of Palestine. The destructive Arab behavior served only to highlight the justice of establishing Israel.

Events That Defy Normal Probability

God's subtle involvement can also be detected when events occur that dramatically defy normal expectations. The very fact that the UN voted to create a Jewish state was a striking defiance of expectations. Benny Morris writes:[57]

> The Arabs were not averse to the [Palestine] problem going before the United Nations, where they anticipated a favorable outcome. With five member states and a handful of reflexive Islamic and third world supporters, they expected an easy victory. Zionist leadership, by contrast, was "wary" (1948, p.38) and quite worried about the United Nations voting on the disposition of *Eretz Yisrael* where a two-thirds majority of the fifty-seven UN members was needed to establish a Jewish state. They had every reason to be worried as many of the UN member states were not initially strongly in favor of establishing a Jewish state.

Morris continues[58]:

> The Zionists faced a major challenge in the twenty-member Latin American bloc, the United Nations' largest, where the anti-Zionist influences of the Catholic Church – the Vatican opposed partition and Jewish statehood – and local Arab and German communities

56. Ibid., 40.
57. Ibid., 37, 40.
58. Ibid., 53-54.

> were strong, and where anti-American feeling, which affected attitudes to Zionism, was widespread.
>
> As late as November 25, 1947 (four days before the critical vote), six Latin American countries abstained, Paraguay absented itself and Cuba voted against in the UNSCOP committee vote.

Regarding Western Europe, Benny Morris writes that it was hardly "in the bag." France was not readily in favor due to its traditional alliance with Britain and the sixteen million Muslims under its rule in North Africa. Moreover, France's vote would affect Belgium, Denmark, Holland[59] and Luxembourg.

The four countries in the British Commonwealth – Australia, Canada, New Zealand and South Africa – were not readily on board either. For example, New Zealand's UN deputy head of delegation, J.S. Reid, was strongly anti-Zionist. These four countries almost always voted in line with Great Britain, which was unsupportive of creating a Jewish state. China was a particularly difficult sell due to its population of twenty million Muslims. Finally, the United States was not strongly in favor of the partition until seventy-two hours before the vote.

With these facts, the Zionist leadership correctly assessed that it did not have the votes for a Jewish state. And yet, the United Nations voted on November 29, 1947 in favor of the partitioning of Palestine into two states. The United States and France voted for the establishment of a Jewish state as did the four commonwealth countries. Astonishingly, thirteen Latin American countries voted for a Jewish state and only one (Cuba) voted against. The five Soviet bloc states voted in favor, which was especially astonishing for reasons explained above. China shifted from outright rejection to benevolent neutrality and ultimately abstained.[60] Liberia, Haiti and the Philippines voted in favor even though they were

59. Holland had to consider the sixteen million Muslims in its colony of Indonesia.

60. Rabbi Marvin Tokayer relates, "The closest friend, adviser, and bodyguard of the first president of China, Sun Yat-sen, was Morris Abraham Cohen, who was called 'Two-Gun' Cohen. He was an unbelievable person. He saved Sun Yat-sen's life several times and was instrumental in getting China not to vote 'no' on the partition of Palestine to produce a Jewish homeland." (*Tales From The Far East: An Interview with Rabbi Marvin* Tokayer, *Jewish Press,* October 1, 2015).

vacillating until the last moment. Eventually Belgium, Denmark, Holland and Luxembourg all voted in favor. Yugoslavia abstained despite its large Muslim population, Argentina abstained despite the many Nazis that took refuge there and its large Arab population, and Ethiopia's abstention was a happy surprise in light of its high percentage of Muslims.

More Evidence of Divine Manipulation

Benny Morris[61] cites a prominent Arab leader who correctly noted that the partition would never have been approved had the vote been conducted in secret as demanded by the Arab states. With God's help, this demand was not accepted by UN leaders.

Moreover, it is reasonable to argue that the divine hand ensured that the UN vote took place in New York (Lake Success to be exact, just outside of Queens which had and still has a very large Jewish community) and not San Francisco (where the United Nations had been founded) or Geneva (the headquarters of the League of Nations). As Benny Morris explains:

> Delegates with no firm instructions from their governments were no doubt influenced by the prevalent atmosphere in New York and Flushing Meadow, where the media broadcast 'that an enemy of partition was an enemy of the American people'.... [At Flushing Meadow the] almost exclusively Zionist audience... applauded declarations of support for Zionism. They hissed Arab speakers. They created the atmosphere of a football match, with the Arabs as the away team.[62]

One could argue that the success of the UN Partition vote was a happy coincidence or a result of massive and wide Zionist lobbying. However, this victory required the coordination of too many delicate factors to attribute the success exclusively to Zionist efforts. Just as the many and varied circumstances that had to work in order for Esther's brilliant plan

---

61. Morris, *1948: The First Arab-Israeli War*, 61.
62. UN officials could well have insisted on moving the vote to a more neutral venue, but did not.

to save the Jews leads us to attribute her success to divine intervention, so too the fact that so many countries were persuaded to vote in favor of a Jewish state must be a result of Hashem's understated, yet influential manipulation of events.

Conclusion

The United Nations was skewed against Zionism and Israel even in its early stages, as illustrated by its staunch anti-Israel stance during the 1956 Suez War. Benny Morris writes that the United Nations cramped the Israel Defense Forces' style and curtailed its battlefield successes in a series of cease-fire and truce resolutions beginning in Israel's 1948 War of Independence. Morris notes that all UN interventions after June 1948 decisively favored the Arabs.[63]

And yet, despite its anti-Israel inclination, the United Nations voted to establish a Jewish state. Perfect timing, unwise Arab behavior and dozens of unfriendly countries voting for a Jewish state (or at least abstaining) were indispensible factors for this amazing outcome. Was it simply coincidence and human effort that brought about this result? The reasonable conclusion is that Hashem was slanting the United Nations to act in a manner contrary to its normal behavior. No one individual or country has that much good fortune or talent. *Baruch she'asa nissim bizman hazeh,* bless God who made this miracle at this time!

Postscript: The Miracle of England's Balfour Declaration and Its Ratification by the League of Nations

Just as there is an extensive basis to argue that God was behind the United Nations establishment of Israel, so too it seems reasonable to conclude that Hashem coordinated the British government's issuance of the Balfour Declaration and its ratification by the League of Nations in 1922.

On November 2, 1917, Arthur Balfour, the British Foreign Secretary, issued the following policy statement:

> His Majesty's government view with favour the establishment in Palestine of a national home for the Jewish people, and will use

63. Morris, *1948: The First Arab-Israeli War,* 403.

> their best endeavours to facilitate the achievement of this object, it being clearly understood that nothing shall be done which may prejudice the civil and religious rights of existing non-Jewish communities in Palestine, or the rights and political status enjoyed by Jews in any other country.

Balfour's Declaration gained the standing of international law when it was ratified by the League of Nations in 1922. The Balfour Declaration paved the way for a fairly large scale Jewish immigration to the Land of Israel from 1920 to 1939, thus setting precedent and paving the way for the United Nations to vote to establish a Jewish state in Palestine in 1947.

Historians endeavor to discover the motivation of Great Britain to issue this document. Some of the explanations defy reason, including the explanation that Britain wanted to curry favor with American Jewry to convince the American government to enter World War I and with Russian Jewry to keep Russia in the war. This would have been a gross error in judgment, as Jews in the United States were hardly a sufficiently potent political force to affect the course of American government policy at the time. The persecuted and downtrodden Jews of Russia were in even less of a position to affect their government's course of action in the Great War.

A more likely explanation is the Bible-centered mindset of Balfour and then Prime Minister Lloyd George, which made them hospitable to the idea of reestablishing a Jewish Home in *Eretz Yisrael*. Here too, the timing was exquisite;[64] before the emergence of a British Foreign Office in 1919 that was hostile to Zionism, and also was most favorable to the adoption of the Balfour Declaration.

---

64. Equally fortuitous was the rise of pro-Zionist Lloyd George to the premiership in 1916 and Zionist leader Chaim Weizmann's introduction to Arthur Balfour in 1906. Weizman gradually drew Balfour closer to the Zionist cause. In addition, Weizmann's discovery – in his role as director of the British Admiralty laboratories during the First World War – of acetone, a critical ingredient in the naval explosive cordite, which played a central role in the British war effort, enabled Weizmann to gain access and influence key British figures such as Sir Mark Sykes, the prominent British Foreign Office diplomat (Gordis, *Israel*, 96-97).

However, even this explanation cannot account for the fact that Balfour's successor as British Foreign Secretary, the stridently anti-Zionist George Curzon, continued to support the enforcement of the Balfour Declaration after assuming his position in 1919. Curzon, who had been opposed to the Balfour Declaration from the start, attributed his implementation of the Balfour Declaration to the imperative of honoring Great Britain's commitments even when he was disturbed that the commitment was originally made. But this explanation is inadequate, as noted by writer Conor Cruise O'Brien in his classic history of Zionism entitled *The Siege.*[65] O'Brien writes that Curzon did not similarly honor other commitments made by the British government, such as the Sykes-Picot agreement with the French and the McMahon letter to Arab leaders. Yet the staunchly anti-Zionist Curzon honored the commitment the British government made to Zionist leaders. Conor Cruise O'Brien makes the following poignant observation:[66]

> If a Zionist, of the pious sort, were to tell me that the true explanation of this phenomenon was that God had decided that it was time for His people to come home, I should no doubt express polite skepticism. But if the same pious Zionist were then to ask me whether I can discern any material interests for the British Government's reinforcement of the Balfour Declaration in the circumstances of the early twenties, I should have to say that I can't find any such explanation.

O'Brien concludes his discussion by noting:[67]

> Efforts were made at the time to show that the Balfour Declaration was, or was not, in conformity with the Covenant of the League of Nations. What mattered far more was that it was felt

65. Conor Cruise O'Brien, *The Siege: The Saga of Israel and Zionism* (New York: Simon and Schuster, 1986), 150.
66. Ibid., 152.
67. Ibid., 153-155.

> to be in conformity with a far older covenant, between God and the Jews, over *Eretz Israel.*[68]

Thus, just as we concluded that the most sensible understanding of the UN partition vote is to recognize that it was the work of Hashem, we can apply that same line of reasoning to understand Britain's issuance and enforcement of the Balfour Declaration as a result of subtle divine influence.

Rav Meir Simcha of Dvinsk, the author of *Or Sameaḥ* and *Meshekh Ḥokhmah,* certainly perceived the Balfour Declaration and its subsequent ratification by the League of Nations as an act of Hashem. In the wake of the League of Nations ratification he wrote the following letter:

> In this century, the rays of light shine forth with a great awakening through the channels of the great men of action such as Montefiore and those like him; and from the rabbis, Rabbi Tzvi Hirsh (Kalisher) from Talyron, and Rabbi Eliahu (Guttmacher) from Gridetz, to build and to develop Jerusalem, and to remove its desolation, almost to the extent which the enthusiasts have widened the cause. Many rabbis stood in opposition, and even many rabbis who praised the matter in their hearts, put their hands to their mouths, in fear of the enthusiast zeal, and in fear of the Three Oaths which Hashem made the daughters of Jerusalem swear. Now, however, Divine Providence has brought together the League of intelligent Nations in San Remo, and a dictate was established that the Land of Israel shall be for the Jewish people. Since the fear of the Oaths has been removed with the permission of the nations, the mitzvah of settling the Land of Israel arises, a

68. O'Brien argues that the power of the Bible held sway over Curzon as well as Balfour and Lloyd George. He writes: "Zionism has shown a capacity to make its opponents do some very strange things." One must ask, however, why this is so. We argue that it is the divine manipulation of Zionism's opponents, much as Hashem manipulated Pharaoh to act in ways counter to his and his country's best interest (see Nahmanides on Ex. 7:3). Indeed, Proverbs 21:1 states, "Like water courses is the king's heart in the hand of the Lord: he directs it wherever he wishes."

> mitzvah equal to all of the other precepts in the Torah, and this mitzvah returns to its place. It is a mitzvah on everyone to help with all of their power to observe this mitzvah, and if Hashem, may His Name be blessed, will allow this to come about, and if the matter will increase and expand, then surely it is a matter which stands at the zenith of the universe.[69]

THE MILITARY MIRACLE OF 1948

Rav Soloveitchik and the Military Miracle

Having perceived Hashem's influence on the United Nations vote to establish the State of Israel, we can further see God's involvement in Jewish history manifest in Israel's War of Independence. Rav Joseph B. Soloveitchik, in his classic essay "Kol Dodi Dofeik," articulates the view that Israel's victory in its War of Independence was miraculous and involved divine intervention:

> The knocking of the Beloved[70] could be heard on the battlefield. The small Israeli Defense Forces defeated the mighty armies of the Arab countries. The miracle of the 'many in the hands of the few' took place before our eyes. And an even greater miracle occurred at that time. God hardened the heart of Ishmael[71] and enjoined

---

69. Printed in *Torat Eretz Yisrael: The Teachings of Rav Tzvi Yehuda Kook* (Jerusalem: Torat Eretz Yisrael Publications, 1991), 234.
70. Rav Soloveitchik alludes to Song of Songs 5:2, which refers to divine intervention in human affairs.
71. There have been numerous instances where Arab intransigence has benefited the Jewish State. Examples that stand out are Hafez al-Assad's rejection of the Barak offer of 99% of the Golan Heights in 1999, Yasser Arafat's rejection of Ehud Barak's extremely generous peace offer at Camp David in 2000, and his rejection of President Clinton's even more generous proposal in December 2000. Dennis Ross documents these proposals, as well as the respective Arab rejections, with pictures of the original maps in the introductory pages to *The Missing Peace* (New York: Farrar, Straus and Giroux, 2004). The ceding of the Golan Heights would have created a grave danger to Israel during the instability in Syria fifteen years after Assad's rejection. Had Palestinian Arab leader Haj Amin al-Husseini accepted the 1937 Peel Partition Plan, Arabs would have controlled more than three quarters of *Eretz Yisrael* (the Land of Israel). Finally, had the Arabs accepted the 1947 UN Partition Plan, the Arab population in

him to do battle against the State of Israel. Had the Arabs not declared war against the state, and instead, agreed to the Partition Plan, the State of Israel would have lacked Jerusalem, a large part of the Galilee, and several areas of the Negev.[72] Had Pharaoh, thousands of years ago, allowed the Israelites to depart from Egypt immediately, in accordance with Moses' original request, Moses would have been bound to keep his promise and would have had to return after three days. However, Pharaoh hardened his heart and did not hearken to Moses. The Almighty took the Israelites out of Egypt with a strong hand and an outstretched arm. Consequently, Moses' pledge that they would return to Egypt was no longer binding. A bilateral contract cannot bind one party if the other party refuses to fulfill his obligations.[73] It is the voice of my beloved that knocketh!

The Big Picture

Detailed knowledge of Israel's War of Independence is not required to recognize God's hand. The very fact that a nation was invaded on three fronts, by five Arab armies, on the day it declared independence, and not only *survived* but managed to acquire considerable territory is

---

the Jewish State, which was very large, could easily have grown to outnumber the Jews and assume control of Israel by democratic means in a few decades or less.

72. It is somewhat surprising that Rav Soloveitchik views the 1948 War of Independence as a positive occurrence. Rav Soloveitchik often stressed the greater importance of human life over *Eretz Yisrael* (Rav Hershel Schachter, *Nefesh HaRav* Jerusalem: Reishit Yerushalayim, 1994, 98). However, Rav Soloveitchik might have felt that the Arab invasion of 1948 worked in the best interest of the Jewish people because the original borders of the 1947 United Nations Partition were indefensible and could have eventually led to far more severe losses than those sustained in the 1948 war.

73. This principle affords justification for the Israelites' not returning to Egypt, despite their pledge to return after three days. For further discussion of this issue, see Rav Elḥanan Samet, *Iyunim B'farshiot HaShavua* (Jerusalem: *Makhon Maaliot,* 2002) 1:178-191. Rav Soloveitchik's insight also justifies the State of Israel expanding its borders, during its War of Independence, beyond the portion allotted to it by the UN in 1947. The failure of the Arab nations to accept these boundaries and instead launch a war of annihilation against the Jews renders the Partition borders moot.

miraculous on its face. Indeed, I am aware of no parallel in history.[74] The fact that Israel was seriously outnumbered and had hardly any heavy weapons at the beginning of the war only underscores the sense of divine intervention. Thus, it is hardly surprising that religious Jews (and many religious Christians as well) believe that a miracle occurred on the battlefields of 1948.

We will examine some of the details in order to clarify and concretize this premise. In this chapter, we will be citing from two excellent works which describe the battles in detail – Chaim Herzog's *The Arab-Israeli Wars* and Benny Morris's *1948*.

Part I of Israel's War of Independence: November 30, 1947-May 13, 1948

In our previous chapter, we noted Paul Johnson's observation regarding the astounding decision of Joseph Stalin to support the founding of the State of Israel. Stalin facilitated the sale of a large amount of arms from Czechoslovakia at a time when the United Nations, with the strong support of the United States, imposed a strict arms embargo on military weapons sale to the Middle East combatants.[75] The timing of the beginning of the arrival of these weapons was absolutely essential to the survival of the Jewish community in Palestine.

The Arabs of Palestine began their assault on their Jewish counterparts the day after the November 29, 1947 UN decision to partition Palestine into Arab and Jewish states.[76] The objective of the Palestinians

74. The closest instance is the success of the American people in its revolution against England. It is, however, not completely parallel since the odds were not stacked as high against the Americans as they were against the Zionists. See John Ferling's *Almost a Miracle: The American Victory in the War of Independence* (New York: Oxford University Press, 2007).

75. The American intention was to avoid war. In reality the absence of weapons in Jewish hands would have resulted, heaven forbid, in the annihilation of the Jewish population of *Eretz Yisrael* in 1948.

76. Israel's War of Independence is divided into two very distinct phases. Palestinian Arabs waged a civil war from November 30, 1947 to May 13, 1948. The Jewish community struggled to survive as its self-defense mechanism, the underground Haganah (the Jewish defense organization in *Eretz Yisrael*), had to fight in a very restrained manner due to the severe limitations imposed by the British who still controlled the country. After the British left and the Jews declared independence, the Jewish

was to prevent the implementation of the UN resolution. As the months progressed, Arab attacks became more intense until the end of March 1948, when the Jewish community was in imminent danger of collapse. The Arabs focused their attacks on the Jewish community's most vulnerable point – the convoys bringing supplies to isolated outposts in the Galilee, Negev and Judea. The Arabs had placed the Jewish community of Jerusalem, which numbered 100,000 residents, under siege, blocking the only available route from the center of the Jewish community, the narrow road.... from Tel Aviv. Benny Morris writes:

> The Arab ambushes during December 1947-mid-March 1948 had taken a heavy toll.... Most of the Palmach[77] was deployed guarding the convoys and the casualty rate was appalling.... It was an unequal struggle between small Haganah units in lightly armed, cramped, highly inflammable, makeshift armored cars and masses of Arabs enfilading the road from behind rocks on surrounding hills. Narrow roads made maneuvers all but impossible.... Once a convoy was ambushed, there was usually nowhere to retreat: Jewish settlements were often far away and unfriendly Arab villages lay in all directions.
>
> In late March, the Haganah had endured a series of major disasters on the roads. They appeared to portend defeat in the war.... In less than a fortnight the Haganah lost most of its armored vehicles and dozens of its best troops... [British High Commissioner Alan] Cunningham noted the Zionists' desperation; 'The balance of the fighting seems to have turned much in favour of the Arabs.' By the end of March the Jewish community had suffered about a thousand dead.
>
> The situation had enormous political implications as well. Even American support for the partition of Palestine was seriously eroding to the extent that the American representative to the UN Security Council expressed the need to withdraw the

---

defense forces were able to operate in an unimpeded manner, but faced the invasion of five regular Arab armies.

77. The standing force of the Haganah.

> partition plan due to the fear of the destruction of the Jewish community in Palestine.
>
> By the beginning of April 1948 the Jewish leadership recognized the need to go on the offensive and attack the bases of Arab militias that were attacking the Jewish community. With an invasion of regular Arab armies on the horizon six weeks after the British withdrawal from *Eretz Yisrael,* the need to destroy the Palestinian militia was vital if the Jewish community had even the faintest chance of surviving large scale invasions of regular armies. During this time period the British were busy evacuating the country and would not seriously hamper Jewish defense efforts. However, the most serious roadblock to a proper Jewish response to insure its survival was the lack of weapons.[78]

Chaim Herzog adds:

> The total armament at the Haganah's disposal in 1947 consisted of 10,500 rifles, 3,500 submachine-guns, 775 light machine-guns, 34 3-inch mortars and 670 two-inch mortars with sufficient ammunition for only three days' fighting – even the standing force, the Palmach, could only arm two out of every three of its active members. At this stage, heavy machine guns, anti-tank guns and artillery were but a dream: not one existed in the Jewish forces.[79]

Benny Morris relates, "The Haganah high command had to 'borrow' weapons from local units for a day or two for specific operations and the units (and the settlements) were generally reluctant to part with weapons, quite reasonably arguing that the Arabs might attack while the weapons were on loan."[80]

---

78. Morris, *1948: The First Arab-Israeli War,* 108-111.
79. Chaim Herzog and Shlomo Gazit, *The Arab-Israeli Wars: War and Peace in the Middle East* (Oxford: Oxford University Press, 2009), 19. All weapons had to be acquired surreptitiously since the British forbade weapons ownership by Jews. The punishment for weapons ownership was, shockingly, death.
80. Morris, *1948: The First Arab-Israeli War,* 117.

The Arrival of Czech Arms Just in Time

On April 1, 1948, the weapons from Czechoslovakia arrived just in time to enable the Haganah to implement a proper plan that would save the lives of the more than six hundred thousand Jews living in *Eretz Yisrael* (the Land of Israel). Chaim Herzog writes: "The arms predicament of the Haganah at the time is emphasized by the fact that the 200 rifles and 400 light machine-guns that were unloaded from the aircraft constituted a major improvement in the Haganah's arms situation."[81] As David Ben Gurion stated at the time, "After we have received a small amount of the [Czech] equipment...the situation is radically different in our favor."[82]

As a direct result of the Czech arms shipments, the Haganah in the six weeks that followed was able to defeat the Arab militias and secure the country to the extent that it stood a chance of surviving the onslaught of five surrounding Arab armies. Moreover, the continued flow of Czech arms during the beginning months of the Arab invasion enabled Israel to deflect the Arab threat and eventually to win the war.

Was this merely a chance set of circumstances? The sensible interpretation is that God's hand was involved. The fact that Joseph Stalin ordered the arming of the Jewish community of *Eretz Yisrael* and the arrival of the arms just in time to avoid collapse seems far too fortuitous to be labeled as mere coincidence. This is bolstered by the other many factors that contributed to Israel surviving its War of Independence, as we shall now set forth.

Enemies' Foolish Mistakes

The Book of Esther depicts Hashem subtly manipulating our enemies to act foolishly so as to avoid our annihilation by the hands of Haman. Israel's War of Independence was replete with rash decisions and actions on the part of Arab leaders. Such actions played an essential part in Israel's survival of this war, in which the declared aim of Arab leaders was to obliterate the Jewish population of *Eretz Yisrael.*

The first great mistake, as noted by Benny Morris, was the Palestinian Arab decision to wage war against the British rulers of *Eretz*

81. Herzog and Gazit, *The Arab-Israeli Wars: War and Peace in the Middle East*, 39.
82. Morris, *1948: The First Arab-Israeli War*, 117.

Yisrael from 1936 to 1939 in what is referred to as the Great Arab Revolt. Morris explains:

> The Arab Revolt ended in unmitigated defeat for the Palestinians. Somewhere between three thousand and six thousand of their political and military activists had been killed, with many thousands more either driven into exile or jailed; the leadership of the Palestine Arab national movement was decimated, exiled or jailed.... Much of the elite was so disillusioned or frightened by what had happened that it permanently renounced political activity. The Palestinians...had prematurely expended their military prowess against the wrong enemy and had been dealt a mortal blow in advance of the battle with the real [perceived] enemy, Zionism. The damage to their war effort in 1947-1948 was incalculable.[83]

The second self-imposed handicap was the severe disunity and disorganization in Palestinian society:

> The Palestinian Arabs, with well-established traditions of disunity, corruption and organizational incompetence, failed to mobilize their resources. They even failed to put together a national militia organization before going to war.... When war came – at their instigation – the Palestinians were unprepared; they lacked a government.... The Palestinians lacked the economic or organizational wherewithal to import arms and ammunition in significant quantities once hostilities commenced, and the Arab states were niggardly with material support.... Almost no villagers came to the aid of townspeople and vice versa. In effect, each [Arab] community was on its own.[84]

Chaim Herzog notes the chaos and distrust among the five Arab armies invading Israel beginning on May 15, 1948, as a result of which "the Arabs

83. Ibid., 21.
84. Ibid., 399-400.

did not have an effective central command: coordination between [the invading Arab armies] was loose and, at times, ineffective."[85] Jordan's King Abdullah headed the most effective fighting force in the Middle East, the Arab Legion, which the British had trained and which employed British officers. Abdullah was appointed the Commander-in-Chief of the invading armies; however, the other Arab leaders suspected him (correctly) of wanting to add land to his kingdom, and so he was allowed to be leader in title only but not in practice.

While the Israelis managed to obtain weapons on the black and gray markets to circumvent the inadequately-enforced UN arms embargo to the Middle East during the War of Independence, the Arab nations inexplicably made little effort to obtain much-needed replenishments for their depleted weapons during this prolonged war.[86]

Arab leaders' suspicion and hatred of the Palestinian Arab leader Haj Amin al-Husseini led them to exclude Palestinians from participating in the Arab armies' invasion of Palestine. Chaim Herzog writes how the Egyptian army leaders led only by the book and their inflexibility and failure to adapt to battlefield fluctuations contributed to their poor performance.[87] Finally, as is well known, the Israeli manufactured Davidka mortars, which were entirely ineffective but made a very loud noise, prompted frightened Arab soldiers to flee the battlefield.[88]

Victory Against All Odds

Without Hashem's intervention it would have been impossible for the Jews to survive the invasion of five Arab armies on May 15, 1948, especially the aggression of the first four weeks of the war. Chaim Herzog outlines the massive disparity in weaponry:

> Facing a multi-pronged Arab attack advancing on all the major routes into Israel were the infant Israel Defence Forces – more

85. Herzog and Gazit, *The Arab-Israeli Wars: War and Peace in the Middle East*, 47-48.
86. Morris, *1948: The First Arab-Israeli War*, 402-403.
87. Herzog and Gazit, *The Arab-Israeli Wars: War and Peace in the Middle East*, 71.
88. The creation of loud noise to prompt our enemies to unnecessary flight is part of Hashem's repertoire, as is clear from II Kings 7:6.

> like a partisan force, with a hodge-podge of various types of non-standard equipment, with a wide range of small-arms, with a primitive communications system, with practically no artillery, armour, or heavy equipment, and with but an embryonic air unit of light liaison aeroplanes.... Such were the unevenly matched forces that were ranged one against the other at the outset.... The Jewish loss of one percent of its population is perhaps the best indication of the intensity of the struggle and its one-sided nature.[89]

Yigal Yadin,[90] the IDF's head of operations during the War of Independence and later its chief of staff, reflected:

> I was suddenly shocked...when I realized...the whole of the north might be lost. In the south, the Egyptian army was advancing on Tel Aviv. Jerusalem was cut off [by the Arab siege], and the Iraqis were putting pressure on the middle of the country. This was a moment when I suddenly felt that the dream of generations was about to disintegrate.

It is well worth reading Chapter Four of Benny Morris' *1948*, which describes in detail how the outnumbered, severely-outgunned and thinly-spread Israeli forces managed to successfully stave off attacks from the invasion of five Arab armies. Read about the desperate, yet successful Israeli stands against the Syrians at Mishmar haYarden and Deganiah, the Iraqi army at Jenin, the Egyptian army at Kfar Darom and Yad Mordekhai and the Lebanese army at the Galilee Panhandle.[91] Most unbelievable was the Israeli resistance to the well-trained and British-commanded Jordanian Arab legion. The only victory of

89. Herzog and Gazit, *The Arab-Israeli Wars: War and Peace in the Middle East*, 24, 48.
90. Martin Gilbert, *Israel: A History* (New York: Haper Perennial, 1998), 192.
91. Not all of these battles ended with an Israeli victory. Sometimes, as at Yad Mordekhai, the vastly outnumbered and outgunned settlers and soldiers held back the Arab invaders long enough to allow the Israeli army to organize defenses of key areas such as Tel Aviv.

note by this formidable force was the conquering of the Old City of Jerusalem.[92]

The well-oiled, well-armed and well-trained Nazi armed forces could not withstand a war conducted on two fronts, as is typical in the course of history. Israel, on the other hand, managed to survive an invasion of five Arab armies (augmented by troops from Sudan, Yemen and Saudi Arabia)[93] on different fronts. Can one reasonably attribute this to coincidence or pure luck?

The Definition of a Hidden Miracle

Rav Yaakov Medan offers a definition of a hidden miracle – in contrast to an obvious miracle – which applies to Israel's War of Independence. He gives the fictional example of a Torah observant Jew led to execution for observing the commandments. The king orders a coin to be tossed. If it comes up heads the Jew will be burnt at the stake, and if it comes up tails he will be guillotined. The coin is tossed but remains suspended in midair, and the Jew is released. This is an open miracle; the laws of nature have been suspended. On the other hand, if the king decrees that a limb will be severed from the Jew each time the coin falls on heads, and it falls on tails one hundred times so that he is finally released unharmed, this is a hidden miracle. None of the tosses of the coin involved suspension of the laws of nature. It is the pattern of one hundred straight tosses that reveals the hand of God. Rabbi Medan writes:

> The victory was comprised of a thousand details, each of which can be explained independently, but when taken together indicate a miracle, a hidden miracle.
>
> Revealed miracles can be discerned by what they lack: the natural order fades away. A hidden miracle is identifiable by what it has: a clear direction and objective such as the salvation of Israel.[94]

92. Rav Moshe Tzvi Neriah offers a spiritual explanation for this defeat of the Zionist forces. Translation is available at ravkooktorah.org/YOM-YER58.htm.
93. Gordis, *Israel: A Concise History of a Nation Reborn*, 170
94. http://etzion.org.il/en/miracles-revealed-and-hidden.

Rabbi Medan was writing about the tiny Hasmonean army's defeat of the mighty Greek forces, but his remarks are equally relevant to Israel's War of Independence. As in the war of the Maccabees, each detail of the military engagements of May and June 1948 can be explained independently, but the landscape that emerges from the collection of details is inexplicable. How is it that the outnumbered and outgunned Israelis prevailed on three fronts, using weapons whose delivery was ordered by arch-villain Joseph Stalin at precisely the right time, while benefitting from numerous and baffling Arab mistakes? The reasonable explanation is that God was managing the situation from above.

Psalm 124 may well be applied to Hashem's involvement in the 1948 war:

> A Ma'alot Poem of David. If not for the Lord who was with us, let Yisra'el now say –
>
> if not for the Lord who was with us, when men rose up against us:
>
> then they would have swallowed us up alive, when their anger was kindled against us:
>
> then the waters would have overwhelmed us, the stream would have gone over our soul: then the proud waters would have gone over our soul.
>
> Blessed be the Lord, who has not given us as a prey to their teeth.
>
> Our soul is escaped like a bird out of the snare of the fowlers: the snare is broken, and we are escaped.
>
> Our help is in the name of the Lord, who made heaven and earth.[95]

The Purpose of the Miracles of 1947-1948

Now that we have outlined the miracles God bestowed upon His people in the years of 1947-1948, we must ask why Hashem specifically chose this time to perform these miracles for our nation.

95. Translation from Koren English Tehillim.

An analogy from the time of the prophet Haggai is instructive. Haggai prophesied in the year 520 B.C.E, a very difficult time for our nation.[96] The Persian emperor Cyrus, in 539 B.C.E., had permitted the Jews to return to Jerusalem to rebuild the Temple. But relatively few Jews had taken advantage of Cyrus' offer, and those who returned struggled with a poor economy while remaining under Persian rule. Moreover, opposition from the local non-Jewish residents had quickly halted the construction of the Temple after the Jews had erected an altar.

After an absence of prophecy since 570 B.C.E.,[97] Haggai emerged with a simple but encouraging message from Hashem: "*Ani itekhem* (I am with you)."[98] The Jewish people were in desperate need of hearing this message sixty-six years after the destruction of the Temple with its accompanying suffering and exile. The widely-anticipated glorious return to Israel was deeply disappointing. Many Jews might have erroneously concluded that Hashem had abandoned us. Along came Haggai with a message from Hashem to counter such a terrible consideration. Perish that negative thought, teaches Haggai! Hashem's commitment to the Jewish people is eternal! Haggai's message was supported and authenticated by the fulfillment of his prophecy in the completion of the building of the Second Temple in 516 B.C.E., against great odds.[99]

Similarly, the years immediately following World War II were a particularly dismal time for the Jewish people. A third of the Jewish people had been brutally murdered by the Nazis and their many accomplices, and hundreds of thousands of Jews languished in displaced persons camps with no country willing to admit them. The doors of Palestine were almost completely sealed to Jewish immigration by its British rulers.

Many Jews at the time identified with the feelings of their ancestors after their return from exile, fearing that God had forsaken his people. Missionaries actively reached out to Jews arguing that the Holocaust and

96. This is according to the approach of the *Da'at Mikra* commentary on Tanakh.

97. See Ezek. 29:17 with the *Da'at Mikra* commentary.

98. Haggai 1:13.

99. The Jews began to build in anticipation of being granted permission once the project was underway. The Persian emperor Darius not only permitted the reconstruction but even financed the effort.

its aftermath proved that God no longer regarded the Jews as His special people. Many Jews, sadly, fell prey to this toxic outreach. It could be argued that Hashem made the political and military miracles of 1947-1948 to clarify to the Jewish people, "*Ani itekhem.*" He is still very much with us.[100]

Conclusion: Our goal

Now that we have outlined the basis for recognizing Hashem's involvement in the political and military establishment of the State of Israel, it is appropriate to articulate our goal in doing so. The object, it is important to emphasize, is not to promote religious Zionism, though I am a fervent religious Zionist, along the lines of the teachings of Rav Soloveitchik. My goal is to point to evidence that Hashem remains involved in the world. I follow in the footsteps of King Solomon, who in the Song of Songs declares in reference to Hashem, "Behold, He stands behind our wall, He looks in at the windows, He peers through the lattice."[101] Each day in our morning prayers we recite the exhortation "*siḥu bekhol nifle'otav* (talk of all his wondrous works)."[102] It is my fervent hope that this extended discussion inspires and sensitizes readers to heed this call and point out Hashem's intimate involvement with the world.

HASHEM AND THE SIX DAY WAR

As with the remarkable and unanticipated establishment of Israel, most believing Jews perceive Israel's stunning victory in the Six Day War as another demonstration of Hashem's hand guiding the course of Jewish history. The result of this war was so implausible that the manifest conclusion is "*me'et Hashem hayetah zot* (This is the Lord's doing)."[103]

Rabbi Lawrence Kelemen writes:

> In 1967, an impatient [Egyptian President] Nasser violated the truce (from the 1956 War between Egypt and Israel) by moving

100. Rav Soloveitchik articulates a similar approach in his essay "*Kol Dodi Dofeik*" (*Fate and Destiny*, 27-31).
101. Song. 2:9.
102. Ps. 105:2.
103. Ps. 118:23.

> 100,000 troops into the Sinai. On May 19, he ordered the withdrawal of the United Nations peacekeeping units, which complied instantly. On May 22, Nasser blockaded the Gulf of Aqaba, and eight days later he signed a military pact with King Hussein of Jordan. The same day, under Jordanian guidance, Iraqi forces took positions on the Israeli-Jordanian border.
>
> On June 5, reacting to intelligence reports that war was again imminent, Israel launched a preemptive strike. In a single day, it destroyed [almost] the entire Egyptian air force. Jordan and Syria both declared war. In six days Israel defeated all three armies, each larger than the size of its own. The Israelis retook Sinai, captured [the Old City of] Jerusalem [and the West Bank] and Syria's Golan Heights. To this day many military experts are at a loss to explain the Jews' 1967 victory.[104]

Rav Yehuda Amital related[105] that before the Six Day War there were American Jewish leaders who pleaded with the Israeli government to evacuate the children from Israel, since the annihilation of Israel was expected. The Chief Rabbinate of Israel had designated public parks as burial sites, with over 80,000 deaths expected. The dramatic and highly-unexpected turn of events instantly took us "from darkness to light." As in the time of Esther and Mordekhai, "The Jews had light, and gladness, and joy, and honour."[106]

We would like to point to some of the specific indications of Hashem's hand in the Six Day War, based on Dr. Michael Oren's authoritative work *Six Days of War* and an insight of the Vilna Gaon.[107] As seen in the events leading to the creation of the State of Israel, we can perceive the hand of God when our enemies act in an inexplicably foolish manner. Similarly, in Judges 3, the Moabite king Eglon and his team of bodyguards foolishly permitted a representative of a conquered nation, Ehud, to speak privately with Eglon. This left Eglon exposed to attack,

104. Lawrence Keleman, *Permission to Believe* (Southfield, Michigan: Targum Press, 1991), 79-81.
105. This author heard Rabbi Amital recounting these events on the Jerusalem Day celebrations at Yeshivat Har Etzion in 1982 and 1983.
106. Est. 8:16.
107. Est. 1:2, 1:8 and 1:20.

defenseless. In addition, the Moabite security guards did not properly check Ehud for weapons, enabling him to sneak in the weapon he used to kill Eglon and thereby end Moabite rule over part of Israel.

Let us now examine some of the foolish actions of the Arab leadership before and during the Six Day War in an effort to perceive how Hashem was hiding behind the latticework, ensuring our victory against all odds. We should clarify that Dr. Oren does not highlight the role of Hashem in the Six Day War, as his work is solely secular.[108] We seek to supplement his excellent book by reiterating that when so many favorable coincidences occur, reason dictates that success should be attributed to Hashem.

The Egyptian Leadership Before the War

The most well-known fiasco was the Egyptian air force leaving almost all of its planes outside their hangars, fully exposed to Israeli attack. Michael Oren records: "Though proposals for constructing concrete hangars had been submitted by the air force and approved, none had ever been implemented."[109] There were many more Egyptian blunders, such as the disorganization of the Egyptian army as it mobilized for an attack on Israel:

> Thousands of [Egyptian] reservists continued to arrive without equipment or food or a sense of either place or purpose. A report prepared by the army's planning wing concluded that Egypt needed another six months at least to shore up its Sinai defenses for battle, but the recommendation went unheeded and perhaps even unread. Instead, chaos reigned. General Tawfiq 'Abd al-Nabi... arrived in Sinai to take command of an antitank brigade only to find that he had no artillery, no mortars and only seven tanks borrowed from another unit. His soldiers, moreover, knew

108. However, in his address to the NORPAC mission to Washington on May 8, 2013, Dr. Oren stated that God made a miracle in the Six Day War. That date was the twenty-eighth of the Hebrew month of Iyar - Jerusalem Day - which commemorates the reunification of Jerusalem.

109. Michael Oren, *Six Days of War: June 1967 and the Making of the Modern Middle East* (New York: Oxford University Press, 2002), 171.

> nothing of tank warfare. Dozens of units had been exhausted, their vehicles worn out, transferring back and forth across the desert.[110]

Moreover, before the Israeli preemptive strike, the Egyptians were planning a surprise attack on Israel which they code-named "Operation Dawn."[111] The Israelis, who suspected that an attack was imminent but were still pursuing diplomatic solutions to the crisis, communicated their fears of an attack to the Americans, who informed the Soviet leaders. The Soviets, in turn, communicated this message to Nasser, who drew the erroneous conclusion that the Israelis had accessed Egyptian secrets. Nasser canceled the offensive only fifteen minutes before it was scheduled to begin, when the Egyptian pilots were already in their planes.[112]

Oren concludes: "The Egyptian offensive was all but dead, struck down by a *chance*[113] intervention just short of the H-hour." Believing Jews do not see this as mere happenstance, but as divine intervention allowing Israel to take control of the crisis with a preemptive strike, rather than be forced to react to an Egyptian attack.

Egyptian Leadership During the War

On the first day of the war, as Israeli warplanes were on their way to destroy the Egyptian planes, the Jordanians (who possessed the most sophisticated radar facility in the Middle East) detected the Israeli attack and communicated the information to the Egyptian defense minister. The Jordanian communication, however, was indecipherable, since the Egyptians had changed their encoding frequencies the previous day, but without updating the Jordanians. Moreover, "even if those messages could have been read, the Egyptian defense minister was not present to read them. He had gone to bed only a few hours before [the Israeli attack] leaving strict orders not to be disturbed. Similarly absent were the officers in charge of decoding and the air operations chief....

110. Ibid., 159-160.
111. Ibid., 92-97.
112. Ibid., 119-121.
113. Emphasis added.

Air force intelligence also reported extensively on the Israeli attack, but the officers at the Supreme Headquarters ... ignored them."[114]

The mishaps continued on the second day of the war. The Egyptian leadership understood the situation as far more desperate than it truly was. "Rather than rallying their still extensive forces, digging in during the day and counterattacking at night when the Israeli Air Force's edge was blunted, Egypt's leaders ordered a wholesale and wildly disorganized retreat."[115]

The Jordanian Leadership

King Hussein of Jordan ignored personal pleas from Israel's Prime Minister Levi Eshkol to end the fighting twice in the course of the war. Hussein's recalcitrance lost Jordan the entire West Bank.[116] Oren explains that Hussein was misled by Egyptian President Nasser, who lied to the Jordanian monarch, reporting massive Israeli losses and the destruction of Israeli airfields.[117] Hussein ignored reports from outside sources that in reality, the Egyptian air force was obliterated.[118] It should be emphasized that King Hussein was a wise leader who ruled Jordan from 1953 until his death in 1999, shrewdly overcoming many existential threats to Jordan as well as numerous assassination attempts. Israelis are fond of saying that King Hussein of Jordan made only two mistakes: attacking Israel in 1967 and refraining from invading Israel during the 1973 Yom Kippur War, when it barely survived a two-front attack by Egypt and Syria. Israel, which was woefully unprepared for the 1973 war, would likely not have survived if Jordan had attacked.

This behavior is reminiscent of the behavior of Naḥash, the king of Ammon (note that the Jordanian capital is the ancient city of Amman), who attacked the Israelites unsuccessfully when King Saul was rising to power,[119] then failed to attack when King Saul's forces had been utterly destroyed.[120]

---

114. Oren, *Six Days of War: June 1967 and the Making of the Modern Middle East*, 172.
115. Ibid., 214.
116. Ibid., 244.
117. Ibid., 185.
118. Ibid., 188.
119. I Sam. 11.
120. I Sam. 28.

Excellent timing worked in favor of the Israeli air force when it found Jordanian fighter planes on the ground refueling. The Israelis were able to eliminate the Jordanian air force within minutes on the first day of the war. By the third day of the war, "Jordanian forces were in total disarray, abandoning vehicles in their rush to reach the East Bank and safety."[121] Among other things, the Jordanians abandoned forty Patton tanks in pristine condition. Oren records that, despite the Jordanian soldiers' "courage and determination," they lost due to their commanders' inability to adapt to changing circumstances.[122] Oren also writes that Hussein's "passions obfuscated reality" and he made poor choices.[123]

The Syrian Leadership

The Syrian leadership also made serious blunders both before and after the war. An example is the Syrians' failure to recognize damage done to their armed forces by Eli Cohen, a famous Israeli spy. Cohen worked in Syria, where he developed close relationships with the political and military hierarchy. The intelligence he gathered is said to have been an important factor in Israel's success in the Six Day War. His most famous achievement came when he toured the Golan Heights and collected intelligence on the Syrian fortifications there. Pretending to feel concern for the Syrian soldiers exposed to the sun, Cohen had eucalyptus trees planted at every position. The trees were used as targeting markers by the Israeli military during the war. Although Eli Cohen was eventually exposed and was executed in Syria in 1965, between that time and the Six Day War the Syrians did not recognize the problem the eucalyptus trees created for them!

During the war the Syrians inexplicably retreated in many instances (although in certain areas they offered fierce resistance). Oren notes instances where Israeli soldiers fired at Syrian tanks which turned out to be abandoned. Oren writes:

> The Syrians were blowing up their own bunkers, burning documents, and retreating en masse. With their forward communications

---

121. Oren, *Six Days of War: June 1967 and the Making of the Modern Middle East*, 247.
122. Ibid., 258.
123. Ibid., 225.

> cut, unwilling to take charge at the front, Syrian commanders had lost all control over the battlefield. Yet even they were nonplussed when Radio Damascus broadcast that Quneitra (the Syrian headquarters on the Golan Heights) had fallen.[124]

A Syrian officer recalled, "The forces that were supposed to block the enemy's advance pulled out without authorization, without coordination. We knew nothing, and had no choice but to fall back."[125]

When the Syrian government tried to correct the mistaken announcement of Quneitra's fall by declaring that Syrian soldiers were still fighting there, the message came too late. The Syrian army was in full flight, abandoning its heavy equipment, jamming the roads. Soviet advisors exhorted the troops to remain at their posts, and orders were issued to shoot deserters on sight. All such efforts proved futile, however; the Soviets were ignored while the commanders charged with executing deserters had themselves abandoned the field. Believing that the entire Golan had already fallen, driven by rumors of Israelis wielding nuclear weapons, some 4,000 Syrian soldiers sought refuge in Jordan and 3,000 in Lebanon.

Indeed, one of Hashem's methods of assisting us is to bring fear upon our enemies.[126] This was certainly in evidence on all three fronts during the Six Day War.

The Soviet Leadership

One of Israel's greatest fears was the possibility of Soviet intervention when they launched their preemptive attack. While Israel could grapple with its neighbors, the Soviet superpower was another matter. Moreover, the American government did not respond to an Israeli request for military assistance in the event of direct Soviet intervention in the war.[127] But the Soviets failed to assist the Arab nations in any substantial way, despite their allies' dramatic losses. Oren explains that there was an

---

124. Ibid., 295.
125. Ibid., 301.
126. See Lev. 26:8, Josh. 2:10, and Judges 7:14 and 21.
127. Oren, *Six Days of War: June 1967 and the Making of the Modern Middle East*, 299.

internal dispute within the Soviet leadership as to whether to confront the United States in the Middle East. In short, "that quarrel, together with the slow pace of Soviet decision making – the government met only once weekly, on Thursdays (the war began on Monday) – had all but paralyzed Soviet diplomacy in the first days of the crisis."[128] Oren writes: "Not only were the Arabs disillusioned with Moscow, but also its allies in Eastern Europe. They were exasperated with Soviet mishandling of this crisis and, to the degree they could, told them so at a summit of Warsaw Pact countries on June 10 [1967]."[129]

Conclusion

Once, while walking in the forest, though deep in thought and meditation, the Baal Shem Tov (according to a frequently recounted Hasidic tale) heard a child crying. Following the cry, the Baal Shem Tov finally found a little boy, frightened and shivering in the dark. "Why are you here in the forest all by yourself?" he asked the child gently. Looking into the man's kind face, the child was calmed. "I was playing hide-and-seek with my friends. I waited and waited for them to find my hiding place but none of them discovered it. Now it is dark and they have all gone home! I am alone and frightened." With that, the boy began to sob sorrowfully once more. "Do not cry, little boy; I will bring you home," comforted the Baal Shem Tov.

The Baal Shem Tov explained that this incident is truly a metaphor for God and the Jews. Since our beginning as a people, we have actively searched for God and sought out a meaningful relationship with Him. Even when we were exiled from our Land and God was forced to "hide" Himself, we still sincerely searched for Him.

But now, God, like the lost child, cries: "I wait and wait for you to look for Me, to find the inherent Godliness and holiness in everything you do. But it seems you have become tired of the search. In the darkness of today's world, in the confusion of the forest of your mundane lives and material aspirations, you have all gone home and I am alone."

---

128. Ibid., 296.
129. Ibid., 296-297.

The attribution of our astonishing victory during the Six Day War to the subtle hand of Hashem coordinating the circumstances to lean in our favor should inspire us to sincerely thank Hashem on Jerusalem Day. More important, it should inspire us to search for Hashem's less obvious actions. The Torah promises that if we sincerely search for Him, we will find Him.[130]

Postscript

In no manner do we wish to minimize the difficulty of many of the Six Day War battles and the heroism of Israel's soldiers. This chapter is dedicated to the elevation of the souls of the more than seven hundred Israeli soldiers, including this author's cousin Noaḥ Rotem, who fell in the Six Day War.

THE MIRACLE OF THE RAID ON ENTEBBE

Rabbi Eli Mansour mentioned in a public lecture that he showed his children a film of the 1976 Israeli hostage rescue at Entebbe, Uganda to reinforce their *emuna*. One who watches a good documentary about the Entebbe rescue must surely notice that this mission was successful despite many potential issues.[131]

The following factors make the mission's success truly extraordinary:

1. Liftoff of the rescue planes was extremely difficult. The weight of the cargo and fuel and the intense desert heat (the planes took off from Sharm el-Sheikh) made it nearly impossible.
2. The overloaded planes had to fly extremely low to avoid detection. This made the flight of the rescue planes extremely dangerous. In the documentary *The Greatest Hostage Rescue in History: Documentary on the Entebbe Raid* (at 26:48-26:53) the pilot recalled that if he had moved the plane's steering wheel just three millimeters improperly, the plane would have crashed into the sea.

130. Deut. 4:29
131. One such film is *The Greatest Hostage Rescue in History: Documentary on the Entebbe Raid,* which is archived at https://www.youtube.com/watch?v=FYU4iOWJ9pU.

3. Refueling the planes was an exceptional challenge. The Kenyan government, at the last moment, surprisingly permitted the rescue planes to land and refuel in its capital city Nairobi. Otherwise, the Israeli planes would have had to remain significantly longer in Uganda to refuel.
4. Landing the plane was an extraordinary challenge due to the extra weight of the plane and the need to avoid detection. The first rescue plane landed just after the last commercial flight landed at the Entebbe airport, and so the landing lights were left on. The soldiers then placed dim lights to allow the other planes to land.
5. The rescuers had to overcome the terrorists and the Ugandan soldiers, while doing everything they could to avoid casualties among the hostages they were trying to rescue.
6. The hostages were housed in a building that was constructed by Israelis, which allowed the IDF to access the plans for the building.
7. Israelis had previously trained Ugandan soldiers and thus knew their nature. This provided the IDF with the knowledge of how to handle the Ugandan soldiers.
8. The Mercedes car used to transport the soldiers from the planes to the terminal was in poor condition. The car easily could have failed to start.
9. The IDF commandos succeeded in destroying the Ugandan Air Force planes located at the airport. Had these planes engaged the very overloaded Israeli rescue planes they would have enjoyed a tremendous advantage.
10. The terrorists were positioned in a manner that made their elimination relatively easy for the Israeli commandos.
11. The terrorists and their Ugandan supporters made many serious errors. For example, holding the hostages in the airport facilitated their quick rescue.
12. The non-Jewish hostages, once released, provided vital intelligence information to the Israeli commandos.
13. The Ugandans permitted the airport to continue operations while holding the Jews hostage, which enabled an Israeli secret

agent to hover over the airport and take pictures of the area while posing as a pilot whose plane was experiencing engine trouble.

14. The Israelis were in the airport for nearly an hour. In that time the Ugandans should have mobilized their Air Force planes located at the airport (before the Israelis blew them up) to destroy the Israeli planes on the ground waiting to take the soldiers and hostages home.
15. Almost all of the hostages were held in one area, making their rescue easier.

That each of these factors worked out as it did, may be explained as coincidence or good fortune. However, the aggregate of so many "coincidences" clearly points to the involvement of Hashem. The Lubavitcher Rebbe wrote about Entebbe:

> One cannot fail to note the extraordinary aspects at both ends of the hijacking. On the one hand, the ease with which the four terrorists hijacked the airbus in Athens, and on the other hand, the extraordinary success of the rescue operation. In other words, both the initial tragedy and eventual deliverance clearly point to the Hand of God. And while every Jew is grateful to, and admires the *Mesirat Nefesh* (dedication) of the brave rescuers, we must not lose sight for a moment of the warning and lesson at the bottom of it all – not just in regard to the danger of hijacking in the ordinary sense, but even more importantly, in regard to the "spiritual hijacking" of so many of our young generation by alien and freak cultures which, unfortunately, capture so many of our innocent boys and girls in *Eretz Yisrael* as in the Diaspora.[132]

CONTEMPORARY APPLICATION: ROCKETS FROM GAZA

The official blog of the Israel Defense Forces states that "since Israel withdrew from the Gaza Strip in 2005, terrorists have fired more than 11,000 rockets into Israel. Over 5 million Israelis are currently living under threat

132. Translation from http://www.chabad.org/therebbe/letters/default_cdo/aid/397865/jewish/The-Miracle-of-Entebbe.htm.

of rocket attacks."[133] Let us ponder this phenomenon for a moment. 11,000 rockets landed in the ten years from 2005 to 2015 – what would one expect the casualty rate to be from such unrelenting fire? In the normal course of events there would be tens of thousands killed and severely injured and billions of dollars of financial loss sustained. While there has been, most unfortunately, some loss of life, limb, and property, it is dramatically lower than one would expect. As I see it, divine intervention to preserve the Jewish people is the only reasonable explanation for this phenomenon. Coincidence, Israeli security skills, or the poor abilities of Arab terrorists can explain some of the incidents, but they cannot adequately account for ten years of unremitting, yet for the most part unsuccessful, attacks. The sensible explanation of ten years of ceaseless rocket fire that has yielded an extraordinarily low casualty rate is divine intervention. These events match the *Arukh Hashulḥan's* description of events that "deviate from the boundaries of naturally occurring events."

WHY HASHEM DOES NOT PERFORM OPEN MIRACLES IN EVERY GENERATION

Nahmanides observes, "Hashem does not make obvious miracles in every generation in the presence of every wicked individual or heretic." Although the absence of obvious miracles may be a source of frustration to some, we shall endeavor to demonstrate that it is also a rich wellspring of religious experience. Nahmanides' approach to this matter will be the focus and basis of our discussion.[134]

The World Functions in a Natural Manner

The following episode recorded by the Gemara[135] illustrates that Hashem wants the world to function in a natural manner. There was a very poor man whose wife had died after having given birth to a child. The widower became frantic, as he had no financial resources to hire a wet-nurse to feed the baby. Hashem made a miracle, and the husband grew breasts from which he nursed the baby. Rav exclaimed, "What a

133. https://www.idfblog.com/facts-figures/rocket-attacks-toward-israel/
134. Ex. 13:16
135. Shabbat 53b

great man this must be that he merited such a great miracle!" Abaye, however, declared that just the opposite is true – if Hashem disrupted the natural order instead of providing him with resources in a natural manner, the man must be on a low spiritual level. Based on Abaye, our challenge in life is to discover Hashem hiding behind the natural processes of life. A miracle performed within the fabric of our daily lives is deeper and more significant than a miracle that disrupts the delicate balance of the world's natural order.

Unfortunately, many neglect their responsibility to seek out Hashem and fail to appreciate His involvement in the world. Nahmanides[136] observes that such a situation prevailed in the years leading up to the exodus from Egypt.[137] Many have noted that Hashem did not directly intervene in any of the events recorded in the beginning of the Book of Exodus until the death of Pharaoh, when we cried out to Him in great anguish.[138] In other words, the great miracles surrounding our departure from Egypt followed many years of *hester panim,* a time in which Hashem concealed Himself.

Nahmanides explains that this motivated Hashem to incontrovertibly demonstrate His existence and divine intervention through the great miracles of the exodus from Egypt.[139] But for subsequent generations the question remains: how does Hashem provide opportunities for people to recognize Him long after the exodus from Egypt?

The Sacred Obligation of the Jewish People to Publicize Hashem's Presence

Nahmanides answers that Hashem has delegated to us the job of publicizing His existence and involvement in the world. Since Hashem will not split the Red Sea or perform the ten plagues in every generation, it is our job to gather and retell these great stories. Nahmanides explains that this is the reason for stressing the exodus from Egypt not only at

136. Op. cit.

137. See, for instance, Pharaoh's exclamation of "Who is the Lord, that I should obey His voice to let Yisra'el go?" (Ex. 5:2). This indicates that Hashem did not make His presence obvious during that era.

138. Ex. 2:23-25.

139. Ex. 13:16.

Passover but every day of the year. The commandments commemorating the exodus from Egypt and all the divine spectacles that accompanied it are meant to refute the claim that Hashem is powerless. He has entrusted the Jewish people of each generation, his "witnesses,"[140] with the sacred task of continuing to publicize and preserve these divine wonders. Indeed, when we recount the details of the exodus from Egypt each year on the Seder night, it is as if we are experiencing the miracles ourselves.

The Jewish people are prepared to serve as Hashem's witnesses, since approximately three million of our ancestors witnessed first-hand the great miracles of the exodus from Egypt and the revelation at Mount Sinai.[141] These three million people included many skeptical individuals who often fought and challenged Moses, except at Sinai when they received the Torah.[142] These millions of Jews related this precious tradition, which has been sacredly protected by every generation, until it has reached our very hands.

This assignment reflects a core mission of humanity, the completion of Creation. Rav Soloveitchik explains that Hashem deliberately refrained from completing Creation.[143] Hashem charges Adam with the job of "conquering" the world.[144] Our job is to complete Hashem's world. In the spiritual as well as the physical realm, Hashem has left the world incomplete. Our job is to complete it by announcing Hashem's presence to all.

Nahmanides states that this task is the central reason and purpose of our existence on this earth, as well as the basic motivation behind all mitzvot. He writes:

> One who purchases a mezuza for a small amount of money, affixes it on his doorpost, and bears in mind the purpose of the mezuza, has already acknowledged divine creation of the world, divine omniscience and providence, prophecy, belief in the pillars of Torah, in addition to thanking Hashem for the enormous

140. Is. 43:10.
141. See Rabbi Judah HaLevi, *The Kuzari* 1:25.
142. Rashi (Ex. 19:2).
143. Rabbi Joseph B. Soloveitchik, *Halakhic Man* (Philadelphia: Jewish Publication Society, 1983), 101.
144. See Nahmanides on Gen. 1:28.

> kindness He bestowed on those who followed His will by delivering us from slavery to freedom.[145]

He also asserts that this is the purpose of gathering in synagogues, "where people acknowledge their Creator and publicize this and proclaim before Him, 'You have created us.'" This explains the deep satisfaction we can experience while participating in communal prayer. By so doing we fulfill the very purpose of our existence, and there can be no greater satisfaction than this.

From Open Miracles to Subtle Miracles

Acknowledging overt miracles *(nissim mefursamim)* leads to recognition of the subtle miracles (*nissim nistarim)* that surround us and we need only be sufficiently alert to identify them. Nahmanides writes that belief in *nissim nistarim* on both the communal and individual levels is the "basis of the entire Torah," for everything we do "involves miracles. There is no nature and way of the world for either the community or individuals."[146] Although Maimonides would not fully subscribe to this statement,[147] he nonetheless agrees that recognizing Hashem's involvement in the world is a key component of a Jew's worldview.[148] There are ample opportunities to perceive Hashem even though He does not openly display His presence as He did during the time of the exodus from Egypt. One who searches in good faith for Hashem will surely encounter Him.

PERCEIVING MIRACLES IN THE PRESENT: JOSEPH AS MODEL

Introduction: Joseph Claims to Know God's Will

Joseph makes the surprising claim that Hashem sent him to Egypt to provide food for his family in the famine. He makes this assertion twice: once when he reveals his identity to his brothers[149] and yet again when

145. Ex. 13:16.
146. Nahmanides on Ex. 13.16.
147. See his commentary to Avot 5:6 and *Shemone Prakim* 8.
148. *Hilkhot Ta'aniyot* 1:1.
149. Gen. 45:8.

consoling his brothers after their father Jacob's death.[150] We are perplexed, though, as to how Joseph became convinced that this indeed was Hashem's intention. After all, unlike the Patriarchs, Yosef never received a direct prophecy from Hashem, so how was he privy to God's will?

This question has ramifications for us. For if Joseph can discern God's will without the benefit of direct communication, then we also might be able to discover Hashem's will even in an age devoid of prophecy (or even the *bat kol* or heavenly voice, the lower degree of prophecy that was sometimes heard in talmudic times).

Joseph's Sweet-Smelling Caravan

An answer to our query emerges from an analysis of an intriguing comment made by Rashi[151]. The Torah records that the caravan that transported Joseph to slavery in Egypt was carrying fragrant spices such as balsam and lotus. Ḥazal and Rashi wonder why the Torah records this seemingly-trivial detail, which appears entirely irrelevant to the story. Why does Hashem feel it is important to know the cargo contents of the caravan?

Rashi, following Ḥazal, explains that normally Arab caravans carried foul-smelling items such as resin and tar. Hashem arranged that the caravan transporting Joseph would feature fragrant spices so that Joseph need not suffer from the malodorous wares.

This teaching is quite puzzling. Joseph is being transported to Egypt to live a miserable existence as a slave. Joseph's privileged life as Jacob's favorite son was transformed instantly to a wretched reality. How would Hashem's arranging for the caravan to carry sweet smells help Joseph in any significant manner? Odoriferous cargo would have appeared to constitute the least of Yosef's newly-encountered problems. The situation would seem analogous to someone who, God forbid, was kidnapped by ISIS and Hashem arranged for the vehicle transporting the victim to be pleasant-smelling. What benefit does the victim in such horrific circumstances have from the pleasant smell?

150. Gen. 50:20.

151. Gen. 37:25, citing Genesis Rabba 84:17.

Discerning Divine Involvement

One answer is that Joseph was a highly intelligent person, as Onkelos and Rashi point out.[152] He therefore realized that it was unusual for an Ishmaelite caravan to be carrying sweet-smelling spices. Joseph realized that this rare occurrence must have been a subtle message from Hashem that He is with him and that He orchestrated his sale to Egypt for a purpose. This message he eventually articulated confidently to his brothers. Joseph did not need a divine revelation to ascertain this information; he needed only a sense of logic and sensitivity to his surroundings to become conscious of Hashem's involvement.

Conclusion: Identifying Hashem's Intervention

Even in a time when Hashem does not perform open miracles and prophetic communication is absent, a reasonable individual can and should discern divine providence. When the inexplicable occurs, whether it is an Ishmaelite caravan transporting sweet-smelling spices or Ishmaelites firing countless rockets at the children of Jacob and doing relatively little damage, it is incumbent upon us to recognize the hand of God. Joseph – whose sophistication, insight and discerning eye in economic matters brought him worldwide recognition and acclaim – unabashedly and frequently spoke of Hashem, whose involvement he discerned using that same acumen.

NOTICING THE 53RD CARD

The Burning Bush vs. the Revelation on Mount Sinai

The revelation on Mount Sinai was undoubtedly a grand event. Exodus 19:16 captures the power of that great moment in Jewish history: "And it came to pass on the third day in the morning, that there were thunders and lightnings, and a thick cloud upon the mountain, and the sound of a shofar exceedingly loud; so that all the people in the camp trembled." By contrast, the revelation at the burning bush in Exodus 3 is surprisingly modest. Hashem's introduction to Moses is a pivotal moment, yet it is conducted in an understated manner.

---

152. Gen. 37:3.

Three Classic Solutions

The classic commentators explain that Hashem was communicating different messages to Moses through this phenomenon. Rashi explains that Hashem chose a meek presentation as a means of showing that He empathizes with the plight and suffering of the Jews in Egypt.[153] An analogy can be drawn to families making a wedding in 1944. While a wedding is a joyous occasion, families felt uncomfortable throwing lavish affairs given the suffering of European Jewry, so their affairs were unadorned compared to normal times.

Other commentators interpret on the extraordinary fact that although the bush was ablaze, it maintained its integrity and shape and was not completely consumed by the fire. The thirteenth-century commentary *Ḥizkuni* explains that the fire represents the Egyptians and the bush symbolizes the Jewish people.[154] The implicit message is that just as the fire does not consume the bush, so too the Egyptians will not succeed in their efforts to annihilate the Jewish people.

A third approach, emerging from Rashi, is that the burning bush actually characterizes Moses.[155] Hashem demonstrates that the burning bush maintains its integrity, unconsumed by the fire, because it is performing Hashem's will. So too, Moses will survive his encounters with Pharaoh because he will be carrying out Hashem's appointed task.

Rabbi David Fohrman's Approach: Noticing the 53rd Card

Rabbi Fohrman offers an interesting approach to this episode, pointing out that the burning bush was a difficult miracle to notice.[156] He presents a social-psychology experiment in which college students were asked to look at playing cards and identify which cards they were seeing. They were shown various cards – an eight of spades, a three of hearts, a five of clubs – and one three of hearts on which one of the hearts had been erased with whiteout. The researchers wanted to see how the students would identify this card. Each student was given the opportunity to look

---

153. Ex. 3:2.
154. Ex. 3:2.
155. Ex. 3:12.
156. https://www.alephbeta.org/course/lecture/seeing-the-hidden-miracle/autoplay.

at the cards for 5-7 seconds. When asked to identify the anomalous card, about half identified it as a three of hearts, and half identified it as a two of hearts. But no one said, "There is no such card in the deck; something is wrong with that card." Their eyes could see the unusual phenomenon, but their minds could not accept what their eyes were seeing.

Similarly, in order to notice that the burning bush was not being consumed, you would have to look at the bush for a certain amount of time before noticing that the bush is not being consumed. And even if you looked at it for a long time, you still might not notice it because that's not the way bushes work. Bushes always get consumed eventually when they burn. And because it's not the way bushes work, even if your eyes see the bush remaining intact despite the fire, your mind might not necessarily accept what your eyes tell you. This, says Rabbi Fohrman, was Moses' test: "Moses had to be someone who could see not with his eyes, but accept with his mind what his eyes saw."

Moses passed the test with flying colors: "And when the Lord saw that he turned aside to see, God called to him out of the midst of the bush," [157] Moshe did notice the 53rd card, proving his worthiness to be the recipient of divine communication and the leader of the Jewish people. Moses' acute sensitivity to the subtle miracle of the burning bush proved his merit to train the Israelites to notice and appreciate the delicate yet powerful divine involvement in our world.

The Bush That Is Not Consumed: Why Does the 'Persecuted People' Survive and Thrive?

Moses' question – "Why is the bush not being consumed" – is a timeless query that can be asked regarding the miraculous survival of the Jewish people. Rabbi Warren Goldstein, the chief rabbi of South Africa, writes:

> These are indeed days of "miracle and wonder." Some 250 years ago, long before these modern miracles, Rav Yaakov Emdin wrote that the miracles performed by God to ensure the survival of the Jewish people throughout the many years of exile are even greater than the awe-inspiring miracles of the Exodus from Egypt – the ten

157. Ex. 3:4.

plagues, the splitting of the sea, the manna falling from heaven and the Clouds of Glory. Jewish destiny defies the normal laws of history.

By any logical and rational assessment, we should not exist as a separate, identifiable people after almost 2,000 years of exile, dispersion and persecution. But God's plan for us rises above the limitations of the physical world. At the heart of His plan is His Torah.

The miracle of the rebirth of Jewish sovereignty in the Land of Israel, which we have been privileged to witness in our time, is a remarkable endorsement of the prescient words of Rav Yaakov Emdin. Torah is flourishing once more, with the great yeshivas of Europe re-established in Israel, America and all over the world; Ponivezh, Mir and Gur[158] are alive and thriving once again.[159]

Conclusion

The intelligent person should ask himself or herself why the State of Israel has not been consumed and why the Jewish people have survived and thrived despite relentless and brutal oppression and attacks. Extraordinary events should not be minimized. If one learns of hundreds of missiles fired by Israel's enemies and little damage is done, he must respond. He should notice God's hand and ask, following the example set by Moses, why the normal laws of nature and history do not apply to the Jewish people. Asking this type of question is an excellent first step in forging a deep connection with Hashem, Torah, and the Jewish people.

PRESENT HIDDEN MIRACLES AND PAST OVERT MIRACLES

Although in our time Hashem seems to work mainly through hidden miracles, the fact that hidden miracles occur today should make us more

158. We should add the remarkable resurgence of the Sephardic Torah world, which in the post-World War Two era was tiny and centered only on Jerusalem's Yeshivat Porat Yosef, then a very small and struggling institution.
159. http://www.jpost.com/Opinion/Op-Ed-Contributors/Days-of-miracle-and-wonder. A beautiful short video presenting Rabbi Goldstein's thoughts is available at https://www.youtube.com/watch?v=oeVMfNQskWc

receptive to belief that overt miracles occurred in the past. Why it was necessary for overt miracles to occur in the past is a question we may address by looking at one of the earliest overt miracles – Sarah's giving birth to Isaac at the age of 90.

A Challenging Question

Avi Ohayon of blessed memory, a congregant at Congregation Shaarei Orah of Teaneck, New Jersey, related to me that a co-worker challenged him with the question: "Do you truly believe that the biblical Sarah gave birth at the age of ninety?" Mr. Ohayon asked me how to respond.

The query is indeed a valid one. Why should, or how could, a reasonable individual believe that a woman gave birth at age ninety? Indeed, Sarah herself asked that question when she laughed on overhearing the prophecy. A proper response requires us to delve deeply into the story of Sarah's laughter, as recorded in Genesis 18.

Sarah's Puzzling Laughter

It has puzzled many commentators that Sarah laughed at the angel's statement that Hashem would send her a child within a year. The angel's response to Sarah's laughter – "Is anything too hard for the Lord?" – is something that should have been very apparent to Sarah.[160] It seems evident from the Book of Genesis that Sarah was a full partner in Abraham's spiritual quest and fully shared Abraham's *emuna*. Indeed, according to Rashi, Sarah's level of prophecy was superior to Abraham's![161] How could someone who was on a higher spiritual level than Abraham have doubted the capabilities of Hashem?

A Hidden Miracle Is Preferable to a Revealed Miracle

An answer to our question lies in Hashem's preference for a hidden miracle, in which He acts in a subtle manner, over an overt miracle such as the splitting of the Red Sea, which involves a violation of the laws of nature. Hashem prefers hidden miracles because they require people

160. Gen. 18:14.

161. Gen. 21:12.

to invest in His discovery, and this enables a legitimate relationship to blossom between humans and their God. The Gemara relates:[162]

> R. Mani was a student of R. Yitzḥak ben Eliyashiv. Once he came crying to his rabbi. "The rich members of my father-in-law's house," he complained, "trouble and afflict me." "May they become poor," R. Yitzḥak told him. Some time later, he again came to complain before R. Yitzḥak. "Now they are pressuring me to support them," he cried. "They tell me they have nothing to eat." "May they become rich," R. Yitzḥak prayed, and so it was. At another time R. Mani came before R. Yitzḥak. "My wife is unattractive," he complained, "and I find it difficult to look at her." "What is her name?" R. Yitzḥak asked. "Ḥanna." "May Ḥanna become beautiful," R. Yitzḥak prayed, and so it was. A short while later, R. Mani again came with a complaint. "She is beautiful now," he cried, "and treats me in an arrogant way." "If so," R. Yitzḥak said, "May she again be plain." And so it was. Two students of R. Yitzḥak ben Eliyashiv once asked him, "Rabbi, pray for us that we should be wise." "Once, I could do this," he answered them. "Whatever I would pray for, the heavens would grant me. Now I have returned this gift to heaven."

Maharsha (Rabbi Shmuel Eidels) explains that R. Yitzḥak ben Eliashiv realized that Hashem prefers to work through natural means instead of through overt miracles.[163]

Understanding Sarah's Laughter

Sarah realized this point as well. This became obvious to her from the fact that Hashem did not intervene on their behalf with a violation of the laws of nature unless it was absolutely necessary.[164] For example,

162. Taanit 23b.
163. R. Yitzḥak ben Eliashiv apparently drew this conclusion from the fact that the violations of nature brought about through his prayers were not helpful.
164. Such as when Hashem saved Abraham from Nimrod's fiery furnace (Genesis Rabba 38:13).

Hashem did not blatantly appear to Abraham and Sarah after they had become completely convinced of His existence. Accordingly, Sarah found it difficult to believe that Hashem would send her a child in her post-menopausal state at age ninety. Sarah reasoned that if Hashem wanted her to have a child He would have sent her a child before she reached menopause, since He acts in a natural manner unless a violation of the law of nature is absolutely necessary.

Thus Sarah reasoned that the three men who visited her family could not be angels, since their prediction did not make sense.[165] This explains Sarah's laughter. But we must still explain why Hashem found it appropriate to bless Sarah with a child in a manner that ran counter to the laws of nature.

The Need for Sarah to Have a Child at Age Ninety

The need for Sarah to have a child at an advanced age may be explained by the principle known as *ma'ase avot siman lebanim*, literally "the acts of the fathers are a sign for the children," which means that the lives of the patriarchs and matriarchs serve as a blueprint for the history of their descendants, the Jewish people.[166]

Sforno observes that Hashem performed a sort of *teḥiyat metim* (revival of the dead) on Sarah's uterus.[167] Hashem felt this was necessary in order to imbed the phenomenon of *teḥiyat metim* into the fundamental fabric of the Jewish people. Our nation has repeatedly rebounded from situations that, given the usual course of history, should have led to our demise long ago. We survived slavery in Egypt, the Egyptian attack at the Red Sea, the Babylonian exile, Haman's decree, the Hellenistic persecutions in the Hasmonean era, the Roman destruction and the Spanish Inquisition – and these are only a handful of the major situations where the Jewish people were close to extinction!

In more recent times, the incredible turning of the tide from the end of the Holocaust in 1945 to the establishment of a Jewish state in

165. Nahmanides (Gen. 18:12).

166. Nahmanides develops this point at length in his commentary to Genesis, beginning with his comments on Genesis 12:6.

167. Gen. 18:12.

the Land of Israel in 1947 is a prime example of how the Jewish people have been "revived from the dead."[168] Another modern-day example is how Orthodox Judaism was heading in the direction of elimination in the mid-twentieth century. Since then, however, Orthodox Judaism has been revitalized and is growing exponentially, while the denominations that deviate from tradition are disintegrating.

Shortly after the establishment of the State of Israel, David Ben-Gurion was willing to grant exemption from army service to yeshiva students, because he saw yeshiva students as a relic that would soon die out. He hardly imagined a scenario where a burgeoning population of hundreds of thousands of scrupulously-observant Orthodox Jews would be clamoring for exemptions from army service in order to devote themselves to fulltime Torah study.

With Isaac's miraculous birth, the Jewish nation was *created* in a manner of *teḥiyat metim* so that the Jewish people would carry the ability to renew themselves when all seems hopeless and foregone.

Thus in reply to the skeptic who argues that a reasonable person should not believe that Sarah had Isaac at age ninety, one need only point out the recurring pattern of "revivals" of the Jewish people that run counter to normal historical and sociological trends. In the light of these events it is reasonable to believe that such a people began in a miraculous manner.

168. Similarly, Ezekiel prophesies about dry bones being restored to life as a metaphor for the revival of the Jewish people after all hope appeared to have vanished (Ezek. 37).

Chapter 5

Humanistic Objections

Another direction from which Orthodox belief is often challenged today is humanism, which assumes that human beings always know what is good.

On the basis of humanism, objections are raised to Torah commandments that are perceived as contradicting current ethical values. Human suffering, especially in the Holocaust, has been a basis for challenging Hashem's justice. And finally, the pursuit of human happiness (or pleasure) as absolute value has led to a view of Torah restrictions as burdensome and oppressive.

We will examine three examples of commandments in the written Torah that have been perceived as clashing with humanistic ethical imperatives, and we will see how the oral Torah, over the centuries, has dealt with these issues. The discussion of *mamzerut*, especially, will offer an extensive example of how the oral Torah interprets the written commandment so as to avoid causing unnecessary suffering. We will also see that there is good reason for these commandments to be "on the books" in the written Torah.

We will address the question of human suffering through an interpretation of the Book of Job.

Finally, we shall see that the Torah way of life is not an obstacle to human happiness but a gateway to it. We shall see the benefits of living one's life according to the Torah's commandments, even when one does not understand the reason for them.

DESTRUCTION OF LIFE: AMALEK AND THE CONDEMNED CITY

The Commandment to Destroy Amalek

Three times a day we recite the verse, composed by King David, which proclaims that "The Lord is good to all: and His tender mercies are over all His works."[1] We also declare that "The Lord is righteous in all His ways."[2]

Hashem acts only with justice and fairness. Accordingly, it is difficult to accept that Hashem commands us to utterly destroy the people of Amalek, including the women and children.[3] In response to this seemingly barbaric mandate, we ask – as did Abraham – "Shall not the Judge of all the earth do right?"[4]

The first steps in resolving the quandary

As a first step in resolving this ethical problem, we may note that the commandment to destroy Amalek is of strictly limited application. The Brisker Rav is said to have held that the commandment to destroy Amalek is limited to a situation where one receives a specific command to do so from Hashem through a prophet of well-established credibility.[5] He cites the fact that Saul attacked Amalek only after Hashem, through Samuel, specifically ordered him to do so. If the command to destroy Amalek applied in all situations, Hashem would not have specifically ordered Samuel to tell Saul to destroy Amalek. Hashem never issued a command to Samuel to tell Saul to respect his parents or place a mezuza on his doorpost. This is because these mitzvot apply at all times, whereas the mitzva to destroy Amalek applies only on specific occasions.

1. Ps. 145:9.
2. Ps. 145:17.
3. Deut. 25:19, I Sam. 15:2.
4. Gen. 18:25.
5. I heard Rav Binyamin Tabory present the Brisker Rav's idea at a lecture at Yeshivat Har Etzion in 1983, but I have not been able to locate a written source for this idea.

Moreover, the *Kesef Mishne* holds that a member of the people of Amalek does not qualify as "Amalek" in regards to the mitzva of elimination if that individual has accepted upon himself the seven Noahide commandments,[6] i.e. the basic rules of humanity such as refraining from murder, adultery, and idolatry.[7]

Amalek contrasted with other nations: Nahmanides' approach

Although we have severely narrowed the application of the commandment to destroy Amalek, one still wonders how Hashem could issue such a command in any circumstances. In order to answer this question we must first resolve another question: why is Hashem more disturbed with Amalek than any other nation? Why is Amalek worse than the Egyptians, whom we are commanded not to hate because they served as our hosts for a long time, even though they tortured and enslaved us for many decades?[8]

Nahmanides offers two answers.[9] The first is based on the timing of Amalek's attack. Amalek was the first nation to attack us in the wake of the splitting of the Red Sea. As noted in the Song at the Sea,[10] the splitting of the Red Sea made an extraordinary impression upon the nations of the world; the nations were in awe of Hashem and us. Amalek attacked us at that point even though we were not even remotely close to their area; Amalek resided in the Negev and the Israelites were much further south in the middle of the Sinai.[11] Nahmanides explains that they attacked us with the deliberate intent of battling Hashem and His reputation.

Rashi compares Amalek to someone who jumps into a burning hot bath which everyone else fears to get into lest he be scalded. The one who jumps into the scorching bath is burned, but he sets a precedent for others to enter the bath, cooling it off in the process.[12] Amalek's action

6. *Hilkhot Melakhim* 6:4.
7. In *Teshuvot Shevet HaLevi* V:149, Rabbi Shmuel Wosner permits accepting converts from Germany despite the connection made by some between Amalek and Germany.
8. Deut. 23:8.
9. Ex. 17:16.
10. Ex. 15:14-16.
11. Num. 13:29.
12. Deut. 25:18.

is severely punishable, first because his aim was to lessen the awe of Hashem, and second because his action was an invitation to others to behave similarly.

Nahmanides' second answer is that Hashem regards Amalek's attack as repulsive since Amalek – unlike Egypt – is related to us; their ancestor was the grandson of Esau.[13] The Torah expects relatives to take responsibility for their kin and views with utmost severity the attack of one relative upon another.[14] Nahmanides offers a similar explanation for Hashem's rejection of Moab and Ammon: Moab hired Balaam, and Ammon refused us bread and water, despite the fact that our ancestor Abraham risked his life to save their ancestor Lot.[15]

Rav Moshe Soloveitchik's approach to Amalek

Rav Joseph B. Soloveitchik quotes his father, Rav Moshe Soloveitchik, as saying that Amalek is more a concept than a nation.[16] He points out that Maimonides presents the commandment to destroy Amalek differently from the commandment to destroy the seven nations of Canaan.[17] Regarding the nations of Canaan, Maimonides writes that they have ceased to exist. The Radbaz (Rabbi David ibn Zimra)[18] explains that their national identities were dissolved by the Assyrian emperor Sennacherib's policy of transferring the populations of the nations he conquered.[19] But Maimonides does not make such a statement regarding Amalek, even though Sennacherib should have upset their national identity as well. Rav Moshe Soloveitchik explains that this is because one may be defined as an Amalekite even if one is *not* a descendant of the biblical nation of Amalek, if he expresses baseless hatred for the Jewish people. Rav Soloveitchik regarded the Nazis as Amalekites.

---

13. Gen. 36:12.
14. Lev. 25:49.
15. Deut. 23:5.
16. Although this idea is commonly attributed to Rav Haim Soloveitchik, the Rav's grandfather, the Rav specifically told me in 1983 that the idea originated with his father, Rav Moshe Soloveitchik.
17. *Hilkhot Melakhim* 5:4-5.
18. *Hilkhot Melakhim* 5:4-5.
19. Berakhot 28a.

Evidence for Rav Soloveitchik's approach to Amalek

Ḥazal seem to agree with this idea. They regard Haman as an Amalekite even though he lived long after the demise of Sennacherib and the Assyrian Empire.[20] Ḥazal make this identification based on the fact that the Book of Esther repeatedly refers to Haman as "Agagi" and that Agag was the name of the Amalekite king upon whom King Saul waged war.[21]

Rav Soloveitchik's definition of Amalek is also supported by Hashem's statement at the end of Exodus 17 that the war against Amalek is "from generation to generation."[22] Hashem knew in advance that Sennacherib would come and disrupt national identities, yet He describes the war on Amalek as perpetual. If the war on Amalek were to be solely based on lineage, it would be impossible to pursue this commandment after the Assyrian exile.

Another proof is a strange phenomenon occurring in I Samuel. In chapter 15 we find Amalek nearly annihilated, yet in chapter 30, only a few years later, Amalek is reconstituted as a nation and attacking King David's camp. We must conclude that the term "Amalek" does not refer to the descendants of the people whose attack on us is recorded at the end of Parashat Beshalaḥ. Rather, "Amalek" is a code-name for any individual or nation who acts with complete disregard of morality and is interested in compromising Hashem's reputation, like the nation that launched an unprovoked attack against us after the splitting of the Red Sea.

Solving the moral difficulty

Rav Soloveitchik's concept answers our question as to why Amalek differs from any other nation. The command to eradicate Amalek transcends the concept of national identity. Any individual or nation has the potential to deteriorate into Amalek. The command to eradicate Amalek includes the eliminating of any hint of Amalek-style behavior (and even thought) from our personalities and our societies. Amalek teaches us that man can descend into the moral abyss if he does not exercise proper care and caution.

---

20. See Megilla 29a with Rashi (s.v. *umafsikin*).

21. I Sam. 15:8.

22. Ex. 17:16.

In regard to Hashem commanding us to wage a war of complete annihilation against Amalek, we assert that it is sometimes an act of kindness to destroy a thoroughly evil nation. Of course, only Hashem can determine when a nation has reached such a nadir and deserves to be eradicated. Nonetheless, there are times when humans must decide, in the course of pursuing a thoroughly evil individual, whether it is acceptable also to kill his wife and children where there is no other option to eliminate the criminal. For example, in the Israel-Gaza War of 2008-2009, a Hamas arch-terrorist who organized and encouraged unprovoked attacks on innocent Israelis realized that the Israelis had finally located him standing alone and were about to kill him. He immediately retreated into his home where his wife and children were located, assuming that the Israelis would not kill him under these circumstances. However, the Israeli military command decided that since the terrorist was so dangerous and thoroughly committed to inflicting great harm upon Israelis, it would obliterate his house, killing the arch-terrorist, his wife and children.

The commandment to eliminate Amalek authorizes a moral nation to eliminate egregious evildoers, even if this cannot be done without causing the deaths of women and children. Israel's responses in the three recent Gaza wars have restored some semblance of normal life to Israel's southern regions after years of living a nightmare. Although women and children were unavoidably killed in these wars, the alternative was an intolerable life for Israel's southern residents. If causing civilian deaths were forbidden in all circumstances, terrorists would simply locate themselves amongst women and children, thereby obtaining legal and moral immunity from any consequences for their attacks on innocents.

The commandment to destroy Amalek is a commandment to resolutely eliminate evil. It rejects granting moral immunity to evildoers who shield themselves among innocents. Israel's attacks on Gaza in 2008-2009, 2012 and 2014, like the Allied attacks on the Nazis during World War II, unavoidably killed some innocents, and yet these attacks were basically acts of kindness because they removed great harm from the world. We pray that all the nations of the world will eradicate the Amalek aspects of their societies, thereby eliminating the need to wage war against them.

The Condemned City

Few commandments in the Torah seem as violent as the rules set forth in Deuteronomy 13 in the case of the condemned city *(ir nidaḥat)* – a city where a majority of the inhabitants serve idols. The Torah demands that we kill all of the city's inhabitants – even the minority who did not serve idols – and burn all of their possessions.

While it is understood that morality requires good people to eliminate evil,[23] the administration of the death penalty to an entire city seems brutal and inconsistent with the characterization of the Torah in the Book of Proverbs: "Her ways are ways of pleasantness, and all her paths are peace."[24] Why, then, did Hashem include this imperative in the Torah?

A question that might unlock the message

A clue to unlocking this mystery lies in the surprising phrase that occurs in Deuteronomy in connection with the condemned city: "and show you mercy."[25] Coming after the commandment to kill all of the inhabitants of a city, this phrase is astonishing. The concept of mercy would appear to be entirely contrary to the idea of a condemned city. How can we explain this?

Classic answers to the question of mercy and the condemned city

Over the centuries Israel's sages have answered this question in a number of ways.

Nahmanides explains that the phrase "and show you mercy" means that we are to spare the children from the punishment of the condemned city.[26]

In a variation on this theme, Rav Zalman Sorotzkin[27] explains that mercy is needed in order to adopt the orphaned children of a condemned city.[28]

---

23. This is why the Torah issues a death penalty for violations of severe transgressions. However, according to the Mishna (Makkot 7a) courts very rarely administered the death penalty.
24. Prov. 3:17.
25. Deut. 13:18.
26. Deut. 13:16; see, however, Maimonides' *Hilkhot Avoda Zara* 4:6.
27. *Oznayim LaTorah* on Deut. 13:18.
28. *Be'er Yosef* (Parashat Vayishlaḥ) similarly interprets Targum Yonatan ben Uzziel on Ex. 13:18 as teaching that the families that left Egypt adopted the children of the many assimilated Jews who died during the plague of darkness.

The Netziv[29] explains that the Torah is concerned lest engaging in violent activity, even when necessary, should negatively transform people into aggressive individuals.[30] Thus, those who administered the death penalty to the residents of a condemned city are in need of Hashem's gift of mercy, so that their justified but extreme actions do not transform them into violent people.

The Gemara presents an opinion that a condemned city would never occur.[31] For the Torah requires that everything in a condemned city be burnt; and if the city contains even one mezuza, then burning the city would involve erasing Hashem's name, which is forbidden[32]. Therefore a condemned city cannot be destroyed if it contains even a single mezuza.[33]

The idea that one small mezuza can spare a city from becoming a condemned city has profound implications. As the first Lubavitcher Rebbe taught, a little bit of light can dispel much darkness.[34] A miniscule drop of positive energy has the power and potential to counter much negativity.

But one may ask: what if a city contains no mezuza? How can the opinion presented by the Gemara claim that a condemned city is an impossibility, if there is a chance that the Jews in the city have strayed so far from Judaism that there remains not even a single mezuza in the city? But according to Rashi, "the Torah will never be completely forgotten

---

29. Deut. 13:18.

30. Therapists throughout the civilized world endeavor to ensure that the personalities of military veterans are not negatively affected by their combat experiences, even when the fighting was undoubtedly morally justified. The Netziv (Rabbi Naftali Zvi Yehuda Berlin) similarly explains that Pinḥas required a covenant of peace (Num. 25:12) lest his necessary violent actions toward Zimri ben Salu and Kozbi bat Tzur affect his personality. The story presented in Josh. 22, where Pinḥas acts as a peacemaker, demonstrates that Pinḥas successfully met this challenge.

31. Sanhedrin 71a.

32. Rashi to Deut. 12:4

33. Torah Academy of Bergen County alumnus Avi Eserner pointed out that this rule would apply even if the mezuza was invalid, since even an invalid mezuza contains Hashem's name.

34. This is one of many of the rich themes expressed by Hanukka candles.

by the Jewish people."[35] Thus, the statement that a condemned city is impossible is an affirmation of faith in the Jewish people, of the belief that there will never be a community among our people that has strayed so far that there is not even one mezuza in the town.[36]

The Lubavitcher Rebbe remarked that if he heard a city was about to be declared a condemned city he would arise at two in the morning and affix a mezuza to a home in that city.[37]

The challenge of the condemned city

Thus, it would appear that the commandment to destroy a condemned city was never meant to be implemented. Rather, it is a deterrent meant to instill a sense of responsibility to safeguard and preserve our traditions. It is the obligation of our broader community to ensure that no single community ever attains the status of a condemned city. Thus the word "mercy" in this context means that the concept of the condemned city must be interpreted in a merciful manner – as a charge of responsibility for each other's spiritual fidelity rather than a summons to violent action.

Support from Nahmanides: a community that sins inadvertently

Support for this contention may be drawn from Nahmanides' comments on Numbers 15:22. Nahmanides asserts that if an entire community does not observe the Torah, its members (though not its

35. Deut. 31:21.

36. Rav Soloveitchik, in a number of his lectures, emphasizes the importance of maintaining faith not only in Hashem, but also in the Jewish people. For example, Maimonides (*Hilkhot Teshuva* 7:5) rules in accordance with the opinion of R. Eliezer that the Jewish people will be redeemed only if they repent. Thus, Maimonides' principle of faith describing the arrival of the Messiah includes a belief that the Jewish people will eventually repent, since the Messiah cannot come otherwise.

37. In other words, should a city be devoid of any authentic Jewish influence and presence, the Lubavitcher Rebbe would create an authentic center of Jewish life. As is well known, this was not a passing sentiment of the Lubavitcher Rebbe but a life's mission for himself and his followers. An examination of www.chabad.org leads one to marvel at the centers of Jewish life established by students of the Lubavitcher Rebbe in almost every corner of the globe, especially in areas that had a dearth of Jewish life. These efforts are part of the happy story of the revitalization of Orthodox Judaism in the late twentieth and early twenty-first centuries.

leaders) are considered to be sinning inadvertently *(beshogeg),* since they are merely swept up by the current of the time. Support for this concept of a *kahal shogeg* (the inadvertently-sinning community) may be drawn from a nearby verse[38] which states: "And it shall be forgiven all the congregation of the children of Yisrael, and the stranger that sojourns among them; seeing all the people were in ignorance." The importance of this principle is expressed by the fact that we recite this verse three times at the conclusion of Kol Nidrei, at the onset of Yom Kippur.

Nahmanides' *kahal shogeg* principle, however, seems to run counter to the conditions of the condemned city, where the death penalty is administered to an entire community for worshipping idols. While inadvertent sinners are not absolved of guilt, they nonetheless hardly deserve the death penalty. If we follow Nahmanides, why should the members of a condemned city deserve the death penalty?

We may answer that in practice the death penalty is not administered to the residents of a condemned city, since the Torah calls upon the broader community to avoid its very qualification as such! The Torah does not intend to punish the residents of a condemned city, but rather challenges the Jewish people to mercifully intervene and strengthen the Jewish identity of a wayward community.

Conclusion

"He is the Rock, his work is perfect: / for all His ways are justice: / a God of truth and without iniquity, / just and right is He."[39] Far from being a brutal and unforgiving *halakha,* the law of the condemned city is in practice a law of mercy and kind intervention, such as is practiced by the Lubavitch community and many other Jewish groups[40] which serve as beacons of Torah light in otherwise dark places, affixing the mezuzas that keep a community from becoming a "condemned city."

38. Num. 15:26

39. Deut. 32:4

40. Among these are the Orthodox Union's National Conference of Synagogue Youth, the Jewish Learning Initiative on Campus, the Aish HaTorah network of institutions and the Torah Links organizations established in many communities.

What we have discovered regarding the condemned city is true of everything in the Torah. What might appear to be unfair at first glance is in reality honorable and just. We are challenged to delve deeply into the text and philosophy to properly analyze passages that we might find incompatible with our moral intuitions, in order to discover the true meaning and implementation of the Torah's rules. With proper investigation and analysis in light of traditional commentary we can discover that all of the ways of Torah are ways of pleasantness and paths of peace.[41]

MORALITY AND *MAMZERUT*

Mamzerut, the halakhic categorization of a child born from an adulterous or incestuous relationship, seems grossly unfair. As a result of a parent's illicit relations,[42] the child suffers undeserved consequences to the extent that he is forbidden to marry most members of the Jewish community.

The Midrash[43] represents the *mamzer* as legitimately complaining to Hashem about his status acquired due to no sin of his own. The Midrash sees a reference to the anguish of the *mamzer* in a verse in Ecclesiastes: "and behold the tears of such as were oppressed, and they had no comforter."[44] The Sanhedrin are viewed as the oppressors because they follow the Torah's mandate, "A bastard shall not enter into the congregation of the Lord."[45] The Midrash continues, "What is this person's sin and why should his father's actions concern him? And yet the *mamzer* has no one to comfort him." God proclaims: "I will comfort him. It is only in this world that he is disqualified. In the world of truth, it will be different. I am with him in his suffering here and I will be with him then as well."

---

41. Prov. 3:17

42. Halakha considers a child a *mamzer* only if he is the result of a relationship that is punishable by *karet* (excision) (Yevamot 4:13). An exception to this rule is a child born from a woman with the status of *niddah* (menstruant). Unlike other law systems, the halakha does not consider a child born from an unmarried man and unmarried woman as illegitimate, so long as the relationship was not incestuous.

43. Leviticus Rabba 32:8.

44. Eccl. 4:1.

45. Deut. 23:3.

Unlike other halakhic situations deemed strictly hypothetical by some opinions that appear in the Gemara,[46] it is clear that *mamzerut* is unfortunately not one of those elusive impossibilities but rather a concrete reality. We know that in talmudic times there certainly were people assigned the status of a *mamzer*. For example, the Mishna records R. Shimon ben Azzai as testifying, "I found a genealogical scroll in Jerusalem, in which was written: So-and-so is a *mamzer* born from a married woman [to a man other than her husband]."[47]

This issue is not merely of theoretical concern to this author, either. In our time, questions about *mamzerut* most frequently arise in cases where a Jewish woman was divorced from a Jewish man without obtaining a *get* (halakhic divorce), then married another man and had children by him. As an active *dayan* (judge) on the *Beit Din* of Elizabeth, I have dealt with some cases of potential *mamzerut* and have worked with Rabbi Gedalia Schwartz[48] to discern possible resolutions. Moreover, I have worked tirelessly (with Hashem's help) and invested great efforts since 1992 – as do many other *get* administrators throughout the world – to eliminate the possibility of *mamzerut* by facilitating *gittin* for Jewish couples who are divorcing.

In this chapter we will first present the issue using the philosophical framework set forth by Rabbi Dr. Walter Wurzburger. Then we shall present examples of how Ḥazal dealt with *mamzerut* in practice and how Rav Moshe Feinstein, Rav Ovadia Yosef, Rabbi Gedalia Schwartz, Rabbi Shlomo Amar and Rabbi Asher Weiss have dealt with *mamzerut* challenges in our time. A thorough examination of this issue will reveal its justice in both theory and practice.

Morality and Halakha: Rabbi Dr. Wurzburger's Ethics of Responsibility

For anyone who is interested in or troubled by the role of ethics in the halakhic process, Rabbi Wurzburger's brief yet illuminating *Ethics of*

46. Sanhedrin 71a.

47. Yevamot 4:13.

48. Rav Gedalia Schwartz is *Av Beit Din*, Chief Justice, of the Beth Din America and Chicago Rabbinical Council.

Responsibility is a must-read. An enlightening review of this work was authored by Dr. David Shatz and appears in the spring 1996 issue of *Tradition.*[49]

Hashem Always Acts Morally

Rabbi Wurzburger echoes Plato's celebrated thesis set forth in the *Euthrypho* dialogue: an action is not right because God commands it, but rather God commands it because it is right. This Platonic idea is undoubtedly congruent with Torah thought, as evidenced by the verse recited thrice daily by Jews, "Hashem is righteous *(tzaddik)* in all His ways."[50] A *tzaddik* is one who chooses to act properly and fairly. Categorizing Hashem as a *tzaddik* means that He chooses only to act well and justly. Hashem can act in any manner, but chooses to act in the finest way possible. Rabbi Wurzburger's point is confirmed by a verse in Deuteronomy: "He is the Rock, His work is perfect: / for all His ways are justice: / a God of truth and without iniquity, / just and right is He."[51]

Our Obligation to Intuit the "Right and the Good in the Eyes of Hashem"

Citing Rav Soloveitchik's statement,[52] "Halakhah is not a ceiling, but a floor," Rabbi Dr. Wurzburger writes:[53]

> Jewish piety involves more than meticulous adherence to the various rules and norms of religious law; it also demands the cultivation of an ethical personality.... We are commanded to engage in a never-ending quest for moral perfection, which transcends the requirements of an 'ethics of obedience'.... The halakhic system serves merely as the foundation of Jewish piety.

49. http://traditionarchive.org/news/originals/Volume%2030/No.%202/Beyond%20Obedience.pdf.
50. Ps. 145:17.
51. Deut. 32:4.
52. Walter S. Wurzburger, *Ethics of Responsibility: Pluralistic Approaches to Covenantal Ethics* (Philadelphia: Jewish Publication Society, 1994), 32.
53. Ibid., 3.

Rabbi Dr. Wurzburger marshals a wide variety of classic authorities who articulate the need for moral intuition, including Rabbi Nissim Gaon,[54] Nahmanides,[55] the *Maggid Mishneh,*[56] Rabbi Joseph Albo,[57] the Maharal,[58] the Netziv,[59] the *Meshekh Chokhma,*[60] and HaRav Kook.[61]

Nahmanides explains the Torah's command "to do the right and the good in the eyes of Hashem":

> The intention of this verse is to teach that while we must keep God's specific laws, we must also institute what is 'the good and straight' in those areas for which God did not issue any specific rules. This is a great matter because it is impossible for the Torah to regulate every area of human behavior on both an individual level and a communal level. After the Torah presents a number of general ethical commands, such as not to gossip and not to take revenge, it commands us to do good and right in all areas.[62]

Ḥazal assign great value to moral intuitions. The Gemara stresses the importance of a *Beit Din* ruling beyond the letter of the law (*lifnim mishurat hadin),*[63] even stating that Jerusalem was destroyed because its courts ruled only according to strict justice.[64] The Gemara[65] also states that God Himself prays that He should act *lifnim mishurat hadin.*[66]

---

54. This is presented in his introduction to the Babylonian Talmud.
55. Deut. 6:18.
56. *Hilkhot Shekhenim* 14:5.
57. *Sefer HaIkarim* 3:23.
58. *Netivot Olam,* vol. II.
59. This is presented in his introduction to Genesis and Exodus 19:6.
60. Deut. 13:4.
61. *Orot HaKodesh* 1:1-35.
62. Deut. 6:18.
63. The *Smak* (Mitzva 49) even includes the mitzva to act *lifnim mishurat hadin,* beyond the letter of the law, in his list of 613 Mitzvot.
64. Bava Metzia 30b.
65. Berachot 7a.
66. The Gemara (Bava Metzia 83a) records a classic application of *lifnim mishurat hadin:* "Some porters [negligently (see Rashi and Maharsha)] broke a barrel of wine belonging to Rabba bar bar Ḥanna. He seized their garments [as a form of payment], so they went and complained to Rav. Rav told [Rabba bar bar Ḥanna], 'Return their

Similarly, the Mishna states that when one acts *lifnim mishurat hadin* (i.e. by doing more than he is strictly obligated to do), "*Ru'aḥ ḥakhamim noḥah heimenu*," "the spirit of the rabbis is pleased with him."[67]

Conflicts between a Divine Command and Our Perception of Morality

However, as a staunch believer in the divine authorship of the Torah, Rabbi Dr. Wurzburger specifies that when our ethical intuitions conflict with the Torah, the Torah enjoys unequivocal priority:

> It would be the height of arrogance to challenge the validity of an explicit divine imperative on the ground that it runs counter to our own ethical intuitions. Indeed, to permit humanistic considerations to override divinely revealed commandments, amounts to a desecration of the Divine Name. In the event of conflict with explicit halakhic requirements, all ethical, aesthetic, intellectual or prudential considerations must be set aside.[68]

Moreover, Rabbi Dr. Wurzburger articulates a profoundly important point regarding this issue, noting that since Hashem represents ultimate righteousness and morality, the Torah can never truly clash with ethical principles:

> Judaism has no need for the Kierkegaardian doctrine of 'the suspension of the ethical' which demands that whenever moral imperatives clash with religious commandments, we must subordinate our ethical concerns to the higher authority of the religious. Once God is defined as the supreme moral authority, obedience to divine imperatives emerges as the highest *ethical*

garments.' [Rabba] asked, 'Is that the law?' Rav replied, 'Yes, (Mishlei 2:20), that you may walk in the way of good men.' So [Rabba] returned their garments. They further claimed [to Rav], 'We are poor men, have worked all day, and are hungry. Are we to get nothing? Rav ordered [Rabba], 'Go and pay them.' He asked, 'Is that the law?' [Rav] responded, 'Yes, and keep the path of the righteous.'"

67. Shevi'it 10:9.

68. Wurzburger, *Ethics of Responsibility: Pluralistic Approaches to Covenantal Ethics*, 29.

> duty. Thus, Abraham's readiness to sacrifice Isaac cannot be invoked as a paradigm of the "suspension of the ethical." On the contrary, it was a perfectly *moral* act. Compliance with the demands of the highest possible moral authority, which combines omnibenevolence and omniscience, is bound to lead to the best possible consequences, even in situations where divine imperatives clash with our ordinary ethical rules that generally bring about the greatest good. Obedience to an omniscient and omnibenevolent God must, by definition, yield the greatest possible good, even if our limited intellectual capacities prevent us from seeing how and why certain divine imperatives engender the most desirable consequences.[69]

The issue of *mamzerut* is one such situation where our moral intuitions seemingly conflict with the divine command. We must yield to the Torah's mandate, and have faith – as did Abraham at the binding of Isaac – that all Hashem does is objectively good.[70]

Minimizing the Gap between the Divine Command and Our Moral Intuitions

Although our moral intuitions do not enjoy veto power over halakha, they do have a vote. Rabbi Dr. Wurzburger explains:

> Conscience.... functions as a hermeneutical principle to help ascertain the meaning and range of the applicability of laws when their formulations contain an element of ambiguity. Since the Torah is characterized in the Book of Proverbs (3:17) as 'its ways are the ways of pleasantness and all its paths are peace,' we should assume that, in case of doubt concerning the meaning of a divine ordinance, the interpretation that is in accordance with our moral sensibilities was intended by the Divine Legislator.[71]

69. Ibid., 19-20.
70. Berakhot 60b.
71. Wurzburger, *Ethics of Responsibility: Pluralistic Approaches to Covenantal Ethics*, 29.

Rabbi Wurzburger cites the Gemara as a source for this important principle.[72] This Gemara supports the traditional identification of "and the boughs of thick leaved trees."[73] one of the "four kinds" taken at Sukkot, with the myrtle. The Gemara rejects the possibility of taking oleander, a stinging plant, based on a moral consideration. The Gemara never would have rejected the use of this plant had the Torah explicitly commanded us to take the oleander. However, since the Torah uses an ambiguous phrase, we presume the intention of Hashem was not for us to take a noxious plant.

Halakhic decisors consistently apply this hermeneutical tool when adjudicating situations of *mamzerut.* Whenever possible, decisors limit the scope of *mamzerut,* adopting an approach in accordance with our moral sensibilities, with the assumption that these decisions are aligned with the intentions of the righteous, Divine Legislator.

We must clarify, however, that Ḥazal and the decisors do *not* indiscriminately interpret the Torah based on our moral intuitions. The hermeneutical tool we speak of applies only to moral sensitivities that are rooted in the values articulated in the Torah and Ḥazal. For example, the moral intuition motivating us to not punish a child for the sin of the parents and brand him with the stigma of *mamzerut* is rooted in Torah thought as expressed in the aforementioned Midrash and the verse "neither shall children be put to death for fathers."[74]

The Torah's respect for moral intuition is conveyed explicitly: "And you shall do that which is right and good in the sight of the Lord."[75] Since we are limited in our ability to determine what is truly "good and right," the Torah therefore clarifies "in the eyes of Hashem" to explain that moral intuitions must emerge from values God articulated in the Torah. As Rabbi Dr. Wurzburger explains, the Torah validates only "the intuitions of a moral conscience formed within the matrix of Torah

---

72. Sukka 32b.

73. Lev. 23:40.

74. Deut. 24:16. Ezekiel (chapter 18) cites a common complaint that it is unfair if "fathers have eaten sour grapes, and the children's teeth are set on edge." For an analysis of Ezekiel 18, see Makkot 24a and Rabbi Hayyim Angel's *Vision from the Prophet and Counsel from the Elders* (New York: Orthodox Union Press, 2013), 153-162.

75. Deut. 6:18. See Rashi and Nahmanides.

teaching"; and "such a conception of the authority of conscience differs radically from the notion that conscience can impose its own laws because it is endowed with independent, autonomous authority."[76]

Rabbi Joseph B. Soloveitchik notes the limitations of moral intuitions:

> The mind certainly condemns murder.... But does this abhorrence of murder also apply when the victim is an old, cruel, miserly woman who in the eyes of society was a parasitic wretch, as in Dostoyevsky's *Crime and Punishment*?.... May euthanasia be practiced to relieve the elderly or terminally ill of further suffering? Here the *logos* hesitates, is uncertain, and imparts no decisive guidance.

Thus the need, explains Rabbi Soloveitchik, for a divine imperative to declare the prohibition against murder to be clear and absolute.[77]

Mamzerut as an Expression of Human Dignity

Now that we have outlined a framework for how to grapple with clashes of halakha and conscience, we are ready to discuss the concept of *mamzerut* both in theory and practice.

While it certainly seems unjust for a child to suffer for the sin of his parents, this is the manner in which the world functions.[78] If a mother uses illicit drugs while pregnant, the child will suffer for his entire life due to no fault of its own. Poor parenting has severe long-term negative consequences. In his book *Unlocking the Torah Text,* Rabbi Shmuel Goldin coins the term "intergenerational reverberation." He writes:

---

76. Wurzburger, *Ethics of Responsibility: Pluralistic Approaches to Covenantal Ethics,* 28.

77. Cited in Rabbi Abraham Besdin, *Reflections of the Rav* (Jerusalem: World Zionist Organization, 1979), 184.

78. It is important to clarify that a *mamzer* is not an outcast from Torah society. He is merely restricted as to whom he is permitted to marry (Yevamot 22b). The *Sefer HaḤinuch* (560) writes: "But to reside in any Jewish community and be fully involved in all communal matters is entirely permissible [for the *mamzer*] just as any other Jew. Ḥazal already taught (Horayot 13a) that a *mamzer* who is a Torah scholar is called to the Torah before an ignorant *kohen.*"

> While Judaism absolutely rejects the Christian concept of "original sin," we cannot deny the reality of "intergenerational reverberation." We are not responsible, in any way, for the transgression committed by Adam and Chava at the beginning of time. We are, however, affected by that sin's ramifications. This is not a punishment, but a reality of life. Had Adam and Chava not sinned, we would now be living a very different existence in the Garden of Eden. Similarly, we are all concretely connected to each other across the generations. Such overarching life issues as where we are born, to whom, into what environment – and, in fact, whether or not we are born at all – are determined not only by God, but also by our parents and by those who came before them as well. Even more importantly, our decisions and actions today will critically affect the lives of our children and their progeny tomorrow.[79]

The Torah's imposition of a severe restriction upon the *mamzer* conveys its perspective on the profound sanctity of marriage and the severity of adultery and incest. While other cultures may view adultery as insignificant, such a world-view essentially belittles marriage and family and ultimately undermines the worth of human beings, the products of marriage and family. Cultures that do not respect marriage and family deteriorate, creating dysfunctional people and misery. Thus, the laws of *mamzerut* fundamentally express respect for humankind, since children thrive when they are born and raised within a healthy and functional family environment.

A casual attitude towards sexual relations – the creation of life and foundation of a marriage – undermines family, marriage and life itself. Thus, the divine restrictions imposed on a *mamzer* are heart-wrenching, but nonetheless indispensible in creating a culture of healthy respect for these institutions, and humanity in general.

Limiting the Application of *Mamzerut* in Ḥazal

As we have mentioned earlier, our moral conscience serves as a hermeneutical tool for interpreting the Torah. Thus, out of sensitivity to the

79. Shmuel Goldin, *Unlocking the Torah Text: Vayikra* (New York: Gefen Publishing House, 2010), p.93-94.

suffering of a *mamzer,* rabbinic authorities make every effort to minimize *mamzerut.* The following are ways in which Ḥazal limit its application.[80]

The most significant reduction of the application of the rules of *mamzerut* is the Gemara's presumption that "most of a married woman's acts of intercourse are with her husband *(rov be'ilot aḥar haba'al).*"[81] This expectation emerges from the Gemara's elemental principle of following the majority. Thus, even if it is rumored that a married woman has been unfaithful to her husband, her children are not classified as *mamzerim.*[82]

The presumption that *rov be'ilot aḥar haba'al* is such a strong presumption that Ḥazal assert that a fetus could spend up to 12 months in the uterus, enabling the attribution of a child's paternity to its mother's husband. Thus, even if a husband had been away from home for up to 12 months before his wife gives birth, paternity is ascribed to him![83]

Another example of Ḥazal's efforts to limit the implementation of the *mamzerut* laws is the Mishna's teaching that "Elijah will not come [in the future] to declare the pure, impure – nor to declare the impure, pure; nor to distance those who are near or to draw near those who were distanced, but only to distance those drawn near by force and to draw near those distanced by force."[84] Rabbi Ovadia ben Abraham of Bertinoro, in his commentary on this mishna, explains that Elijah will distance only those who are publicly known to be *mamzerim* but were forcibly mixed

---

80. One may ask why then Ḥazal expand the categories of *mamzerut* to include the *shetuki* and *asufi* (where the identity of the child's father or both parents is unknown and there is concern that either parent is a *mamzer* or that the relationship that created the child was adulterous or incestuous). An answer is that Ḥazal are given the mandate to fully develop the Torah in a manner similar to the obligation humanity has to develop the world (Gen. 1:28 and 2:3). Hashem made the world incomplete and we are commanded to complete it. Similarly, Hashem left room for us to complete the Torah. This is explained by Nahmanides regarding the need for Ḥazal's restrictions regarding Shabbat (Vayikra 23:24). Thus, since Hashem includes the category of *mamzer* in the Torah, Ḥazal are mandated to fully develop this category. Nonetheless, in practice, Ḥazal seek to limit the practical implementation of this rule.

81. Ḥullin 11b.

82. Sotah 27a.

83. Yevamot 80b.

84. Eduyot 8:7.

among the Jewish people, "but where there is an individual *mamzer* in a particular family, but this is not publicly known, owing to the family having intermingled [into the Jewish community], Elijah will let it remain so and let the family retain its presumption of legitimacy."

This is one basis[85] for Rabbi Moses Isserles' ruling that if a person learns that one of the ancestors of a particular family is a *mamzer* he may not reveal this, "but rather he should allow the family's presumption of legitimacy to remain intact, for all the families that have become assimilated into Israel are legitimate in the future."[86]

Limiting *Mamzerut* in Modern Times: Rav Feinstein and Rav Ovadia Yosef

Decisors throughout the generations continued the tendency of Ḥazal to limit the implementation of *mamzerut*.[87] In the twentieth century Rav Moshe Feinstein and Rav Ovadia Yosef were the exemplars par excellence of this tradition. Rav Feinstein famously ruled that non-Orthodox and civil marriages were invalid.[88] This landmark ruling removed the status of *mamzerut* from tens of thousands of individuals (if not even more) whose mothers remarried without receiving a *get* from their first husbands.

Rav Feinstein was by no means the only decisor who adopted this approach, but he greatly expanded this ruling. For example, he invalidated a marriage ceremony conducted by a non-Orthodox rabbi even if valid witnesses had been present in the audience, as long as they did not see the actual delivery of the ring from groom to bride. Moreover, in the context of a ruling regarding *mamzerut*,[89] Rav Feinstein decided that even a Conservative rabbi who fully observes Torah and believes in Maimonides' thirteen principles of faith is an invalid witness because he is defined as an *apikores* (heretic). Rav Moshe argued that the rabbi's

85. Kiddushin 71a is also a source for this important ruling.

86. *Even HaEzer* 2:5.

87. See *Pitḥei Teshuvah* and *Otzar HaPosekim* on *Even HaEzer* chapter 4 for a summary of the classic responsa literature on *mamzerut*.

88. See, for example, *Igrot Moshe, Even HaEzer* 1:75, 1:135, and 3:25, and a summary of this topic in *Gray Matter* 1, 63-90.

89. *Igrot Moshe* E.H. 4:13.

mere affiliation with the Conservative movement – which endorses and promotes heretical viewpoints – renders him an *apikores* and therefore an invalid witness.

Another landmark judgment by Rav Feinstein is his conclusion that a child conceived via artificial insemination is not a *mamzer* even if the sperm donor is not the husband.[90] Rav Feinstein rules that *mamzerut* is created and transmitted only through actual relations. This leaves open the possibility of a *mamzer* producing children through artificial means with his wife and avoiding the transmission of his status to the next generation.[91]

While Rav Moshe served as the primary authority regarding questions of *mamzerut* in North America, Rav Ovadia Yosef paralleled his role in Israel.

Rav Ovadia clarifies that just as the consensus view among *dayanim* (rabbinic judges) is to consider blood tests inadmissible evidence in rabbinic court, so too *dayanim* should reject DNA tests as proof in rabbinic courts.[92] In this ruling, Rav Ovadia Yosef closed the floodgates of *mamzerut* that could have opened as a result of the acceptance of DNA evidence of paternity.[93] He applies the Gemara's principle that "most of a married woman's acts of intercourse are with her husband" even against DNA evidence,[94] and his ruling has become the accepted practice of Israel's chief rabbinate.

Another major ruling of Rav Ovadia Yosef is a long responsum,[95] written at the behest of the Ashkenazic Chief Rabbi Yehuda Unterman, permitting marriage of non-Karaite Jews to Karaite Jews. Karaites are a sect of Jews who more than a thousand years ago broke from mainstream Judaism, arguing that only the written Torah is binding. Halakhic concern for *mamzerut* has arisen in connection with the Karaites because, while their form of *kiddushin* (marriage) may be valid according to Jewish law, their *get* deviates from the form dictated by Ḥazal. Therefore

90. *Igrot Moshe* E.H. 1:10.

91. See Kiddushin 69a and *Teḥumin* 28:58-62.

92. *Yabia Omer* 10 E.H. 13.

93. For more discussion of this issue, see Rabbi Chaim Jachter, *Gray Matter* 3 (Teaneck, New Jersey: Kol Torah Publications, 2008), 168-181.

94. Rabbi Yosef Shalom Eliashiv issued a similar ruling in *Kovetz Teshuvot* 1:134.

95. *Yabia Omer* 8 E.H. 12.

a Karaite woman divorced by a *get* administered by a Karaite court is not properly divorced and might remain a married woman, so that any child she bears to another husband on the basis of a Karaite *get* is a *safek mamzer* (possible *mamzer*).

Since it is impossible to determine who, throughout the generations, remarried on the strength of such invalid divorces, Rabbi Moses Isserles[96] casts the suspicion of possible *mamzerut* on all members of that community. Rabbi David ben Solomon ibn Zimra (the Radbaz),[97] however, did permit marriages between Karaites and non-Karaite Jews on the grounds that the *kiddushin* of the Karaites is also halakhically invalid, because Karaite witnesses to the *kiddushin* are disqualified due to their heretical views and observance of holidays on the wrong dates. Thus, according to Radbaz, *mamzerut* does not attach to a child of a woman who married, was divorced, and then married another man, all in accordance with Karaite practice, since she is regarded as never having been married at all.

Rav Ovadia Yosef argues at length in support of the Radbaz's determination, and his ruling has been adopted as policy by Israel's chief rabbinate. In a similar fashion, Rav Ovadia Yosef ruled that Ethiopian Jews are not considered *mamzerim* despite the fact that their *gittin* did not conform to halakha.[98]

Continuing the Tradition: Rav Gedalia Dov Schwartz, Rav Shlomo Amar and Rav Asher Weiss

The present generation of decisors has continued in the path set by their predecessors. Rabbi Gedalia Schwartz is an extraordinary Torah scholar, exemplary in his fear of God, and a gentleman of the highest order. He is often called upon to adjudicate potential situations of *mamzerut,* and I have posed at least a dozen such questions to him in the past twenty years.

Rabbi Schwartz rules in the tradition of Rav Moshe Feinstein regarding *mamzerut*. In one memorable case, Rabbi Schwartz spared two

96. E.H. 4:37.

97. *Responsa numbers* 73 and 796.

98. *Yabia Omer* 8:11.

children whose mother had married without obtaining a *get,* from the status of *mamzerut,* because the mother's first marriage was conducted by a Conservative rabbi. Rav Schwartz ruled that this rabbi was a halakhically invalid witness due to his membership in the Rabbinic Assembly (the Conservative rabbinic organization), despite the fact that the rabbi told me that he observed Jewish law and believed in Maimonides' thirteen principles of faith.

In another case, a daughter reported that her mother told her that she had married in a secret[99] wedding ceremony in Vilna during the early 1970's and subsequently married another man without having received a *get* from her first husband. The daughter was born from the second marriage and wondered if she was a *mamzer.* Rabbi Schwartz, invoking the Gemara,[100] noted that if the mother had no witnesses to support her claim that she was married in a halakhic wedding ceremony, then she lacked halakhic credibility regarding her daughter's personal status. Moreover, Rabbi Schwartz said that it was highly unlikely for a wedding conducted in Vilna in the early 1970's to have been performed in accordance with halakha. Thus, Rabbi Schwartz concluded that the daughter was not a *mamzer.*[101]

In Israel, Rav Shlomo Amar, the former Sephardic Chief Rabbi, and Rav Asher Weiss continue the tradition of Rav Ovadia Yosef. Examples of Rav Amar's rulings on *mamzerut* may be found in his responsa work *Teshuvot Shama Shelomo;*[102] examples of Rav Weiss' approach to *mamzerut* appear in *Teshuvot Minchat Asher.*[103]

---

99. Religious ceremonies were forbidden in the former Soviet Union.

100. Yevamot 47a. The Gemara also relates the following incident: A man who was accepted as a legitimate convert in the Jewish community confided to R. Yehuda that a rabbinic court was not present at the time of his conversion (and therefore his conversion was invalid). R. Yehuda asked if there were witnesses who could corroborate his assertion. The gentleman answered "no." R. Yehuda asked if he had children. The man answered "yes." R. Yehuda then said, "You are believed [as a witness] to disqualify yourself but not your children."

101. Rav Moshe Feinstein *(Igrot Moshe, Even Haezer* 4:22 and 24) rules similarly in comparable circumstances.

102. *Shama Shlomo* 4: *Even Haezer* 2 and 6 and 5: *Even Haezer* 5.

103. *Minhat Asher* 1:72-75.

When a Solution is Unavailable

Nonetheless, Ḥazal and later decisors did not entirely eliminate the application of *mamzerut,* since there have been clear cases where leading halakhic authorities were unable to avoid ruling that a certain individual was a *mamzer.*[104] Once Rav Moshe Feinstein was presented with the following tragic question: A husband had refused to give a *get* to his wife and the woman subsequently remarried in a civil ceremony and had a child with her second husband. A rabbi proposed to Rav Moshe Feinstein a ruling that the child was not a *mamzer* because the woman and her first husband engaged in intense fights and the husband was incarcerated immediately following the marriage. The rabbi proposed that the first marriage should be considered invalid because had she known that the husband would engage in such serious misbehavior she never would have married him. Rav Feinstein rejected this proposal as untenable and ruled that the child was certainly a *mamzer*. Rav Feinstein writes that the proposal was "certainly incorrect because any problem that arises subsequent to the marriage cannot serve as a reason to view the marriage as having been entered on a fraudulent basis."

Rav Joseph B. Soloveitchik's position illuminates the complexity of such troubling halakhic decisions. As Rabbi Steven Weil summarizes:[105]

> Judaism has historically been and continues to be responsive to the needs of both the community and the individual. But, the Rav taught, it has its own orbit and its own speed, it responds to a challenge with its own criteria and principles. The Rav followed the rabbinic traditions of his grandfather, Rav Chaim, who believed in striving for leniency based on the personal needs of the inquirer. However, even Rav Chaim's skills had limits. When

104. *Igrot Moshe, Even Haezer* 1:53.

105. This is cited in Rabbi Steven Weil's synopsis of a speech delivered by Rav Yosef Dov Soloveitchik in 1975. The synopsis was printed in the April 2013 issue of *Jewish Action.* (https://www.ou.org/jewish_action/04/2013/the_rav_speak/).

> you reach the boundary of halakhah beyond which you dare not pass, you must say: "I surrender to the will of the Almighty."[106]

Conclusion

The issue of *mamzerut* weighs very heavily on those involved with matters of personal status, such as *get* administrators. It is our responsibility to honor and insure fidelity to God's law to the best of our ability while trying to be kind and sensitive to a fellow Jew's need. We must and do take extraordinary proactive steps to avoid *mamzerut* and leave no stone unturned in our efforts to resolve questions of status.

Our moral conscience drives us to determine that someone is not a *mamzer* whenever it is halakhically justifiable to do so. However, just as not every physician is able to cure every patient and, occasionally, must bow to the divine decision, so, too, we are not always able to find halakhic basis to relieve someone of the status of *mamzerut*. In such cases we must submit in the belief that – again in the words of Rabbi Dr. Wurzburger – "compliance with the demands of the highest possible moral authority, which combines omnibenevolence and omniscience, is bound to lead to the best possible consequences, even in situations where divine imperatives clash with our ordinary ethical rules that generally bring about the greatest good."

JOB, THE HOLOCAUST, AND THE JEWISH STATE

Most people have only a vague concept of the Book of Job. The primary barrier to understanding is the difficult language it employs, as even Ibn Ezra notes.[107] However, the basic messages of the Book of Job are relatively simple and straightforward, in contrast to Ecclesiastes, which is written in relatively simple language but whose message is exceedingly difficult to decipher. The lessons of Job enable us to form a healthy perception of – and relationship with – Hashem; therefore it is worthwhile

106. There have been, similarly, some situations I have submitted to Rav Gedalia Schwartz, where he was unable to arrive at a lenient ruling. In addition, a number of years ago I was notified by the London Beth Din (rabbinical court) that a particular woman was a *mamzer*.

107. Job 2:11.

to be aware of the essence of this life-altering text. It is especially relevant for our generation to grasp and internalize the teachings of this unique book, because during the Holocaust the Jewish people collectively experienced unprecedented suffering, parallel to Job's ordeal.

Recently the *Da'at Mikra* commentary on the Book of Job has made this text comprehensible to the broader Hebrew-speaking community. Based on this commentary, we will present Job's messages. We will also summarize Rav Soloveitchik's application of these messages, in his influential essay "*Kol Dodi Dofeik*," to the Holocaust and the subsequent establishment of the State of Israel.

Job's Sufferings

The beginning of the book introduces Job as a righteous man who is blessed with ten children and is financially and socially successful. The book thus begins with the paradigm of the *tzaddik vetov lo,* the righteous man who receives the reward he justly deserves for following in God's ways.

Job's fate begins to shift when Satan issues a challenge to Hashem, arguing that Job serves Hashem solely for reward.[108] Hashem concedes to Satan, allowing him to remove these rewards but not to harm Job.[109] Satan quickly eliminates Job's wealth and children. Job reacts to these dreadful events with equanimity: "the Lord gave, and the Lord has taken away; blessed be the name of the Lord."[110]

Satan

The interactions between Hashem and Satan are astonishing. In order to explain these exchanges, we must first clarify that the Book of Job shows Satan as operating only within Hashem's mandate. The Gemara emphasizes this point when R. Isaac states that Satan experienced worse torment than Job because he had to restrain himself and not kill Job.[111] This stands in contrast to other nations' philosophies that regard Satan as a force operating independent of Hashem's will.

108. Job 1:6-11.
109. Job 1:12.
110. Job 1:21.
111. Bava Batra 16a.

Nahmanides explains: "Hashem opened the mouth of Satan in the manner of a king and his servants."[112] In other words, Hashem entirely controls the situation. Satan is not a sort of "gadfly angel" or "loose cannon" in the heavens who starts trouble. Rather, Satan plays the role of the "prosecutor general" of the world. Hashem employs angels to play this role in order to make His deliberations comprehensible to us; as Nahmanides puts it,[113] the Torah speaks in human language.

Satan, under Hashem's supervision, becomes the representation of Hashem's strict attitude in decision-making, or what is commonly referred to as Hashem's *middat hadin* (attribute of judgment). This explains the surprising fact that Samuel II[114] and Chronicles I[115] use Hashem and Satan interchangeably! Satan is a personification of God's attribute of judgment, not a mean-spirited angel who manipulates Hashem into harming people. For this reason, when Hashem appears to Job at the conclusion of the book, He does *not* explain that He was manipulated by Satan into treating Job badly.[116] Indeed, Satan is not even mentioned when Hashem reveals himself to Job to offer insight as to how one deals with suffering in this world. Thus, as noted in the *Da'at Mikra* introduction to the Book of Job, Satan is absolutely *not* the explanation for Job's suffering, nor is he a force operating beyond Hashem's jurisdiction.

Satan communicates two vitally important messages: First, he acknowledges that Job is an unparalleled *tzaddik.* As Nahmanides notes, this contrasts with the opinion of Job's three friends, who ascribe Job's suffering to sins that he must have committed either publicly or privately.[117] Second, Satan's questioning of Job sheds light on a fundamental truth: if the world functions in a manner where every *tzaddik* is rewarded immediately and visibly and every *rasha* (wicked person) is punished in an equally transparent fashion, righteousness would be inauthentic. In such a world, one's service to God would stem from promise of

112. Job 1:8 and 2:3.
113. Job 2:3.
114. II Sam. 24:1.
115. I Chron. 21:1.
116. Job 42.
117. Job 1:9.

reward; authentic righteousness emerges from unconditional devotion to our Creator.

In fact, Job's wife precisely represents this type of shallow righteousness. After Job is struck with a miserable case of boils, she tells him to curse God and die.[118] Nahmanides explains that Job's wife fallaciously believed that one worships Hashem exclusively for the reward,[119] so once Hashem eliminated the reward, she reasoned that continued service would be useless![120]

Job's Crisis

In the second chapter, Satan argues that if Job's body were harmed, he would insult Hashem. Hashem permits Satan to *afflict* Job but not to kill him.

When Job was faced with the tragic loss of his ten children, he was able to make sense of it; as Nahmanides explains, Job suspected that perhaps his children had sinned in their hearts, and he could attribute their deaths to this.[121] However, when Job's own body is afflicted, he is thrust into a theological crisis. At this point he can no longer rationalize the justice of Hashem's actions, since he knows for certain that he was free of sin. True, he rebukes his wife with the words "shall we receive good at the hand of God, and shall we not receive evil?"[122] But although Iyov does not curse Hashem, he does not bless him either, because his

118. Job 2:9.

119. Job 2:9

120. Torah Academy of Bergen County alumnus Matthew Wexler adds that this point sheds light on the talmudic principle of *mitzvot lav lehanot nitenu* (we perform mitzvot not because we enjoy performing them and/or derive benefit from them, but rather because we are commanded to do so; see Rosh Hashana 28a with Rashi s.v. *lo lehanot*). Although performing mitzvot is for our benefit and we aspire to enjoy them, mitzvot are essentially means of serving Hashem. If one performs mitzvot only when he feels it is to his benefit, then one is essentially serving himself! This is a vital lesson to bear in mind. As Rav Soloveitchik taught, not every halakhic problem has a solution. Sometimes we are summoned and challenged to submit to the divine will. Ultimately, though, all that God does is in our interest, and often what we think is in our interest is illusory.

121. Job 1:21.

122. Job 2:10.

entire understanding of how Hashem operates has been shaken and undermined. In the third chapter, Job curses the day he was born. Job again restrains himself from actually cursing Hashem, but we see him becoming more vulnerable to his emotions.

It is important to note that Job's cursing the day he was born is expressed in an excruciatingly long (twenty-four-verse) soliloquy. This stands in contrast to Jeremiah's relatively brief expression of the same notion.[123] In fact, painfully long speeches prominently characterize the Book of Job. The economy of words we are so accustomed to in the rest of Tanakh (and the writings of Ḥazal) is completely abandoned in this book. Such unusually verbose dialogue exists because the Book of Job is not simply a philosophical analysis of why bad things happen to good people. It is also a book that offers profound psychological insight into the experience of suffering, both by those afflicted and by the friends and families of the victims. The long-winded speeches of the Book of Job are intended to not only teach us philosophy but also to help us gain insight into the complex emotional states of the characters.

Challenging Hashem

Throughout the book, Job questions Hashem rather forcefully. He demands that Hashem explain why he has been targeted. Later, Job boldly declares, *Hashem has wronged me!*[124]

Do those who have suffered terribly – like Job or Holocaust survivors – have the right to speak this way to Hashem? Interestingly, towards the conclusion of the book, Hashem tells Eliphaz that he, Bildad and Tzofar, "have not spoken of me the thing that is right, like my servant Iyov."[125] According to the *Metzudat David* commentary, Hashem means that the three friends have spoken improperly just as Job has spoken improperly.[126] On the other hand, *Da'at Mikra* explains that Hashem

123. Jer. 20:14-18.

124. Job 13:3, 19:6.

125. Job 42:7.

126. Job 42:7; this reflects the opinion of Rava in Bava Batra 16a.

is implying the opposite, that He *accepted* Job's harsh questioning, as opposed to the unrefined approach of Iyov's friends.[127]

Although the Book of Job does not offer a conclusive resolution to our query, the Book of Lamentations offers support for the latter view. In Lamentations we direct harsh statements towards Hashem such as, "He has bent his bow like an enemy: with His right hand set like an adversary,"[128] "You have killed, and not pitied."[129] And He is to me like a bear lying in wait, and like a lion in secret places."[130] I heard Rav Soloveitchik explain that while normally we follow Ḥazal's directive to "bless Hashem for the bad as well as the good,"[131] on the Ninth of Av we are allowed to vent our frustration with Hashem. Interestingly, Yemenite Jews study the Book of Job on the Ninth of Av and incorporate the entire book in their liturgy for that day.[132]

Job's Three Friends

Job's spiritual turmoil shocks his three friends – Eliphaz, Bildad and Tzofar – who come to comfort him. When they see him they at first do not recognize him.[133] Rashi explains that Job's face changed due to his suffering. *Da'at Mikra* adds that the sickness of boils is especially

127. In his commentary on this verse, Nahmanides adopts a compromise position between the *Metzudat David* and *Da'at Mikra*, holding that Job sinned with outspoken speech but had repented, unlike his friends who did not repent for speaking harshly to Job during his time of sorrow.

128. Lam. 2:4.

129. Lam. 2:21.

130. Lam. 3:10.

131. Berakhot 9:5.

132. The question to what extent we are allowed to question HaShem is a complex one. Our tradition holds that Hashem is both our King and our Father. As He is our King, we have no right to ever question Him; but as He is our Father, He understands our frustration and therefore sets aside one day for us to air our grievances. It is possible that the Book of Lamentations gives us license to vent frustration *as a community* over the mass suffering of the community, whereas individuals are not granted this license. It is also possible to suggest that Job expressed himself too harshly against Hashem, but a milder expression of individual frustration might be condoned on the Ninth of Av.

133. Job 2:12.

prone to change the appearance of one's skin.[134] However, we may suggest that they are not only taken aback because of Job's change in *physical* appearance but also because of the *theological* change he experienced on being physically afflicted. He has begun a spiritual journey in which his perception of how Hashem runs His world undergoes a major paradigm shift. This is what shocks his three friends and draws them too into the theological maelstrom experienced by Job; he and his three friends become partners in navigating this religious upheaval. From chapter 4 through chapter 31, Job and his friends struggle with his transformation, engaging in three rounds of intense debate. His friends strive mightily to return Job to his old outlook, while Job steadfastly clings to his new-found, refined perspectives on Hashem and how one should relate to Him.

The perspective of Job's friends, although presented in lengthy speeches, is very simple. They argue that Job's suffering is a result of his sins and that it is entirely unacceptable for Job to express his anger toward God despite his enormous suffering. They contend further that Job's outbursts at Hashem substantiate their claim that Job is a sinner. Ironically, this matches Job's suspicions of his children, mentioned earlier. Job, on the other hand, insists upon his righteousness, even swearing and describing his piety at great length.[135]

The progression in the debate between Job and his friends manifests an escalating level of tension and hostility. They ultimately end up insulting one another, as Tzofar tells Job, "Know therefore that God exacts of you less than your iniquity deserves."[136] and Eliphaz shockingly accuses Job of manifold evil acts such as stealing the clothes of the poor, afflicting orphans and withholding food from starving individuals. Eliphaz even outrageously claims, "Is not your wickedness great? and your iniquities infinite?"[137] Job, in turn, voices sharp criticism against Hashem, and tells his friends they would be wiser if they refrained from talking. Job insists that his friends are the ones who insult Hashem by

134. Job 2:12.
135. Job 27-31.
136. Job 11:6.
137. Job 22:5.

clinging to the model of "the righteous are always rewarded," since it is manifestly untrue.[138] Job insists that he remains a righteous man despite his protests, and that his friends' theology is impious.[139] The friends eventually abandon the argument that Job has suffered due to his sins; Eliphaz's accusations are so absurd that even he realizes this and refrains from speaking again. The end of their conversation marks the disintegration of the simplistic and flawed theology that one's deeds are rewarded immediately in a transparent manner.

Job's three friends were not evil individuals. Although Ḥazal portray Iyov's friends as paradigmatic violators of the prohibition of cruel speech,[140] their intentions were pure. We must recall that the Book of Job records that when they first visited Job after the calamities that befell him, they sat with him in utter silence for no less than seven days![141] Indeed, their actions are the source of the well-known halakha that comforters are forbidden to speak until the mourner begins to speak, as sometimes the mourner prefers silence to speech.[142]

Despite their good intentions, Job's friends were not only theologically misguided, but also mistaken in their approach to someone who has experienced tragedy. As previously noted, the Book of Job teaches not only philosophy, but also psychology. A therapeutically sound response to Job's trauma would have been to listen attentively and to validate his emotions.

Elihu: A Third Approach

The debate ends in a stalemate, but one in which Job twice expresses his desire for wisdom.[143] Job realizes that there is a need for a new voice to emerge that will explain his suffering in a manner that will differ from both his earlier approach and that of his friends, as they have all reached the limits of their wisdom.

138. Job 13:4-5.
139. Job 13:16.
140. Bava Metzia 58b.
141. Job 2:13.
142. *Moed Katan* 28b and *Shulḥan Arukh, Yore De'a* 376:1.
143. Job 28:12, 28:20.

Elihu is the young man who appears and articulates the anticipated third approach to Iyov's suffering.[144] Although there is much debate as to the role of Elihu[145], *Da'at Mikra* suggests that Elihu's four speeches prepare Job for the two monologues Hashem will address to him. The fact that Job does not respond negatively to Elihu's speeches, coupled with the fact that Hashem does not criticize Elihu,[146] clearly distinguishes his approach from the shallow and counterproductive approach of Job's friends.

Elihu's Insights

Elihu rejects both the friends' simplistic view that suffering is always explained by sin *and* Job's strident words of complaint. He lends insight into Hashem's masterful operations, clarifying that Hashem is always just – as evidenced by His crushing extremely powerful evil leaders[147] – and that Hashem uses suffering as a way to communicate with us.[148] While Elihu does *not* deny Job's complaint that some evil individuals prosper – at least temporarily – the collapse of seemingly invincible leaders proves that there is justice in this world.

Elihu states that Hashem is not influenced by man's good or evil acts. This is a vitally important point as it explains that when Hashem rewards or punishes, He does so not out of personal vengeance or remuneration.[149] Isaiah expresses this exact point when he quotes Hashem as saying, "For my thoughts are not your thoughts, nor are your ways my ways."[150] Elihu thus introduces Job to the paradigm shift he must experience in regard to his relationship with, and understanding of, Hashem. Elihu instructs Job to ponder the greatness of Hashem's actions and the magnitude of His abilities to demonstrate that we cannot understand everything that Hashem does. Elihu teaches that just as we are content to live without understanding the specifics of Creation, so too, we should

---

144. Job 32-37.
145. *Da'at Mikra: Iyyov*, pp. 287-288, summarizes the debate.
146. Job 42:7.
147. Job 34; examples include the fall of Pharaoh, the defeat of the Assyrian emperor Sennacherib, and the collapse of the Babylonian empire.
148. Job 33:19.
149. Job 35:6-7.
150. Is. 55:8.

make peace with the notion that while Hashem is just, we cannot always *comprehend* Hashem's justice.[151]

Hashem's Two Speeches

Although Job does not react negatively to Elihu's speeches, he does not express agreement either. Nahmanides explains that at this point Job is ambivalent and needs Hashem's words to solidify his change in attitude.[152] Hashem appeases Job with two long speeches promoting one explicit message: a human being does not understand much of how the world operates.[153] Job eventually accepts this truth foreshadowed by Elihu, embracing his limitations in discerning Hashem's judgments.[154] Our relationship with Hashem differs from the simple quid-pro-quo exchange a slave expects from his master. In order to truly connect to Hashem, we submit our will to His and respect His omnipotence.

Thus one who suffers should not engage in a pointless exploration of *why* Hashem has afflicted him, as Job and his friends did. Rather, one should accept Hashem's judgment and concede that understanding the divine verdict is often beyond human comprehension. Rav Soloveitchik is said to have opined[155] that full knowledge of why people suffer would detract from our humanity. If we knew why others suffer we would simply regard them as receiving their due justice rather than empathizing with them as we should. The hurtful behavior of Job's well-meaning friends exemplifies the apathy that would emerge if we completely grasped Hashem's judgments, as Job's three friends believe they do.

After Hashem's Speeches

After Hashem criticizes Eliphaz, Bildad and Tzofar, He states that they must offer sacrifices as atonement and asks Job to pray for them. In an astonishing turn of events, Job's health, wealth, and family are restored after he prays for his friends.[156]

---

151. Job 36:22-37:14.
152. Job 38:1.
153. Job 38-41.
154. Job 42:5-6.
155. I heard this idea presented in the name of Rabbi Soloveitchik.
156. Job 42:10.

In the view of *Da'at Mikra,* Job's return of good fortune is due to his prayers for his friends.[157] This seems, after all, to establish a causal connection between Job's sufferings and a fault on his part – a failure to adequately empathize with others' needs. In Chapter 1 he offered *korbanot* (sacrifices) exclusively for his family members, not on behalf of others. We can view Job – in his struggles with his friends in chapters 3-31 – as being inappropriately self-centered, and now that he has ameliorated that character flaw by acting on behalf of others, Hashem removes his suffering.

Rav Soloveitchik's Explanation of the Book of Job

It is quite astonishing that the Book of Job ultimately seems to present an explanation for Job's misery, since the goal of chapters 38-41 was to emphasize that we cannot grasp the reason for Hashem's judgment. Providing a formula for Job's suffering – and subsequent blessing after he remedies his flaw – seems to undermine the objective of Hashem's speeches!

Rav Soloveitchik addresses this matter in his celebrated essay "*Kol Dodi Dofeik*." He explains that once Hashem establishes that a human being cannot completely comprehend the divine will, He teaches Job a *lesson* about suffering. Although this does not explain the global reason for suffering, affliction is a *message* from Hashem telling us that we must improve. This is precisely the idea Ḥazal seek to convey when they state, "One who is confronted with affliction should examine his deeds."[158] Ḥazal instruct us to avoid engaging in the fruitless exercise of trying to determine *why* Hashem sent afflictions, as Job does with his three friends. Instead, we should use the suffering as an opportunity for introspection and spiritual improvement.

Once Job emerges from his psychological stupor of self-pity and confusion, deciding instead to use the situation as a springboard for growth, he flourishes. The conclusion of the Book of Job, which records how Job prospers for the remainder of his long life, emphasizes the great benefit that accrues to one who, instead of passively reflecting, actively seeks to improve himself in the wake of tragedy and affliction.

157. Job 42:10.
158. Berakhot 5a.

The Holocaust and the State of Israel

Rav Soloveitchik applies this lesson to our nation's collective reaction after the Holocaust. He cautions us not to repeat the mistake of Job and his friends but rather to courageously accept the fact that we cannot explain why Hashem allowed the Holocaust to be perpetrated upon His special nation. Instead, we should view our collective and individual suffering as a catalyst for change, and reform ourselves accordingly.

Indeed, many Jews followed this exact formula after experiencing the pain of Auschwitz. Instead of exhausting their energies with futile questioning, they resolved to focus on their betterment and the future of the Jewish people. This helped many to preserve their *emuna* and encouraged them to marry and raise large families after the war. Many Jews channeled an enormous amount of energy into creating the State of Israel and into building communities and yeshivas in the Land of Israel that reflected the ideals of their spiritual centers before the war. The Lubavitcher Rebbe commented that just as the evil Nazis sought to eradicate Jews everywhere in the world, so he, the Rebbe, resolved to establish beacons of Torah and Judaism in every corner of the globe.

Conclusion

As we stated at the outset, the message of the Book of Job is direct and relevant, despite its challenging language. The trial of suffering is widely debated and explored, especially in instances where it challenges the development of a healthy relationship with Hashem. It is thus incumbent upon every Jew to study the Book of Job and internalize its vitally important themes so that we can use our *nisayonot* (tests) to facilitate growth, rather than letting them consume our *emuna*, God forbid.

The story of Job mirrors the story of our people for the last eighty years. After World War II the Jewish people stood at the brink of both physical and spiritual destruction. Yet through the heroism of hundreds of thousands of Jews, we have succeeded in rebuilding our nation and in substantiating our physical and spiritual resilience and unparalleled invincibility. Just as Job prospered after he revised his approach to his affliction, so too we have thrived in rebuilding Jewish families, yeshivas, Torah centers throughout the world, and the State of Israel.

Unfortunately, our suffering has not ended. We remain, however, steadfast in our commitment to grow as individuals, families, communities, and a people. The efforts of Rabbi Yehoshua Fass – after his cousin was murdered in a Palestinian attack in the year 2000 – are legendary. Instead of philosophizing about his cousin's death, the young rabbi used the tragedy as a powerful motivator to establish the Nefesh B'Nefesh organization, which has facilitated the immigration of more than fifty thousand Jews to Israel. Our success both as individuals and a people depends to a great extent on our adhering to the lessons of the Book of Job; we ignore its messages at our peril.

IT'S GREAT TO BE A JEW: FIVE ARGUMENTS IN FAVOR OF TORAH RESTRICTIONS

Among Jews who regrettably choose not to observe the Torah, there are those who attribute their decision to a distaste for the host of restrictions imposed by the Torah. While the core of this distaste may be an unwillingness to *submit* to the discipline and limitations of the Torah's rules, the rejection is often accompanied by rationalizations. Thus, it is important to present practical, rational, and compelling explanations for the restrictions Hashem created for the Jewish people.

Argument #1: Creating a Relationship with Hashem Through Self-Contraction

First and foremost, acceptance of Torah restrictions must be viewed as a way of establishing and maintaining a relationship with Hashem.

In order for any relationship to flourish, each party must submit to certain limitations on their behavior. In a successful marriage, one spouse does not unilaterally decide where to go and what to do during a vacation. Decisions are made collaboratively, with each spouse compromising their desires for the sake of the other. Practically, making concessions to one another is not burdensome, since the benefit derived from the relationship far outweighs any personal frustration caused by the need to compromise.

Hashem, surprisingly, also limits Himself for the benefit of others. The masters of Kabbala teach that Hashem contracted Himself – in order for the world to exist – in a phenomenon known as *tzimtzum*.[159] Because Hashem is infinite, He must minimize Himself in order for anything else to exist. He must also engage in *tzimtzum* in order for human beings to have free will.[160] Thus, Hashem places limitations on Himself to afford us the opportunity to live and thrive in His world.[161]

Accordingly, it is reasonable for us to reciprocate this gesture, to accept limitations on our behavior and lifestyle in order to create a space for Hashem in *our* lives. Just as both members of a loving couple must accept restrictions in order to create a healthy relationship, the same expectations apply to our bond with Hashem. The result is a satisfying, mutual exchange. We both engage in *tzimtzum* in order to create space for each other. Thus, Torah restrictions should not be viewed as a nuisance, but rather a wonderful opportunity to help us cultivate a relationship with our Creator and Father in heaven. A relationship with Hashem, as Rabbi Ḥaim Moshe Luzzatto notes in the first chapter of his *Path of the Just,* "is true joy and the greatest pleasure that can be found."

The Ashkenazic practice regarding the placement of the mezuza reflects the necessity of compromise in family relationships. In Ashkenazic tradition, the top of the mezuza is inclined towards the inside of the room, and the bottom towards the outside. The *Tur* explains[162] that this is a compromise position between the positions of Rashi, who writes that a mezuza should be placed vertically,[163] and Rabbeinu Tam, who

159. The Gemara (Yoma 69b) provides another example of Hashem exercising restraint: Hashem refrains from immediately punishing those who insult Him, in order to give even those who act impudently toward Him opportunity to mend their ways and repent. Hence Hashem is described as *erekh appayim* (slow to anger) as one of the 13 attributes of mercy (Ex. 34:6).

160. The *Meshekh Ḥokhma* (Gen. 1:26) uses the idea of *tzimtzum* to resolve the classic paradox of human free will and divine foreknowledge.

161. Wikipedia states: "An Israeli professor, Mordekhai Rotenberg, believes the kabbalistic-hasidic *tzimtzum* paradigm has significant implications for clinical therapy. According to this paradigm, God's 'self-contraction' to vacate space for the world serves as a model for human behavior and interaction. The *tzimtzum* model promotes a unique community-centric approach which contrasts starkly with the language of Western psychology." (https://en.wikipedia.org/wiki/Tzimtzum, accessed June 25, 2015)

162. *Shulḥan Arukh, Yore De'a* 289.

163. Menaḥot 33a.

holds that placing the mezuza in a "standing" position is not respectful and that it should be placed horizontally, like the Tablets and the Torah scroll in the Ark in the Temple.[164] The *Tur* concludes that those who are careful to perform the commandments in the best way possible fulfill both opinions by placing their mezuzot on a slant. Rabbi Moses Isserles writes that the position of the *Tur's* "careful ones" has since become prevalent in Ashkenazic communities.[165] This practice persists until today.

The compromise between Rashi and Rabbeinu Tam's opinions holds a critical message for families. Compromise is essential; family members must accept limitations to their behavior in order to function happily together. By accepting limitations (and obligations), family members are able to form a loving family unit. This idea is so fundamental and central that it needs to be emphasized and "advertised" from the doorpost in (almost) every room in one's home.

Rabbi Emmanuel Vinas eloquently describes the incomparable joy and benefit of cultivating a deep and personal relationship with Hashem:

> A relationship with Him is above all other things. It provides so many blessings that they are innumerable and indescribable. The person who lives according to the Torah following its teaching and lifestyle lives as if on another planet from everyone else. Friday is no longer Friday for it becomes Erev Shabbat Kodesh. Saturday is no longer Saturday; it is the Holy Shabbat. Time is sanctified by observance of the days and moments commanded to us in the Torah. Every day we recite the "*Shir Shel Yom*" (the Psalm of the day) recognizing that it is a blessed day because it and we are in a covenant with God that has uplifted us from the rest of society. Saying one hundred blessings every day, eating only kosher, marrying only permitted spouses, having sexual relations only with those permitted to us uplifts the human condition and imbues it with great meaning. It alters your consciousness – you

164. *Tosafot* on Menaḥot 33a (s.v. *Ha*)

165. *Shulḥan Arukh, Yoreh De'a* 289:6. Sephardic Jews, however, follow Rashi's opinion and affix their mezuzot vertically.

feel God's love surrounding you all the time even when there is trouble. It makes life so much sweeter and makes difficulty so much easier to handle.[166]

Argument #2: Torah Restrictions as a Vehicle of Human Empowerment

Rabbi Mordechai Kaminetzky relates the following poignant story:

> I once sat on an overseas flight next to a talkative executive who was skeptical about his own Jewish heritage. During the first hours of the flight, the man peppered me with questions, mostly cynical, about Judaism.
>
> Then the meal came. I was served a half-thawed omelet that seemed to be hiding under a few peas and carrots. The half-cooked egg was nestled between a small aluminum pan and its quilted blanket of tape and double-wrapped aluminum foil. Next to me, the executive was served a steaming piece of roast pork on fine china, with a succulent side dish of potatoes au gratin and a glass of fine wine.
>
> As if to score big, the executive tucked his napkin into his collar and turned to me. He stared at my pathetic portion and with sympathetic eyes sarcastically professed, "I'd love to offer you my meal, but I'm sorry you can't eat it!"
>
> I did not buy into his gambit. "Of course I can eat it!" I smiled. "In fact I think I'll switch with you right now!" His smile faded. He was famished and in no way did he want to give away his portion. But he was totally mystified at my response. I saw the concern in his face. He was looking forward to eating this meal.
>
> "I can have it if I want it. And if I don't want it I won't eat it. I have free choice and control over what I eat and what I don't. The

166. Rabbi Emmanuel Vinas, *Divrei Emmanuel* (Yonkers, New York; Lincoln Park Jewish Center, 2008), 51.

> Torah tells me not to eat this food and I have made a conscious choice to listen to the Torah. I therefore choose not to eat it."[167]
>
> Then, I went for broke: "Now let me ask you a question. Can you put the cover back on the food and hold yourself back from eating it?"
>
> He smiled sheepishly and said, "You are not allowed to eat it. I, however, cannot *not* eat it." And with that he dug in.[168]

Reflecting upon this anecdote, one realizes that though the non-observant executive may appear to others as a powerful individual, in truth he is a pitiable slave to his biological urges. His own words – "he cannot not eat it" – reveal his lack of self-mastery. A human being is a composite of an animal and an angel.[169] Humans must satisfy both elements of their personality in order to experience authentic fulfillment.

In a similar vein, a rabbi who was raised as a non-observant Jew relates the following incident, which he says convinced him to live a life of Torah observance:

He had decided to experiment and experience one Shabbat during his visit to Israel. He stayed at a yeshiva for *baalei teshuva* (returnees), where he greatly enjoyed the Friday night prayers, dinner, and discussions. When he returned to his room, he was confronted with a dilemma: the main light had not been turned off before Shabbat.

The young man was conflicted. On one hand, he was not yet observant, so he was inclined to turn off the light in order to get a proper night's rest, as he would have on any other Friday night. On the other

167. Rabbi Kaminetzky's approach is in line with Rashi's comments (Lev. 20:26; citing R. Elazar ben Azaria) that one's attitude to *kashrut* should be that he wishes to eat non-kosher food but chooses not to in order to conform to Hashem's command.
168. Rabbi Mordechai Kaminetzky, *Parasha Parables,* volume 4 (Nanuet, New York: Feldheim Publishers, 2003), 37-38.
169. Rabbi Efrem Goldberg articulates: "In Jewish thought, man lives in two dimensions simultaneously. On the one hand, the Talmud observes, we are members of the animal kingdom who share in common the three basic physical activities of animals: eating, elimination, and reproduction. On the other hand, we have been endowed with a *Tzelem Elokim,* a Godly soul, providing us the capacity to be disciplined, exhibit self-control, and reign sovereign over our instincts and impulses" (http://rabbisblog.brsonline.org/please-god-help-us-empowered-lessons-sacred-sacrifices/).

hand, he had promised to give Shabbat an authentic effort. He decided to leave the light untouched.

The next morning he woke up tired from lack of proper sleep but exhilarated over his ability to control himself. Never before had he experienced such a profound sense of satisfaction! The "angel" side of his personality was finally gratified. This thrill became his prime motivation to become a Torah-observant Jew.

Such deep satisfaction can be experienced when one refrains from an activity that is forbidden, such as eating that which he should not eat, speaking *lashon hara* (derogatory words about others), or inappropriate sensuality. Elation emerges from the empowerment of being able to master one's physical urges. One who observes the Torah knows the joy of being able to control himself; he is not a slave to his passions. Indeed, Ḥazal teach that "the only truly free individual is the one who is immersed in a Torah lifestyle *(ein lekha ben ḥorin ela mi she'osek baTorah).*"[170]

Rav Soloveitchik's Essay "Catharsis"

The ideas presented in this section are discussed most elegantly and profoundly by Rav Joseph B. Soloveithchik in his seminal article "*Catharsis,*" printed in the spring 1978 issue of *Tradition*. This brief essay, one of Rav Soloveitchik's most important works, is an essential read for every Jew interested in probing the fundamental philosophical underpinnings of Torah observance. Rabbi Reuven Ziegler's cogent analysis of this essay is archived on the website of Yeshivat Har Etzion.[171]

The essay expounds upon Ḥazal's saying "The commandments were given to purge mankind."[172] This implies that man is born unrefined and thus requires improvement. The mitzvot are necessary to facilitate the indispensable refinement of the human being. Without such modification the individual is unredeemed.

Rav Soloveitchik identifies four areas of human life in need of redemption: carnal drives, emotional life, intellectual life, and religious

170. Avot 6:2.

171. http://etzion.org.il/en/topics/thought-rav-soloveitchik.

172. Midrash Gen. Rabba 44:1.

life. Essential to redemption is the ability to retreat and withdraw from situations. For example, a hungry individual who resists eating delicious food due to *kashrut* (Torah dietary laws) regulations, or one who refrains from a business deal due to its incompatibility with Torah law and values, has redeemed an aspect of his personality. Rav Soloveitchik also explains that halakha challenges us to engage or be prepared to engage in such redemptive and heroic actions on a regular basis.[173]

Without rectification, one remains an incomplete individual.[174] The profound sense of satisfaction experienced by the young man who refrained from extinguishing the light in his room on Shabbat emerged from his deeply felt need to redeem his human personality. In contrast, the wealthy businessman who could not resist his urge to eat in the story related by Rav Kaminetzky is living an unredeemed life.

Argument #3: God's Way of Acting in Our Best Interest

The businessman's behavior recalls the Torah account of Esau's selling his birthright for lentil soup. Regrettably, the Western culture by which we are surrounded today has become a culture of Esau, glorifying immediate gratification. Rav Efrem Goldberg puts it poigniantly:

> In the area of the battle between the animal and the Godly soul, the temptations of the physical world versus the quest for spirituality, we not only have not progressed, but a survey of advertisements, websites, themes of movies and TV, and behavior of politicians and celebrities shows that we have regressed.

173. See also Rav Soloveitchik's book *Family Redeemed* (New York: Toras HoRav Foundation, 2000), 73-104, which argues that redemptive actions lend dignity to the body. In a beautiful and sensitive chapter, "The Redemption of Sexual Life," Rav Soloveitchik explains the vital importance of transforming the sexual act from a self-centered pursuit of pleasure to an activity expressing respect, love and an everlasting bond between the married couple.

174. Rav Soloveitchik's observations do not merely highlight the deficiencies of living a life without Torah; they also urge religious Jews to consider whether their mitzva observance is truly redeeming their personalities. Ḥazal's teaching that the Torah was given only to refine our character is a sobering reminder of the ultimate goal of Torah observance. Every Jew must engage in serious introspection and examine his progress in achieving this lofty aspiration.

> The world of marketing seeks to exploit the animal impulse inside us all with messages like "Obey your thirst" and "Just do it." Look at the infidelity rates and the obesity statistics and you cannot help but conclude that for many modern people, the animal instinct is defeating the Godly, disciplined soul.[175]

The problems created by this culture of immediate gratification lend ample support to Moses' recurring reminder that observance of the Torah is *letov lakh* (for our benefit).[176] Ultimately, moreover, Torah observance actually increases the pleasures of life. A classic illustration of this is given by R. Meir, who explains that Torah restrictions on marital relations during the time a wife is impure exist "because if the husband would become accustomed to his wife, he would loathe her, therefore the Torah made her impure for a certain amount of time so that she would be as beloved to her husband as at the moment she entered the *ḥuppa* (wedding canopy)."[177]

Indeed, every healthy Torah observant couple reaps the benefit of observing the laws of family purity, as they relive each month the excitement of the wedding night and the anticipation leading up to it.[178] Couples who observe *nidda* laws are eager to be intimate during permitted times since they know that their opportunity is limited. This explains reports from therapists I have consulted that, in the long term, observant couples engage in marital relations more often (which, in turn, continuously strengthens the marital bond) than non-observant couples. Moreover, the time spent abstaining from their physical relationship allows a couple to develop other aspects of their bond, as during their courtship.

Similarly with other restrictions the Torah imposes on sexual activity. Refraining from physical relations before marriage allows the

175. (http://rabbisblog.brsonline.org/please-god-help-us-empowered-lessons-sacred-sacrifices/)
176. Examples include Deut. 4:40, 5:16, 6:18, and 6:24.
177. Nidda 31b.
178. The information in this paragraph comes from discussions conducted with a variety of observant family therapists and from my and my wife's experiences as halakhic guides to bridegrooms and brides before and after marriage.

personal relationship to be nurtured before the physical relationship begins. Marital intimacy is most impactful when the husband abides by the Torah discipline of *shmirat einayim* (guarding the eyes, or not looking at sexually stimulating sights) and *shmirat habrit* (guarding the covenant, or refraining from impure actions). Failure to observe these halakhic precautions habituates one to a selfish attitude about satisfying biological urges instead of a healthy approach of mutuality and love.

The dramatically lower incidence of divorce among fully-committed Jews as compared with less observant Jews constitutes cogent evidence of the efficacy of the Torah's laws regarding male-female relationships.[179]

The laws of family purity have been aptly compared to parents' restrictions on the amount of cake and candy their children eat. Parents are not trying to reduce the children's pleasure but rather to make it possible for them to enjoy instead of becoming sick. I read[180] of a non-observant Jew who stated that he began engaging in intimate relations with his wife on their second date and did not observe the laws of family purity during their marriage. He noted that he and his wife began to develop their personal relationship only when working together to raise their children after their divorce, when refraining from intimacy. What a tragedy!

Those who conduct their lives in accordance with the rules designed by our Creator for our benefit are likely to succeed, whereas failure to adhere to the divine guidance leads to disaster. As Hosea put it, "O Yisrael, return to the Lord your God; for you have stumbled in your iniquity."[181]

The benefit of observing Torah law is also apparent in other realms of halakha. Keeping Shabbat brings the priceless treasure of a natural

---

179. The Spring 2017 issue of the Orthodox Union's *Jewish Action* reports (https://www.ou.org/jewish_action/03/2017/data-divorce-g-dr-yitzchak-schechter) a study by Dr. Yitzchak Schechter (a clinical psychologist and director of the Center for Applied Psychology at Bikur Cholim in Monsey, New York) that reveals that the overall divorce rate in the American Orthodox community appears to be around ten percent.

180. This appeared in the comments section to a Jerusalem Post article.

181. Hos. 14:2.

vacation and a day to unplug from electronics. The halakhic prohibition of driving on Shabbat and holidays also compels us to reside within walking distance of a synagogue, which leads to the creation of clusters of observant Jews living within a concentrated area. *Kashrut,* similarly, helps build and create a cohesive community because the restrictions require us to live in an area where kosher food is readily available. When traveling, *kashrut* and Shabbat regulations lead us to meet the local observant Jews for lodging and dining.

In 2003, Dr.Ismar Schorsch, then chancellor of the Jewish Theological Seminary, declared during a speech at the biennial convention of the United Synagogues of Conservative Judaism that the Conservative movement made a mistake in its 1950 sanctioning of driving to synangogue on Shabbat.[182] By sanctioning travel on the Sabbath, he said, the Conservative movement "gave up on the desirability of living close to the synagogue and creating a Shabbos community."[183] This, tragically, proves the truth of Moses's warning, "And Moshe said, Why now do you transgress the commandment of the Lord? It shall not prosper."[184]

A root of all sin is thinking that one will benefit from the sin. Eve thought that by eating the forbidden fruit from the Tree of Knowledge she would become as great as Hashem.[185] She regarded the forbidden fruit as "good for food, and that it was a delight to the eyes, and a tree to be desired to make one wise." In reality it led only to exile and death.[186]

It is tempting to believe we know what is best. However, Moses cautions us against these attitudes when he says, "You shall also consider in your heart, that, as a man chastens his son, so the Lord your God chastens you."[187] My wife and I heard an elderly relative express his regret

182. Nacha Cattan, *Conservative Head Calls Sabbath-Driving Rule a 'Mistake,' Jewish Daily Forward,* November 7, 2003. http://forward.com/news/6998/conservative-head-calls-sabbath-driving-rule-a/.

183. I have heard non-Jewish clergy praise the beauty of Jewish families walking back and forth from synagogue on the Sabbath. A Catholic priest commented half-jokingly that he should raise with his colleagues the need to forbid driving to their house of worship on Sunday, to induce families to walk together to worship.

184. Num. 14:41.

185. Gen. 3:5.

186. Gen. 3:6.

187. Deut. 8:5.

that he did not provide a Jewish day school education for his children, despite his wife's pleas that he do so. He admitted that the reason he had no Jewish grandchildren was his stubborn insistence, against the advice of his rabbi and his wife, on his children attending public school. Failure to abide by the Torah way leads only to disaster, as repeatedly taught in Tanakh.

From an early age we must realize that everything Hashem has commanded us is in our best interest and for our long-term pleasure. Hashem instructs Abraham "*Lekh lekha* (Get for yourself out)" to the Land of Canaan.[188] Rashi[189] explains that the seemingly unnecessary word *lekha* ("for you") means that the journey is intended for your benefit and pleasure.

We can draw an analogy to car ownership. If one follows the manufacturer's instructions on how to drive and maintain the car, one will enjoy the car for a long time. One who does not adhere to the manufacturers' instructions will suffer the consequences in the long term and regret his decision. Hashem is our Manufacturer and the Torah is the user manual. Strict adherence to the Manufacturer's user manual is undoubtedly the prudent approach to life.[190] As we say in the *viduy* (confession) recited on Yom Kippur and other occasions, "We have turned away from Your good commandments and it has not been worthwhile."

The above are only examples of the benefits of observing the mitzvot. The classic *Sefer HaHinukh,* which is available online in English, gives a survey of the benefits of all the mitzvot and is warmly recommended.

Besides the benefits of adhering to each and every mitzva, there is a benefit to adhering to the tradition as a whole. Rabbi Efrem Goldberg cites a study[191] by Dr. Marshall Duke of Emory University, who tested children on their knowledge of their family backgrounds and then administered psychological tests. He reached an "overwhelming conclusion": "The more children knew about their family's history, the stronger

188. Gen. 12:1.

189. Gen. 12:1.

190. This theme is emphasized throughout the Book of Proverbs. We neglect this book, which is brimming with wise advice, at our loss.

191. Reported in "The Stories That Bind Us," *The New York Times* (March 15, 2013).

their sense of control over their lives, the higher their self-esteem and the more successfully they believed their families functioned." Rabbi Goldberg writes:

> When I saw this article and read about Duke's research, all I could think of is the Pesach Seder and the wisdom of our sacred tradition. This new research simply affirms what we knew and have practiced for millennia. When we sit at the Seder and tell the story of our people, our children feel part of something larger than themselves. When they hear our personal stories of ups and downs, bitterness and sweetness, they feel part of something larger and greater than themselves. They don't see their own circumstance in a vacuum or feel the need to face their challenges alone. When they see themselves as part of our collective history and our family's personal narrative, they are encouraged, strengthened and uplifted.[192]

Torah living certainly promotes a sense of belonging to something larger than ourselves. As Torah Jews, we see ourselves as links in a chain stretching back nearly four thousand years to Abraham and Sarah and forward to the Messianic Age. When we think we are living for ourselves alone, we actually diminish ourselves.[193]

Argument #4: Healthy Acceptance of Human Limitations

Human beings are capable of grasping the reasons for many mitzvot. However, there are certain mitzvot, classified as *ḥukim,* that are either very difficult to understand or whose explanation rests beyond human comprehension.[194] Although Maimonides encourages exploring the

192. http://rabbisblog.brsonline.org/have-you-told-your-children-your-family-narrative/.
193. I often tell youngsters that only if they care about their grandparents' traditions will their grandchildren care about their traditions.
194. The Rishonim disagree as to whether *ḥukim* are merely difficult to understand (Maimonides, *Hilkhot Me'ilah* 8:8 and *Guide to the Perplexed,* 3:31) or whether the reasons are beyond human comprehension and known only to Hashem (Rashi and Nahmanides on Leviticus 19:19).

reasons for all mitzvot, he cautions that just because one fails to discover the reason for a mitzva he may not disregard or disparage the commandment.[195]

The *Be'er Yosef* explains that there is great value to our inability to comprehend every mitzva.[196] Observance of *Ḥukim* helps us recognize and internalize that human beings are of limited intellectual capacity and are incapable of understanding all of God's ways. *Ḥukim* train us to accept Hashem's judgments even when they appear unjust to our eyes. Our adherence to Hashem's commands even when we do not understand them can help us effectively manage our emotions if and when tragedy strikes.

One may ask, however, why Hashem withholds information from us. This question is especially poignant in an age such as ours, which aggressively asserts man's rights to know all. Rav Soloveitchik's essay "*Catharsis*," discussed earlier at some length, offers an answer to this question.

As we saw, the central idea of this essay is that man is in need of redemption, which is accomplished by man's internal growth process – conquering his inclinations. We noted that Rav Soloveitchik identified four aspects of the human personality that require such refinement. The intellect is one of these four human traits in need of improvement.

Man is certainly encouraged and even mandated to explore and know as much as possible about this world.[197] This is true not only in regard to scientific endeavor but to religious inquiry as well. The Gemara boldly discusses and develops Torah thought and halakha to the point even of daring to disagree with Hashem.[198] However, just as there are limits to scientific knowledge, there are limits to religious pursuits as well.[199]

---

195. *Hilkhot Me'ila* 8:8.
196. *Parashat Ḥukat.*
197. This mandate emerges from Hashem's command to Adam upon his creation to conquer the world (see Gen. 1:28 with Nahmanides' commentary).
198. Bava Metzia 59b.
199. Rabbi Reuven Ziegler explains, in his analysis of "*Catharsis*": "In the scientific realm, cognitive catharsis implies recognizing the ultimate mystery of being. To begin with, we must recognize that every problem we solve engenders a more complex and

Humanity achieves its intellectual (and perhaps even religious) catharsis and redemption when it humbly acknowledges it cannot understand the reason for Hashem's every command and cannot justify God's every action. When we respectfully accept Isaiah's teaching of "For My thoughts are not your thoughts, neither are your ways My ways,"[200] we admit that while we *are* partners with Hashem in creation,[201] we are junior partners. Such healthy acceptance of our limitations ultimately allows us to flourish and develop our personalities to the greatest extent possible. Failure to reconcile and accept such limitations can lead only to frustration, since man is not fated to know all. Ḥazal say that the first three mitzvot Hashem introduced to us at Marah after the splitting of the sea were honoring parents, Shabbat, and the law of the red heifer.[202] While it is understandable that Hashem would introduce Shabbat and honoring parents – these are foundations of Torah life, included in the Ten Commandments – why did He give the law of the red heifer at Marah? It hardly seems to constitute an appropriate introduction to the Torah we were to receive in a few weeks. An answer is that by introducing the red heifer, the commandment most often cited as impossible to understand, at an early stage of our national development, Hashem communicated a basic and critical lesson: the human being must reconcile himself to the reality that he is incapable of comprehending everything.

Rabbi Yehuda Amital once said that he instructed those just setting out on the path of Torah observance to follow the example Hashem set at Marah and choose three mitzvot to observe – one that is between us and Hashem, one that is between us and our fellow man, and one mitzva whose reason we do not grasp. Rabbi Amital explained that a mitzva from each category should be chosen because Torah is not only

inclusive problem than the first," (http://etzion.org.il/en/16-catharsis-intellect-and-religious-experience). Dr. Jeremy England, an Orthodox professor of physics at MIT eloquently states: "*Dvekut baShem* (clinging to Hashem) and taking hold of Torah is a choice in attitude about how to decide when you don't know everything." (*Orthodox Jewish All Star, Dr. Jeremy England, 'The Next Darwin,'* archived at https://www.youtube.com/watch?v=crJ7cPFN5ug&t=58s).

200. Is. 55:8.

201. Shabbat 10a.

202. See Rashi Ex. 15:25.

about fostering our relationship with Hashem but improving our relationships with other people as well. In addition, by choosing a mitzva they did not understand, the learners would adjust their psyche to recognize that it is not necessary to fathom every command of Hashem in order to function as a fully-committed Jew. Rabbi Amital used the example of a plastic cup. He noted that we use it even though we do not understand how it is made or how it maintains its integrity. Similarly, Rabbi Amital explained we can and should observe mitzvot even if we do not appreciate the reason for everything we do.[203]

Argument #5: "It's Great to Be a Jew"

Rav Moshe Feinstein bemoaned the fact that many of the generation of European Orthodox Jews who came to the United States made a grave mistake in raising their children. Encountering the difficulties of being observant in "the New World," they raised their children on the saying "*es iz shver tzu zein a Yid* (it is difficult to be a Jew)."[204] They tried to implant in their children the willpower to serve Hashem even under trying conditions. While this may have worked in "the old country," where everything was hard for everyone anyway, it was ineffective in North America, where the option of living a difficult life as an observant Jew had to compete with the opportunity to live a "stress-free" life of non-observance. In the New World both options were readily available.

Instead, Rav Feinstein explains that they should have shown their children the beauty and thrill of serving Hashem and observing His mitzvot. They should have emphasized the profound satisfaction and the spiritual and emotional tranquility of the religious Jew as opposed to the confusion and instability the non-observant experience. Needless to say, it is similarly essential for Torah educators to present their lectures in a joyful manner that makes Torah learning attractive to their students.[205]

---

203. Rav Amital delivered this message to a group of Yeshivat Har Etzion alumni, meeting at Yeshiva University in 1986.

204. *Igrot Moshe Yore De'a* 3:71.

205. The Midrash (Song of Songs Rabba 4:11) cites a statement from Reish Lakish: "Whoever says words of Torah and they are not pleasant like a bride is to her groom under the wedding canopy, it is better that he not say them."

Rav Feinstein's idea is hardly revolutionary. Our prayers are replete with similar ideas. Here is a sample: *"May the words of Your Torah be sweet in our mouths." "This thing is beloved and pleasant for us." "Happy are we, how good is our lot." "Serve Hashem with gladness." "Those who keep Shabbat will rejoice in Your kingdom."* Instead of complaining about Torah restrictions, we should feel pleased that Hashem has blessed us with them! We should be sure to communicate this message to peers, children and students. It is wonderful to hear high school students singing a newly popular song "it's *geshmack* to be a *Yid* (it's great to be a Jew)"!

One of the great satisfactions of living a Torah life is the dignity and self-esteem that emerge from knowing that one is living the mission that God has set for him. The Midrash Rabba on Lamentations (1:30) states: "Every being seeks to fulfill its divinely assigned mission." This explains why Jews observed Torah in Nazi concentration camps and Soviet gulags. The inner sense of having a divinely ordained mission and purpose in life impelled them to perform the mitzvot even in those extremely trying circumstances. The joys of Torah observance are far greater than the instant – yet ultimately fleeting and destructive – gratification ubiquitously peddled in western culture. The Torah's restrictions facilitate a relationship with Hashem, empower the individual, steer people away from toxic behavior and instill a healthy sense of balance and perspective on one's role in this world.

Conclusion

There Is a God

The well-known Hasidic master Rabbi Levi Yitzhak of Berdichev once summoned the entire Jewish population of his town to the main square, to hear an important announcement. Everyone eagerly gathered to hear the famous rabbi issue a message of great import. Anticipation grew as Rabbi Levi Yitzḥak began to speak. Finally, he annonounced with a loud voice, "There is a God!"

Rabbi Levi Yitzḥak was following the example set by our forefather Abraham. As Rashi notes,[1] before Abraham annonounced to all that there is a God, Hashem was only the God of heavens. After Abraham's (and Sarah's, as noted by Rashi)[2] outreach efforts, Hashem was not only the God of heavens but also the God of the earth. Hashem does not make His presence obvious, as we discussed at length, so without a human partner, Hashem remains only the God of heaven. Once Abraham partnered with Hashem and publicized His subtle involvement in the world, Hashem became the God of the earth as well.

In the words of Rashi, Abraham facilitated recognition of Hashem amongst humanity and made His reputation commonplace throughout

1. Gen. 24:7.
2. Gen. 12:5.

the world. We, as Abraham's biological and ideological descendents, continue the mission initiated by our forefather.

Nevertheless, just as there were those who seek to extinguish the light of Abraham and Sarah, great efforts have been made in the past century and a half to invalidate the message of Orthodox Judaism. However, just as Abraham was saved from Nimrod's burning fire,[3] Orthodox Judaism has successfully emerged from the cauldron of criticism. It has emerged stronger than ever from its encounter with the manifold intellectual, psychological and social challenges of the modern age. *Emuna* shines ever more brightly, not despite but specifically because of the developments of the past one hundred years.

There are individual heroes that have enabled a vibrant contemporary Orthodoxy. These individuals include Rav Joseph Soloveitchik and Rav Aharon Lichtenstein, who created a very sophisticated intellectual framework that demonstrates that one need not hide from the advances of the modern world to thrive as an Orthodox Jew. Rav Moshe Feinstein and Rav Ovadia Yosef are among the brilliant rabbinic decisors who applied the ancient rabbinic writings to the myriad of new issues that have emerged in our time. Orthodox scientists have articulated a variety of paths to resolve the apparent contradictions between Torah and science. Orthodox Bible scholars such as the contributors to the *Da'at Mikra* series and Rabbi Amnon Bazak offered a resounding Orthodox response to Bible critics, both regarding the biblical text and regarding archaeology. Jewish thinkers have refined classical arguments for the divine origin of the Torah.

Hashem, of course, provides ample opportunity for us to discover His ongoing presence in the world, especially through the establishment and continued flourishing of the State of Israel. Scientific discoveries afford a magnificent opportunity for spiritual inspiration for those with an eye for spirituality.

The most potent response to the criticism of Orthodoxy, though, lies in the strength of the Orthodox communities. Orthodoxy can never and will never be defined merely by its leaders and ideology. Vibrant centers of Orthodoxy whose members are intelligent, well-educated and

3. According to rabbinic tradition, Genesis Rabba 38:13.

paragons of kindness, spirituality and moral living, represent the ultimate goal of Abraham and Sarah.[4] Thus, the ultimate responsibility is upon every individual Jew and every Jewish community to serve as a bastion of faith and living a life that conveys the message "It's great to be a Jew."

Maimonides, as presented earlier, explained that Abraham discovered God at age three but arrived at a more complete faith at age forty. In light of our earlier distinction between belief through *tvi'at ayin* (intuition) and *simanim* (rational arguments), it is reasonable to suggest that Abraham began his journey with an intuitive recognition of God at age three but bolstered his faith through rational argument as he matured. An example of such argument is the parable presented by the Midrash of one

> who was traveling from place to place when he saw a palace full of light. He pondered, "Is it possible that this edifice has no one who looks after it?" The owner of the building peeked out at him and said, "I am the owner of the palace." Similarly, because our forefather Abraham pondered, "Is it possible that that this world has no one who looks after it?" Hashem looked at him and said, "I am the owner of the world."[5]

The spiritual journey of every Jew can follow the model set by our illustrious ancestor. We begin with an intuitive recognition and reinforce it through the passing of time with cogent arguments.

Why did Abraham and Sarah discover Hashem and almost everyone else in their time fail to recognize the King of kings? The answer is simple – one cannot find something if one does not engage in a sincere and earnest search. Abraham and Sarah modeled for us a life of searching for and connecting to Hashem. Rabbi Soloveitchik has expressed that a Jew must be a seeker of God ("*uvikashtem misham et Hashem Elokekha*"), in line with the teaching of Deuteronomy 4:29, which presents the quest for God as a sine qua non for redemption. In fact, Rabbi Soloveitchik composed a full essay entitled "*Uvikashtem Misham*," outlining the parameters of the quest for the Divine.

---

4. See Maimonides, *Guide to the Perplexed*, 3:51.
5. Genesis Rabba 12:1.

It is my fervent hope that this book can serve as a stimulus for many to be alert to the "still small voice" (I Kings 19:12) and the Beloved "standing behind our wall, looking through the windows, peering through the lattice." I hope I have adequately lived up to the model of Abraham and Sarah, who called out in the name of God and spread His reputation near and far (Genesis 12:8 with Nahmanides).

The Bible presents us with many portals and paths to relate to and connect with our Creator. The opening chapters of Genesis present us with the potential to connect to God through nature and science. The centerpiece of the Book of Exodus, the revelation narratives, allow us to relate to Him by connecting to what Rabbi Soloveitchik refers to as the covenantal community, the Jewish people, who are the descendants of the nation that witnessed the great Sinaitic revelation. The many mitzvot of the Pentateuch allow us to approach Him by adhering to His code of conduct. The Book of Esther paves a path to perceive God as revealed in history. The prophetic proclamations throughout the Bible create the enthralling opportunity to see their fulfillment. The Book of Psalms models relating to God in both triumphant and disappointing moments. Finally, the Song of Songs models a passionate drive to bond with our Beloved Creator.

Hashem provides us with manifold opportunitites to recognize that there truly is a God, that the Torah is undoubtedly a divine document, and that the Torah is indeed a blueprint for the best possible communal and individual life.

About the Author

Rabbi Chaim Jachter has earned an international reputation as a *get* (Jewish divorce) administrator, consultant for community *eiruvin* and a prolific writer. His publications include a series of four well-received books entitled *Gray Matter* on contemporary topics in Jewish law. He is a veteran teacher of Judaic Studies at Torah Academy of Bergen County, Rabbi of Congregation Shaarei Orah (the Sephardic Congregation of Teaneck), and Dayan on the Beit Din of Elizabeth. Rabbi Jachter has lectured on topics of significance at a wide variety of venues worldwide. Rabbi Jachter lives with his wife and five children in Teaneck, New Jersey.

Acknowledgments

Many people have contributed to making this book a reality.

The most important contributors to the content of *Reason to Believe* are my students and congregants. Their questions, concerns, and insights in discussions over the past twenty-two years of teaching at Torah Academy of Bergen County are the basis of this work. Discussions with my beloved congregants at Congregation Shaarei Orah, the Sephardic congregation of Teaneck, have also added immesurably to this work. Its writing began with my weekly column in the TABC's weekly Torah newsletter, *Kol Torah*. The editors-in-chief of *Kol Torah* – Alex Feldman, Avi Hirsch, Matthew Wexler, Hillel Koslowe and Yehuda Koslowe – helped create the document from which *Reason to Believe* developed.

In the spring of 2015 the process of shaping the *Kol Torah* articles into a book was begun by Moshe Pahmer and Matthew Wexler as part of Torah Academy of Bergen County's work-study program for graduating seniors. Matthew and Moshe's efforts and insights provided an excellent start for *Reason to Believe*. I am especially grateful for their recommendations regarding the Torah and Science section, all of which have been incorporated into this work.

In that same spring Mimi Fuchs, an outstanding Torah educator with a sincere desire to bolster the level of faith in our community, began the work of transforming the collection of articles into a book. Mimi has exceeded my expectations and has collaborated in producing an excellent product. The high quality of this work is a reflection of the many hours of hard work Mimi invested in *Reason to Believe.*

I thank Dr. Elliot Prager for devoting many hours to carefully reviewing and editing the text. His countless insights and recommendations made a great impact on the work.

It is a great pleasure and honor to reunite with my old friend Rabbi Reuven Ziegler to publish this work, together with Ashirah Yosefah, editor-in-chief of Menorah Books, an imprint of Koren Publishers Jerusalem. Koren has emerged as the leading publishing house of thoughtful Jewish works in our community. It is an honor to be welcomed into the Koren Publishers' circle. Esther Cameron did an outstanding job of very carefully reviewing *Reason to Believe.* Her insights and comments have dramatically enhanced the quality of this work. A special thank you is due Matthew Miller of Koren Publishers for translating the concept of *Reason to Believe* into concrete reality.

My deepest gratitude is due to Marcia and Barry Levinson for their constant encouragement and gracious support for the creation of this work. Without their support this dream would never have been translated into reality. As Ivy League graduates and very successful professionals who live fully devoted lives of Torah belief and observance, Marcia and Barry set an example of *kiddush Hashem* (sanctifying God's name). The Hebrew title of this book, *Zichron David,* honors Mr. David Wagner z"l, Marcia Levinson's father, who departed this world in May 2016. May this work serve *l'ilui nishmato,* to elevate his soul.

I thank the administrators, board, and staff of the Torah Academy of Bergen County, where I have had the honor of teaching Torah to precious Jewish young men for the past twenty-two years, for their encouragement and support. In particular, I thank TABC's Mrs. Teri Norman for providing the support necessary for the production of this work, and Mr. Arthur Poleyeff for his warmth, wisdom and constant encouragement. Above all, the support of Torah Academy's *Rosh Yeshiva,* Rabbi Yosef Adler, has been indispensable. May Hashem grant him a *refuah sheleima* in light of his manifold merits. A special welcome to our new head of school, Rabbi Asher Yablok.

A special thank you to my *Rebbe*, Rabbi Mordechai Willig, for his support and guidance through the years, and for specific encouragement in the production of this work. I am always amazed how Rabbi Willig, a Torah giant of towering proportions, finds time for each of his thousands of *talmidim*. I also owe a special debt of gratitude to Rabbi Elazar Meyer Teitz, chief justice of the Rabbinic Court of Elizabeth, who is a constant fount of wisdom and kind support. Finally, I thank the leadership and membership of Congregation Shaarei Orah, the Sephardic Congregation of Teaneck, for providing me with the great joy of serving as their rabbi. Jack and Heidi Varon, the central pillars of our community, are owed special gratitude.

My parents, Ben and Shirley Jachter of blessed memory, encouraged me to write books. My father urged me when I was only fifteen years old to record every *ḥiddush* (novel idea) that I developed. My mother, as we sat on our Brooklyn porch one summer night discussing my future, remarked, "You will write books." I am eternally grateful to my mother for having instilled in me at an early age the knowledge that Hashem is a reality and that we must live life in the light of that reality. May this work be *l'ilui nishmatam,* for the elevation of their souls. It is due to their encouragement and vision that *Reason to Believe* has come to light.

I also extend a heartfelt "thank you" to my in-laws, Rav Shmuel and Chana Tokayer, for all of their continued encouragement and support. May Hashem send a *refua sheleima* to my father-in-law, in the merit of the help he has given to many people over the years as a rabbi and a psychologist.

I cannot thank Hashem enough for the privilege of being married to my wonderful wife, Malca. Her wisdom, kindness, warmth, and patience are the joy of my life. I have been able to grow in Torah learning and write Torah essays and books only because of her self-sacrifice, encouragement, and dedication. I am deeply grateful to Malca and our children. May Hashem merit us to continue to raise our wonderful and outstanding children, Bracha, Binyamin, Chaya Zipporah, Atara, and Hillel, in the path of Torah study, careful observance of mitzvot, and contributions to *Am Yisrael.* I thank Malca for raising our children with firm *emuna* and commitment to Torah. I also thank Malca, Bracha, Binyamin, Chaya Zipporah, Atara, and Hillel, whose many insights have been incorporated in this work.

Above all, I thank Hashem for giving me the strength and guidance to teach Torah to His children, the members of *Am Yisrael.*

Teaneck, New Jersey
5777/2017

English Language Works Cited

Aviezer, Nathan. *Fossils and Faith: Understanding Torah and Science.* Hoboken: Ktav Publishing House, Inc., 2001.

______, *In the Beginning: Biblical Science and Creation.* Hoboken: Ktav Publishing House, 1990.

Avner, Yehuda. *The Prime Ministers: An Intimate Narrative of Israeli Leadership.* London: The Toby Press, 2010.

Besdin, Abraham. *Reflections of the Rav,* 184. Jerusalem: World Zionist Organization, 1979.

Berger, Motti and Resnick, Asher. *The Seven Wonders of Jewish History.* http://www.aish.com/jl/h/h/48965856.html.

Brands, H.W. *The First American: The Life and Times of Benjamin Franklin.* New York: Random House, 2000.

Carmell, Aryeh and Domb, Cyril, eds. *Challenge: Torah Views on Science and Its Problems.* Jerusalem: Association of Orthodox Jewish Scientists, 1978.

Eban, Abba. *Israel: The Birth of a Nation Part One,* available at https://www.youtube.com/watch?v=bdHQ6NTvqo0&t=1760s

England, Dr. Jeremy. "Jewish All Star, Dr. Jeremy England, 'The Next Darwin.'" Archived at https://www.youtube.com/watch?v=crJ7cPFN5ug

______, "The Partly Predictable World." *Commentary* (December 2015): 27-33.

Eliach, Yaffa. *Hasidic Tales of the Holocaust.* New York: Oxford University Press, 1982.

Ferling, John. *Almost a Miracle: The American Victory in the War of Independence.* New York: Oxford University Press, 2007.

Freedman, Daniel. "The World's Deadly Obsession with Israel." *Forbes* (June 24, 2010), http://www.forbes.com/2010/06/23/israel-hamas-middle-east-opinions-columnists-daniel-freedman.html

Gilbert, Martin. *Israel: A History.* New York: Harper Perennial, 1998.

Gordis, Daniel. *Israel: A Concise History of a Nation Reborn.* New York: Harper Collins, 2016.

Harary, Charlie. *The Six Constant Mitzvos with Charlie Harary: Mitzvah #1,* https://www.youtube.com/watch?v=dv2PgYw2W7g

Herzog, Jacob David. *A People that Dwells Alone: Speeches & Writings of Yaacov Herzog.* New York: Sanhedrin Press, 1975.

Herzog, Chaim and Gazit, Shlomo. *The Arab-Israeli Wars: War and Peace in the Middle East.* Oxford: Oxford University Press, 2009.

Hort, Greta. "The Plagues of Egypt." *Zeitschrift fur die Altestestamentliche Wissenschaft* 70 (1958): 48–59.

Johnson, Paul. *A History of the Jews.* New York: Harper Collins, 2009.

———, "Israel: The Miracle." *Commentary* (May 1998): 21-27; re-published online in 2011 http://www.jewishideasdaily.com/878/features/israel-the-miracle/.

Kelemen, Lawrence. *Permission to Believe.* Southfield, Michigan: Targum Press, 1990.

———, *Permission to Receive: Four Rational Approaches to the Torah's Divine Origin.* Southfield, Michigan: Targum Press, 1996.

———, "Rational Approach to the Divinity of the Oral Tradition." https://www.youtube.com/watch?v=V4OzkVQte6g.

———, "A Rational Approach to the Divine Origin of Judaism." https://www.youtube.com/watch?v=PEg_Oys4NkA.

Kreeft, Peter. "God vs. Atheism: Which is More Rational?" https://www.youtube.com/watch?v=4T_P14JjMcM

Lichtenstein, Aharon. "The Source of Faith is Faith Itself." https://www.ou.org/jewish_action/04/2015/the-source-of-faith-is-faith-itself/.

Mann, Daniel. *A Glimpse of Greatness: A Study in the Works of Giants of Lomdus* [halakhic analysis]. Jerusalem: Eretz Hemdah Institute for Advanced Jewish Studies, 2013.

McCullough, David. *Truman.* New York: Simon and Schuster, 1992.

Meiselman, Moshe. *Torah, Chazal and Science.* Lakewood: Israel Bookshop Publications, 2013.

Miller, Merle. *Plain Speaking: An Oral Biography of Harry S. Truman,* New York: G.P. Putnam's Sons, 1974.

Morris, Benny. *1948: The First Arab-Israeli War.* New Haven: Yale University Press, 2008.

O'Brien, Conor Cruise. *The Siege: The Saga of Israel and Zionism.* New York: Simon and Schuster, 1986.

Oren, Michael. *Six Days of War: June 1967 and the Making of the Modern Middle East.* New York: Oxford University Press, 2002.

Pew Survey of American Jewry 2013, http://www.pewforum.org/2013/10/01/jewish-american-beliefs-attitudes-culture-survey/.

Sacks, Jonathan. *The Great Partnership: Science, Religion, and the Search for Meaning.* London: Hodder & Stoughton, 2011.

Schneerson, Rabbi Menachem M. "A Letter on Science and Judaism." Printed in *Challenge: Torah Views on Science and Its Problems.* Jerusalem: Association of Orthodox Jewish Scientists, 1978.

Schroeder, Gerald. *Genesis and the Big Bang: The Discovery of Harmony between Modern Science and the Bible.* New York and Toronto: Bantam Books, 1992.

______, *The Science of God: The Convergence of Scientific and Biblical Wisdom.* New York: Broadway Books, 1998.

Senor, Dan and Singer, Saul. *Start-Up Nation: The Story of Israel's Economic Miracle.* Toronto: McClelland & Stewart, 2011.

Siegel, Seth M. *Let There be Water: Israel's Solution for a Water-Starved World.* New York: Thomas Dunne Books, St. Martin's Press, 2015.

Schachter, Hershel. "Science and the Sages." Printed in *Jewish Action,* New York: Orthodox Union, Winter, 2014, available online at https://www.ou.org/jewish_action/12/2014/science-sages/.

Slifkin, Natan. *The Challenge of Creation.* Brooklyn: Yashar Books, 2006.

Soloveitchik, Joseph B. *Abraham's Journey: Reflections on the Life of the Founding Patriarch.* Jersey City: Ktav Publishing House, Inc., 2008.

______, "Catharsis." *Tradition,* Spring 1978, 38-54.

______, *The Emergence of Ethical Man.* Jersey City: Ktav Publishing House, 2005.

______, *Family Redeemed. Toras HoRav Foundation, 2000.*

______, *Fate and Destiny: From the Holocaust to the State of Israel.* Hoboken: Ktav Publishing House, 2000.

______, *Halakhic Man.* Philadelphia: Jewish Publication Society, 1983.

______, *The Lonely Man of Faith.* Northvale, New Jersey: Jason Aronson, 1997.

———, *The Lord is Righteous in All His Ways: Reflections on the Tish'ah be-Av Kinot.* Jersey City: Ktav Publishing House, 2006.

Steinberg, Milton. *As a Driven Leaf.* New York: Behrman House Publishing, 1939.

Tuchman, Barbara. "Israel: Land of Unlimited Impossibilities" in *Practicing History.* New York: Ballantine Books, 1981.

Twain, Mark. "Concerning the Jews." *Harper's Magazine,* March 1898, 527-535.

———, *The Innocents Abroad.* New York: Oxford University Press, 1996.

Weinglass, Simona. "Meet the Orthodox Jewish Physicist Rethinking the Origins of Life." *The Times of Israel,* October 29, 2015, http://www.timesofisrael.com/meet-the-orthodox-jewish-physicist-rethinking-the-origins-of-life/.

Wurzburger, Walter S. *Ethics of Responsibility: Pluralistic Approaches to Covenantal Ethics.* Philadelphia: Jewish Publication Society, 1994

———, *God is Proof Enough.* New York: Devora Publishing, 2000.

Biographical Notes of Major Torah Personalities

Abarbanel, Don Isaac ben Judah (1437-1508): commentator on the Bible who lived in Spain, Portugal and Italy.

Avraham ben David (ca. 1120 - ca. 1197): scholar living in Posquieres, France, who wrote many works, including critical comments to Maimonides' *Mishneh Torah.* He is often referred to by the acronym Ravad.

Abraham ben Moses ben Maimon (1186 – 1237): son of Maimonides. He succeeded his father as leader of the Egyptian Jewish community.

Amital, Rabbi Yehuda (1924-2010): founder and head of Yeshivat Har Etzion, Israel.

***Arukh Hashulḥan*:** a halakhic work on the *Shulḥan Arukh* authored by Rav Yeḥiel Mikhel Epstein (1829-1908), Rav of Novardok, Russia.

Auerbach, Rabbi Shlomo Zalman (1910-1995): renowned halakhic authority and author of *Minḥat Shlomo.* He resided in Jerusalem and served as head of Yeshivat Kol Torah.

Bahya Ibn Paquda (first half of the eleventh century): Jewish philosopher and rabbi who lived in Spain; author of the classic *Duties of the Heart* (*Ḥovot Halevavot).* He is often referred to as Rabbeinu Bahya.

Berlin, Rabbi Naftali Tzvi Yehudah ("The Netziv") (1817-1893): head of Yeshivat Volozhin in Russia; author of the Torah commentary *Ha'amek Davar* and many other works.

Breuer, Rabbi Mordechai (1921-2007): German-born Israeli Tanakh expert. Author of many books and articles that present Orthodox responses to biblical criticism.

Elitzur, Dr. Yehuda (1911-1997): Orthodox Israeli Bible scholar who served as an editor of the *Da'at Mikra* Bible commentary and wrote many books and articles that present Orthodox responses to biblical criticism.

Emden, Rabbi Jacob (1697-1776): a major rabbinic figure who lived in Emden (western Germany). He published a commentary on the prayerbook as well as responsa and other halakhic works.

***Ein Yaakov*:** a compilation of all the aggadic material in the Talmud with commentaries. It was compiled by Jacob ibn Habib and (after his death) by his son Rabbi Levi ibn Habib in the fifteenth and sixteenth centuries.

Feinstein, Rav Moshe (1895-1986): a renowned halakhic authority who authored *Igrot Moshe* and served as head of Mesivta Tifereth Jerusalem in New York.

Halevi, Rabbi Haim David (1924-1998): Rav of Tel Aviv-Yafo, author of *Aseh Lecha Rav* and many other works.

Hirsch, Rabbi Samson Raphael (1808-1888): leading German rabbi who authored many works, including a commentary to the Torah.

Ḥizkuni (13th century): Ḥezekiah ben Manoaḥ, a French rabbi who authored an authoritative commentary on the Torah.

Ibn Ezra, Rabbi Abraham ben Meir (1089-ca.1167): a great commentator on the Torah who lived in Spain.

Ibn Gikatilla, Moshe: poet and grammarian who lived in eleventh-century Spain.

Isserles, Rabbi Moshe (1520-1572): author of glosses on the *Shulḥan Arukh*, most of which are considered authoritative by Ashkenazic Jewry. He served as Rav in Cracow, Poland and wrote other works such as the *Darkhei Moshe* commentary on the *Tur* and response. He is often referred to by the acronym Rama.

Judah Halevi (ca.1086-1141): major twelfth-century Jewish pihilosopher who lived in Spain and authored *The Kuzari* and other works.

Kanievsky, Rav Yaakov Yisrael (1899-1985): Rav in Bnei Brak, known as the Steipler Gaon, author of *Birkat Peretz* and many other works.

Karo, Rabbi Yosef (1488-1575): great halakhic authority who lived in Safed; author of the halakhic code *Shulḥan Arukh* as well as *Kesef Mishneh, Beit Yosef*, and responsa.

Kook, Rabbi Avraham Yitzhak Hakohen (1865-1935): Ashkenazic Chief Rabbi in Israel from 1921 through 1935 and the author of numerous halakhic and philosophical works.

Kotzker Rebbe (1787-1859): Menachem Mendel Morgensztern of Kotzk, who was a leading Hasidic rabbi and leader.

Lichtenstein, Rav Aharon (1933-2015): head of Har Etzion Yeshiva in Alon Shevut, Israel, holder of a doctorate in English literature from Harvard University, and son-in-law of Rav Yosef Dov Soloveitchik. He wrote numerous books and essays, including *Leaves of Faith*.

Lipshitz, Rav Yisrael (1782–1860): leading German rabbi who authored the authoritative *Tiferet Yisrael* commentary to the Mishna and the essay entitled *Drush Or Hahayim* which grapples with the discovery of dinosaur fossils.

Maharsha (ca. 1555 - 1632): acronym for Moreinu Harav Shmuel Eidels. He authored a commentary to the Talmud and the commentaries of Rashi and Tosafot to the Talmud.

Maimonides (Moshe ben Maimon) (ca. 1135 -1204): rabbi, philosopher and physician. Born and raised in Spain, he later moved to Egypt. He authored a halakhic code called the *Mishneh Torah*, a commentary on the Mishna, and a philosophical work, *Moreh Nevuchim* (*Guide to the Perplexed*). He is often referred to by the acronym Rambam.

Malbim (1809-1879): acronym for Meir Leibush ben Yeḥiel Mikhel Wisser, a major biblical commentator who served as a rabbi in Eastern Europe.

Meir Simha of Dvinsk, Rabbi (1843–1926): major Eastern European rabbinic figure who wrote *Meshekh Hokhma* and other works.

Nahmanides (1194 -1270): Rabbi Moshe ben Naḥman, often referred to by the acronym Ramban. He authored major commentaries to the Torah and Talmud as well as other works. He lived in Spain and in Israel.

Netziv: see **Berlin, Rabbi Naftali Tzvi Yehuda**.

Ohr HaḤaim: major commentary on the Torah authored by Ḥaim ben Moshe ibn Attar who was in Morocco and died in Jerusalem (1696-1743).

Pitḥei Teshuva: summary of the responsa literature from the 17th century to the early 19th century presented as a commentary to the *Shulchan Aruch*. It was written by Rav Tzvi Hirsh Eisenstadt, Rav of Utian, Russia (1812 - 1868).

Rabbeinu Tam (1100 - 1171): Rabbeinu Yaakov ben Meir, Rashi's grandson, who lived in France and was the most prominent of the Tosafists.

Radak (1160- 1235): acronym for Rabbeinu David Kimchi, author of a major Bible commentary.

Ralbag (1288-1344): acronym for Levi ben Gershon, also known as Gersonides, who was a philosopher and astronomer who lived in France and wrote a highly regarded commentary to the Bible.

Rama: see **Isserles, Rabbi Moshe.**

Rambam: see **Maimonides.**

Ramban: see **Nahmanides.**

Ran (ca. 1290-1375): acronym for Rabbeinu Nissim, who authored a commentary to the Talmud and a compilation of sermons entitled *Drashot HaRan*.

Rashbam (ca. 1085 - 1174): acronym for Rabbeinu Shlomo ben Meir. He authored a commentary to the Torah and certain tractates of the Talmud. He was a grandson of Rashi and the older brother of Rabbeinu Tam and lived in France.

Rashi (1040 - 1105): acronym for Rabbeinu Shlomo Yitzḥaki, author of the premier commentaries to the Bible and the Talmud, who lived in Troyes, France.

Saadia Gaon (882-942): Jewish philosopher who lived in Baghdad, author of *Emunot VeDei'ot.*

Salant, Rabbi Yosef Zvi (1885-1981): author of *Be'er Yosef,* an acclaimed work on the Torah. He lived in Jerusalem.

***Seder Olam*:** Ḥazal's chronology of biblical events.

Schachter, Rav Hershel: contemporary leading American rabbi who authored many works including the essay *Science and the Sages* (born 1941).

Schneersohn, Rabbi Menaḥem Mendel (1902-1994): the seventh Lubavitcher Rebbe, who had an extraordinary impact on the Jewish community.

Schwab, Rabbi Shimon (1908-1995): German rabbi who immigrated to the United States and headed the German Jewish community in the Washington Heights section of Manhattan. His works include the essay "How Old is the Universe?"

Sefer Haḥinukh: enumeration and discussion of the 613 *mitzvot* written in the 13th century by an unknown author (attributed by some to the Ra'ah, Rabbeinu Aharon Halevi).

Seforno (Sforno), Rabbi Ovadia (1470 - 1550): Italian rabbi, Torah commentator, philosopher and physician.

***Smak*:** acronym for the *Sefer Mitzvot Katan,* written by Rav Yitzhak ben Yosef of Corbeil, France (d. 1280).

***Shulḥan Arukh*:** see **Karo, Rabbi Yosef.**

Soloveitchik, Rav Ḥaim (1853-1918): the Rav of Brisk, Lithuania and author of commentaries on Maimonides' *Mishneh Torah* and parts of the Talmud.

Soloveitchik, Rav Moshe (1879 -1941): son of Rav Ḥaim who served as head of the Rabbi Isaac Elchanan Theological Seminary at Yeshiva University.

Soloveitchik, Rav Joseph B. (Yosef Dov) (1903 - 1993): son of Rav Moshe who was a Rav in Boston, MA, and succeeded his father as head of the Rabbi Isaac Elchanan Theological Seminary at Yeshiva University. His students refer to him as "the Rav." He earned a doctorate in philosophy at the University of Berlin.

Sorotzkin, Rabbi Zalman (1881-1966): noted Israeli rabbi who wrote a Torah commentary entitled *Oznayim LaTorah.*

Steipler Gaon: see Kanievsky, Rav Yaakov Yisrael.

Tosafot: talmudic commentaries of the Tosafists, talmudic scholars in France and Germany in the 12th and 13th centuries.

***Tur (Arba'a Turim)*:** a halakhic code which served as the prototype of the *Shulḥan Arukh.* It was authored by Rabbi Jacob ben Asher (ca. 1275-ca. 1340).

Tzitz Eliezer: responsa authored by Rabbi Eliezer Waldenberg (1915-2006), member of the *Beit Din Hagadol* (Supreme Rabbinic Court) of the Israeli Chief Rabbinate who resided in Jerusalem.

Vilna Gaon (1720-1787): Lithuanian Rav who is regarded as one of the leading Torah authorities of the past five hundred years.

Wasserman, Rabbi Elḥanan (1874-1941): leading rabbi in pre-war eastern Europe who authored *Kovetz Maamarim* and many other works.

Wosner, Rabbi Shmuel (1913-2015): a leading Israeli rabbinic authority, author of the responsa collection *Shevet Halevi.*

Wurzburger, Rabbi Dr. Walter (1920-2002): American rabbi and noted philosopher who received a doctorate in philosophy at Harvard University. He authored *Ethics of Responsibility* and *God is Proof Enough.*

Yerushalmi: the Jerusalem Talmud, redacted in northern Israel sometime between 350 and 410.

Yisraeli, Rav Shaul (1909-1995): a leading Israeli rabbi, author of *Perakim Bemaḥshevet Yisrael.*

Yore De'a: one of the four sections of the *Shulchan Aruch,* which discusses the laws of *kashrut,* family purity, mourning, and other matters.

Yosef, Rav Ovadia (1920-2013): Sephardic halakhic authority in Jerusalem and former Sephardic Chief Rabbi of Israel. He wrote *Yabia Omer, Yeḥaveh Da'at,* and countless other works.

Zohar: the foundational work of Jewish mysticism (*Kabbala*).

The fonts used in this book are from the Arno Koren family.

Menorah Books
At the Heart of Judaism
Koren Publishers Jerusalem Ltd.